Cognitive Style

COGNITIVE STYLE

FIVE APPROACHES AND RELEVANT RESEARCH

KENNETH M. GOLDSTEIN

Staten Island Children's Community Mental Health Center
of the Staten Island Mental Health Society

SHELDON BLACKMAN

St. Vincent's North Richmond Community Mental Health Center
of the St. Vincent's Medical Center of Richmond

A WILEY-INTERSCIENCE PUBLICATION

JOHN WILEY & SONS, New York · Chichester · Brisbane · Toronto

To our wives

ELAINE and SHERRY

Library of Congress Cataloging in Publication Data

Goldstein, Kenneth M.   1940-
  Cognitive style.

  "A Wiley-Interscience publication."
  Bibliography: p.
  Includes indexes.
    1. Cognitive style.   I.   Blackman, Sheldon, joint
author. II. Title.

BF311.G583   153.4   78-1378
ISBN 0-471-31275-4

Printed in the United States of America

10 9 8 7 6 5 4 3

Series Preface

This series of books is addressed to behavioral scientists interested in the nature of human personality. Its scope should prove pertinent to personality theorists and researchers as well as to clinicians concerned with applying an understanding of personality processes to the amelioration of emotional difficulties in living. To this end, the series provides a scholarly integration of theoretical formulations, empirical data, and practical recommendations.

Six major aspects of studying and learning about human personality can be designated: personality theory, personality structure and dynamics, personality development, personality assessment, personality change, and personality adjustment. In exploring these aspects of personality, the books in the series discuss a number of distinct but related subject areas: the nature and implications of various theories of personality; personality characteristics that account for consistencies and variations in human behavior; the emergence of personality processes in children and adolescents; the use of interviewing and testing procedures to evaluate individual differences in personality; efforts to modify personality styles through psychotherapy, counseling, behavior therapy, and other methods of influence; and patterns of abnormal personality functioning that impair individual competence.

IRVING B. WEINER

Case Western Reserve University
Cleveland, Ohio

Preface

In the last few years there has been renewed interest in cognitive psychology in general and in cognitive style in particular. Cognitive style, emphasizing the structure rather than the content of thought, refers to the ways in which individuals conceptually organize their environments. A number of approaches to the study of cognitive style have been made. We choose to review five of these approaches in detail. They are approaches selected to illustrate the movement from a content-oriented to a structure-oriented emphasis. We view the five approaches as representative of an evolutionary process in the study of cognitive style. The five approaches also illustrate a concern with the structure of thought from the point of view of differentiation and integration. Differentiation refers to the number of dimensions used in structuring the environment and the gradations along these dimensions. Integration refers to the relationships among these dimensions.

A number of themes appear repeatedly in the various approaches to the study of cognitive style. These include the relationship of cognitive style to intelligence, rigidity and intolerance of ambiguity, and performance under stress. We attempt to trace the origins of such interests from the early content-laden research on authoritarianism to the more avowedly stylistic approaches represented in the work of George A. Kelly and Herman A. Witkin. We also attempt to locate parallel themes among the various research interests.

The book is intended to be of use to advanced undergraduates, graduate students, and professionals interested in cognitive psychology. There have been thousands of studies involving cognitive style variables, and one of our major problems was to delimit the material covered. To this end we are concerned with cognitive style primarily as it relates to differentiation and integration, within the five major areas reviewed. In particular, we do not review studies in which the central concern is the relation of cognitive style to personality variables such as dependency or extraversion or studies relating cognitive style to psychopathology. For the most part, we limit our review to studies involving English-speaking populations.

A book of this type involves a considerable amount of tedious work on the part of research assistants and secretaries. The task of acquiring copies of, and keeping track of, the many hundreds of references that were consulted in the preparation of this manuscript required patience, skill, and dedication. For this we are indebted to Mrs. Frances Brown, Mrs. Ellen Fischer, Mrs. Grace Gross, and Mrs. Lucile C. Hausheer. The arduous job of typing and retyping most of the material was admirably undertaken by Mrs. Fischer, to whom we are extremely thankful. A number of our colleagues bore with us while we were engaged in the preparation of this book, and we would especially like to thank Mr. James J. Mahoney, Dr. Lawrence C. Miller, Mr. Howard Safar, and Dr. Nora Smith. A debt of gratitude is also due the many investigators who were kind enough to respond to our requests for copies of published and unpublished research reports. Especially helpful in this regard were Dr. Alvin W. Landfield and Dr. Herman A. Witkin.

Finally, we must acknowledge the origin of our interest in cognitive style in the stimulation provided to us as students of Harold M. Schroder and the late George A. Kelly.

Kenneth M. Goldstein
Sheldon Blackman

Staten Island, New York
February 1978

Contents

Cognitive Style

CHAPTER ONE

Introduction

Although students of behavior are generally interested in the relationship between stimulus input and the organism's response, they differ in the conceptual models they apply in an attempt to understand and predict this relationship. Two broad approaches have been distinguished, the stimulus-response (S-R) and the stimulus-organism-response (S-O-R) models. S-R theorists maintain that behavior is best predicted by studying functional relationships between stimuli and responses. The adherents of the S-O-R model maintain that relationships between stimuli and responses are best predicted from information about the intermediary processes that occur within the organism.

A number of theorists have posited mediating structures. Freud's concept of the ego is one such structure that is conceptualized as mediating between the environment and the organism's responses to the environment. Guilford (1959) noted that most psychologists reject the S-R model and posit mediating processes between directly observable stimuli and responses. Among the mediating processes discussed by Guilford are motives, abilities, interests, and temperament, none of which are directly observable but are inferred from behavior.

Cognition is a mediating process that is the center of a resurgence of interest. Mahoney (1977) noted: "There are numerous indications that psychology is undergoing some sort of 'revolution' in the sense that cognitive processes have become a very popular topic." He pointed out that one characteristic of the current cognitive–learning perspective is that the organism responds to its cognitive construction of the environment rather than to objective reality. Zajonc (1968) noted that, in social psychology, the cognitive representation of social

1

stimuli and incentives is assumed to be more important than the physical and objective properties of such stimulation and incentives. The current importance of cognitive psychology has also been discussed by McKeachie (1976) in his historical overview of the status of psychology. Specifically, he cited a return to an interest in "the psyche," mental processes, and consciousness. The relationship between research in personality and in cognition was cited in a recent paper by Mischel (1977).

One manifestation of the trend toward increased interest in cognition is the attention paid to cognitive style in such recent publications as those of Kogan (1976), Landfield (1977), and Messick and associates (1976). Brody (1972) noted several common characteristics among the cognitive approaches to personality that have become popular during the last 20 years: (1) individual differences in *styles* of thinking (not motivation, emotion, or biological processes) as a starting point, (2) an emphasis of style over content, (3) the assumption that "cognitive styles are related to other personality characteristics of individuals," and (4) the treatment of cognitive styles as traits (i.e., the characteristics are independent of situational influences, a position leading to an emphasis on the consistency of the style).

NATURE AND DEFINITION OF COGNITIVE STYLE

Cognitive style is a hypothetical construct that has been developed to explain the process of mediation between stimuli and responses. The term *cognitive style* refers to the characteristic ways in which individuals conceptually organize the environment. Harvey's (1963) view that cognitive style refers to the way an individual filters and processes stimuli so that the environment takes on psychological meaning is representative of this use of the term. As such, cognitive representations modify the one-to-one relationship between stimulus and responses. If it were not for these cognitive representations, Harvey pointed out, stimuli would be irrevelant for the individual, or the individual would respond to stimulation in a robotlike fashion.

Bieri (1971) too noted that a process of information transformation is a basic assumption of the cognitive theorist. He maintained that individuals learn "strategies, programs, or other transformation operations" to translate *objective* stimuli into meaningful dimensions. Bieri termed these strategies "cognitive structures."

Messick (1976) also defined cognitive style in terms of consistent patterns of "organizing and processing information." Zajonc (1968) similarly maintained that cognitive structures mediate between environmental input and the organism's output. He added the idea that cognitive structures organize behavior as well as input.

Coop and Sigel (1971) used the term cognitive style "to denote consistencies in individual modes of functioning in a variety of behavioral situations." In this definition cognitive style is equated with behavior rather than mediating processes. This definition is, as Coop and Sigel pointed out, similar to the use of the term style by Gordon Allport (1937) to describe consistencies in behavior.

Coop and Sigel (1971) pointed out similarities between the construct cognitive style and the earlier concept of *silent organization,* a term used by the Gestaltists to describe cognitive structures that are not tied to specific content but rather guide behavior (Scheerer, 1954). Investigators who used related constructs include Tolman, who utilized the concept of *cognitive maps,* and Bartlett and Piaget, who utilized the concept of *schemata.* Lewin's concepts of *differentiation* and *hierarchical organization* are also important.

Common to all theory and research on cognitive style is an emphasis on the structure rather than the content of thought (e.g., Suedfeld, 1971). Structure refers to *how* cognition is organized; content refers to *what* knowledge is available. In this book the term cognitive style refers to the ways in which thought is structured. Behavioral consistency is viewed as the product of this structure.

Numerous approaches to the study of cognitive style have been made. Messick (1970) attempted to conceptualize this work in terms of nine categories. The first four derive from the work on cognitive controls by Gardner, Klein, and their colleagues (e.g., Gardner, Holzman, Klein, Linton, & Spence, 1959). Messick used these cognitive controls as his first four categories: scanning, leveling–sharpening, constricted–flexible control, and tolerance for incongruous or unrealistic experience. A fifth approach was originated by Witkin and his coworkers (e.g., Witkin, Lewis, Hertzman, Machover, Meissner, & Wapner, 1954), who use the term *field dependence.* Workers in the area of cognitive controls also investigated this variable, terming it *field articu-*

lation. A sixth approach noted by Messick is cognitive complexity. Messick included in this category the work of Kelly (1955), Bieri, Atkins, Briar, Leaman, Miller, and Tripodi (1966), and Harvey, Hunt, and Schroder (1961). The final three categories are reflection-impulsivity (Kagan, Rosman, Day, Albert, & Phillips, 1964), styles of categorization (Pettigrew, 1958), and styles of conceptualization (Kagan, Moss, & Sigel, 1963). Recently, Messick (1976) modified these nine categories, added new ones, and listed a total of 19 approaches to the study of cognitive style. This reflects both increasing research interest in cognitive style and Messick's continuing attempt to organize and integrate a wide variety of research efforts.

Kogan (1973, 1976) distinguished three types of cognitive styles. Cognitive styles of the first type refer to an ability to perform, with performance judged against a standard. For example, an individual who is field independent is better able to locate figures embedded in a surrounding context than is a field-dependent person. In Type II cognitive styles, greater value is placed on one of the stylistic categories by the investigator. For example, Kelly (1955) and Bieri et al. (1966) view the cognitively complex person as having an advantage over the cognitively simple person in processing information about his environment. The Type III cognitive style does not relate to ability. Further, the investigator does not attribute superiority in performance to an individual at any particular pole or in any category. Kogan (1976) cited Pettigrew's (1958) category width approach as an example of this type of cognitive style.

Despite the elements of common interest in the study of cognitive style, various investigators disagree on the details of the approach to the study of cognitive style and the use of measuring instruments. This has resulted in a body of literature from which it is difficult to extract general principles. Kagan and Henker (1966) pointed out the need for systematization at the levels of theory and research. Studies designed to relate the variables used by one investigator to those used by other investigators are needed.

APPROACHES TO THE STUDY OF COGNITIVE STYLE

In this section a number of approaches to cognitive style are surveyed. They are cognitive controls, category width, conceptual styles, and reflection–impulsivity. In the remainder of the book five other approaches are examined in detail. These other approaches were selected to reflect a shift in emphasis from content-oriented to stylistic-oriented approaches. The plan for the succeeding chapters is considered at the conclusion of this chapter.

COGNITIVE CONTROLS

George Klein (1954) introduced the term "cognitive control." According to Klein, a cognitive control is a hypothetical construct that directs the expression of need in socially acceptable ways, as required by the situation. In many ways this conceptualization is similar to Freud's conceptualization of a social ego controlling primitive id urges. Hence cognitive controls delay the gratification of needs, leading to their description as "delay mechanisms." Gardner and Long (1962a) noted that cognitive controls were conceived within a framework of psychoanalytic ego psychology. According to the authors, ". . . controls are viewed as enduring cognitive structures that, like defense mechanisms, presumably emerge in the course of development from the interaction of genetic and experiential determinants."

Based on studies in the area of thirst and color interference, Klein distinguished between constricted and flexible control. Individuals who manifested constricted control over the expression of need were characterized in a manner similar to compulsive people. They were precise and meticulous, overvalued order, were uncomfortable with disorder, and tended to pigeon-hole reality rather than deal with it in affective terms. The characteristics of the flexible individual were less clear. Klein suggested that such individuals function by allowing more information, including affect, to be used in decision making.

This line of research, which was conducted by members of the "Perception Project" at the Menninger Foundation (Gardner, 1962), led to a concern with the "conceptual and empirical delineation of the various cognitive controls and the examination of their relationships and patterning within individuals" (Kagan & Kogan, 1970).

Gardner (1962) noted that in the initial work, Klein and his associates used the term "perceptual attitudes." This term was later replaced by the terms "cognitive attitudes" and "cognitive system principles." The terms "cognitive controls" and "cognitive control principles" were adopted to denote the idea that a delaying, controlling function was involved.

Gardner, Jackson, and Messick (1960) differentiated cognitive controls from cognitive style. According to these authors, the former term refers to the specific dimensions investigated as part of the Perception Project and includes leveling–sharpening, scanning, field articulation, conceptual differentiation, and constricted–flexible control. Cognitive style refers to the organization of these dimensions within an individual. However, as Kagan and Kogan (1970) noted, the distinction between cognitive control and cognitive style has not been strictly adhered to.

A review of the early work in the study of cognitive style is contained in Gardner (1959). In another overview of some of the work on cognitive control, Gardner (1970) reiterated that behavior cannot be understood without consideration of the role of cognitive structures in adaptation (cf. also Wachtel, 1972). Klein (1970) collected a set of seminal papers on cognitive controls.

The dimensions of cognitive control that have been explored include:

1. *Tolerance for unrealistic experiences.* Klein and Schlesinger (1951) showed that individuals who tended to give literal, concrete, and unelaborated responses to Rorschach inkblot stimuli also tended to have difficulty perceiving movement in the phi phenomenon. They termed this behavior "intolerance for instability." Klein, Gardner, and Schlesinger (1962) later hypothesized that such behavior was an aspect of a broader cognitive control labeled "intolerance for unrealistic experiences." This dimension was defined as ". . . the subject's readiness to accept and report experiences at variance with conventional reality or with what they [sic] knew to be true." The measure of tolerance for unrealistic experiences is the perception of movement in the phi phenomenon (Segal & Barr, 1969).

2. *Conceptual differentiation.* This dimension of cognitive control was first termed "equivalence range." It was investigated by Gardner (1953), who hypothesized that individuals would be consistent in ". . . what they will accept as similar or identical in a variety of adaptive tasks." Gardner, Jackson, and Messick (1960) defined equivalence range as ". . . the degree of differentiation in individuals' experiencing of similarity and difference. . . ." Gardner and Schoen (1962) ex-

tended the concept of equivalence range to that of "conceptual differentiation," the term that is currently used (Gardner & Moriarity, 1968). An individual with a narrow equivalence range is also high in conceptual differentiation. In a free sorting task, such an individual utilizes many categories.

Gardner (1953) used an Object Sorting Test to measure equivalence range. This task requires the subject to sort 73 objects into as many categories as he believes the objects warrant. Clayton and Jackson (1961) developed a 50-item form of the Object Sorting Test. The Size Constancy Test is a second instrument for assessing equivalence range. The subject is required to match a stimulus with standards on the basis of retinal image size. To perform well the subject must retain a set developed in previous training for distinguishing between real and apparent size (Gardner, Jackson, & Messick, 1960).

Sloane, Gorlow, and Jackson (1963) administered a variety of tests designed to measure equivalence range to 60 female undergraduates. The data indicated a similarity of scores based on the sorting of diverse stimulus materials and that group-administered tests often yielded results comparable to those obtained from individually administered tests.

3. *Constricted-flexible control.* Smith and Klein (1953) provided the first report of the constricted-flexible dimension of cognitive control. Some of the initial research that led to the study of this dimension was reported by Klein (1954). Individuals are ordered along the dimension in terms of their susceptibility to distraction.

Constricted–flexible control is assessed with the Color-Word Test (Gardner, Jackson, & Messick, 1960). This test is Thurstone's (1944) modification of a test developed by Stroop (1935). The subject is presented with four color names—red, green, blue, yellow—each of which is printed many times. These names may be printed in red, green, blue, or yellow ink. For example, the word red may be printed with yellow ink. The task is to name the color of the ink with which the word is printed. To perform well, the subject must disregard one of the two conflicting cues. The individual who is able to disregard the conflicting cue and perform the task quickly and accurately is designated flexible.

Broverman (1960a, b) used the Stroop test as the basis for developing measures of two dimensions of cognitive style: perceptual-motor versus conceptual dominance and automatization. A group-administered version of the Stroop test (Golden, 1975) relates well with an individually administered version. The Fruit-Distraction Test (Santostefano & Paley, 1964) is a measure of constricted–flexible control that is suitable for use with children. Jensen (1965) reviewed some of the psychometric properties of the Stroop test and found that the more common indices were satisfactorily reliable. Jensen and Rohwer (1966) and Dyer (1973) reviewed the Stroop Color-Word Test and related research. In their review of the literature, Jensen and Rohwer (1966) found a general improvement in performance on the Stroop test until about the teenage years, with some evidence of a decrement in performance beyond the age of 60 years. They found no consistent evidence of a relationship of performance on the Stroop test to intelligence.

4. *Leveling–sharpening.* This dimension of cognitive control was defined by Gardner, Jackson, and Messick (1960) as ". . . the characteristic degree to which current percepts and relevant memory traces interact or assimilate in the course of registration of the current percepts and memories. . . ." As an event is perceived, there is an interaction between events already perceived and stored in memory and the new event that is being perceived. This interaction, or "assimilation," is a coming together of memory traces and the new perception.

Holzman and Klein (1954) studied individual consistency in assimilation (Gardner & Moriarty, 1968), terming individuals who demonstrated great assimilation "levelers" and those who did not "sharpeners." They found that leveling results in the maximum simplification of the cognitive field, whereas sharpening results in maximum complexity and differentiation.

The Schematizing Test, based on a procedure developed by Hollingworth (1913), is the principal measure of leveling–sharpening. Following a period of dark adaptation, subjects are required to judge the sizes of squares of light of increasing size. It has been found that subjects tend to underestimate the sizes of the squares as new squares of light of increasing size are added. This occurs because of ". . . assimilation among percepts of new squares and the trace aggregate of smaller squares seen earlier" (Gardner, Jackson, & Messick, 1960). Levelers perform poorly on this task, making large underestimates. Several scores have been derived to measure performance on this test. Pritchard (1975) recommended the use of a ranking-accuracy score rather than a lag score, whereas Levine (1976) suggested using both lag and accuracy scores in a multiple-regression approach. Instruments for the measurement of leveling–sharpening in children were devised by Santostefano (1964) and Santostefano, Rutledge, and Randall (1965).

5. *Scanning.* The cognitive control principle of scanning is defined as the extent to which an individual attempts to verify the judgments he makes (Gardner & Moriarity, 1968). The dimension is assessed by two size-estimation tests. In one, the subject is instructed to match a projected circle of light to each of three standard disks. In the second test, the subject is required to adjust a variable light circle to each of two projected disks. The extent to which an individual compares the stimulus with the standard is the extent of his scanning. Presumably, the more extensive the comparing, the better should be the performance on these tasks (Gardner, Jackson, & Messick, 1960). A number of scores derived from these tests have been shown to correlate highly (Gardner & Long, 1962a, b). The Circles Test (Santostefano and Paley, 1964) was developed to measure scanning in children. This test is also a size-estimation task.

6. *Contrast reactivity.* The cognitive control dimension of contrast reactivity was introduced by Gardner, Lohrenz, and Schoen (1968). The principal measure of this dimension is the Lines Contrast Test. This task requires the subject to estimate the lengths of pairs of lines, the ratio of the estimates being used as a measure of contrast reactivity. In his discussion of the reliability of the measure, Gardner (1973) proposed that the test be lengthened.

7. *Field articulation.* The cognitive control dimension of field articulation (Gardner & Long, 1960a) is the same as that of field dependence (Witkin et al., 1954). The latter is reviewed in detail in Chapter 6. Gardner and Long maintained that field articulation is a broader concept than field dependence. The person who is high in field articulation is selective in attention. He can attend to either the figure or the embedding context. Gardner, Jackson, and Messick (1960) view the individual who is high in field articulation as able to selectively attend to relevant rather than compelling irrelevant stimuli. The operational distinction between field articulation and field dependence is unclear, a fact that Gardner (1962) finds troublesome.

The assessment of field articulation is based on the work of Witkin (Gardner, Jackson, & Messick, 1960). The measures, the Embedded Figures Test (EFT) and the Rod-and-Frame Test (RFT), are considered in detail in Chapter 6. In the EFT the subject is required to find a geometric figure located in an embedding context. In the RFT the subject is required to bring a rod into a vertical position when presented with a variety of disorienting cues. A size-estimation test has also been used as a measure of field articulation (Gardner & Moriarty, 1968).

CATEGORY WIDTH

The results of the work of Bruner and co-workers (cf. Bruner, Goodnow, & Austin, 1956) were cited by Pettigrew (1958) as evidence of intraindividual consistencies in the range in which individuals consider events likely to occur. That is, individuals who estimate a wide range for the width of windows are likely to estimate wide ranges for other phenomena. Pettigrew developed a paper-and-pencil measure of category width, the C-W scale, to measure this stylistic dimension. In its final form, the 20-item test presents the subject with a central measure and requires that he select one of four alternatives as the highest end of the range and one of four as the lowest.

Pettigrew gave two explanations for the observed consistency in judgments of category width. One, risk taking, is that broad categorizers are willing to risk being overinclusive. The second explanation uses the cognitive control concept of equivalence range and posits that narrow categorizers make fewer differentiations. Research on these two points of view has been reviewed by Bieri (1969) and Touhey (1973) and is not conclusive.

CONCEPTUAL STYLES

Cognitive style was viewed by Kagan, Moss, and Sigel (1963) as ". . . stable individual preferences in mode of perceptual organization and conceptual categorization of the external environment." These investigators studied cognitive style by analyzing how individuals group objects. They postulated that individuals could be dimensionalized on the basis of their proclivity ". . . to analyze and to differentiate the stimulus environment. . . ." Kagan, Rosman, Day, Albert, and Phillips (1964) also discussed this point of view.

Kagan et al. (1963) developed the Conceptual Style Test (CST). This test initially consisted of 44 triads of pictures. Shorter versions are more commonly used. The subject is asked to select the two pictures from a triad that could go together. The reasons for the groupings are considered in terms of analytic, relational, and inferential styles. An individual whose style is analytic-descriptive groups pictures on the basis of common elements, such as people without shoes. An individual whose style is relational utilizes functional, thematic relationships in his groupings; for example, two people are grouped together because they are married. An individual whose style is inferential-categorical makes his groupings on the basis of a more abstract similarity between the pictures; for example, two individuals may be seen as poor. The latter category is observed infrequently, a fact that Stanes (1973) attributed to the simplicity of the stimuli.

One modification of the CST was made by Sigel (1967) and is known as the Sigel Conceptual Styles Test (SCST). The Sigel Object Categorization Task (SOCT), another modified CST, uses three-dimensional objects (Sigel & Olmsted, 1970). This latter instrument was reviewed by Lindstrom and Shipman (1972). Kogan (1976) reviewed the use of the various CST instruments with young children.

The approach by Kelly (1955) and Bieri et al. (1966) is reviewed in detail in Chapter 4. The various versions of the CST are similar in concept to the instruments used by Kelly and Bieri. The latter investigators, however, defined cognitive complexity as the *number* of different ways in which objects are grouped. In the CST the rationale for the groupings forms the basis for assessing cognitive style. In Kogan's (1976) classification system, conceptual style is a Type III approach, whereas cognitive complexity is a Type II approach.

REFLECTION–IMPULSIVITY

A popular approach to the study of cognitive style in children is reflection-impulsivity. Originally introduced by Kagan, Rosman, Day, Albert, and Phillips (1964), reflection-impulsivity allows an ordering of children in terms of the differences in the speed with which they make decisions under conditions of uncertainty. Kagan and Kogan (1970) made a second major contribution to the conceptualization of reflection–impulsivity.

The Matching Familiar Figures (MFF) Test (Kagan et al., 1964) is used to assess reflection–impulsivity. The subject is presented with 12 test pictures. For each picture he is asked to choose which of several almost identical alternatives exactly matches the stimulus picture. A child who responds rapidly and with errors is labeled impulsive; a child who responds slowly and accurately is labeled reflective.

The adequacy of the MFF Test has concerned a number of investigators. Although the definition of reflection–impulsivity involves the time taken to reach a decision, the MFF Test measures both time and accuracy (Block, Block, & Harrington, 1974). Kagan and Messer (1975) noted that both speed and accuracy are involved in the definition of reflection–impulsivity, but Block, Block, and Harrington (1975) remained unconvinced. The psychometric properties of the MFF Test were recently criticized by Ault, Mitchell, and Hartmann (1976) and Egeland and Weinberg (1976). Messer (1976) presented an important overview of research on reflection–impulsivity. A review by Kogan (1976) examined literature dealing with reflection–impulsivity during infancy and early childhood.

APPROACHES TO BE REVIEWED IN DETAIL

In the following chapters five approaches to the study of cognitive style are reviewed. The five approaches were selected as representative of a continuum from emphasis on content to emphasis on structure.

Authoritarianism is the first of these approaches considered in detail. This is the most content-laden approach to the study of cognitive style that is reviewed. Adorno, Frenkel-Brunswik, Levinson, and Sanford (1950) were interested in the individual whose structure of thinking was expected to make him especially susceptible to antidemocratic propaganda. The researchers approached the question by studying anti-Semitism, ethnocentrism, and political-economic conservatism. They next considered the personality variables underlying these attitudes and values. Eventually they studied some of the behavioral correlates of authoritarianism, especially rigidity and intolerance of ambiguity. These two classes of behavior are manifestations of an underlying cognitive style.

The second approach to be reviewed is Rokeach's (1960) work on dogmatism. This work represents efforts to develop a structurally-based measure of authoritarianism to replace the content-based measure developed by Adorno and his colleagues.

In Chapter 4 we turn to the work on cognitive complexity by Kelly (1955) and Bieri et al. (1966). In this approach the investigators are concerned with the psychological dimensions that individuals use to structure their environments. The various measures of cognitive complexity are less content laden than the measures used in the study of authoritarianism and dogmatism.

Next we review the work of Harvey, Hunt, and Schroder (1961) on integrative complexity. A sentence-completion method is used to assess the differentiation and integration involved in information processing. This represents a further development of content-free measurement.

The theory and research of Witkin and his associates (Witkin, Dyk, Faterson, Goodenough, & Karp, 1962; Witkin, Lewis, Hertzman, Machover, Meissner, & Wapner, 1954) is reviewed in Chapter 6. Here cognitive style is measured with tests in the perceptual domain.

The final chapter presents a summary and integration of the five approaches. A number of investigators have noted common elements among them: Warr and Coffman (1970) commented on expected similarities in functioning among individuals classified as authoritarian, dogmatic, and cognitively simple. Bieri et al. (1966), Witkin et al. (1954), and Harvey, Hunt, and Schroder (1961) were considered by Klein, Barr, and Wolitsky (1967) to be concerned with the degree to which experience and judgment are differentiated. They point out the need for additional research to determine the common aspects of the various positions.

ORGANIZATION OF EACH CHAPTER

Each of the next five chapters is devoted to a review of a major theory and body of research about cognitive style. Each chapter begins with a brief summary of the aspects of the approach that relate to cognitive style. Next we consider the instruments that were developed to measure the cognitive style aspect of the theory, later modifications of these instruments, and their reliability and validity. In the next section of each chapter, the developmental aspects of each theory are presented. We then review the research derived from the theory that has implications for cognitive style. The final section of each of the chapters is a critique.

CHAPTER TWO

Authoritarianism, Rigidity, and Intolerance of Ambiguity

During the years of Adolph Hitler's rise to power, the extent of people's inhumanity shocked the civilized world. In an attempt to grapple with Nazism, social scientists like Kurt Lewin and his associates (Lewin, Lippitt, & White, 1939; Lippitt & White, 1943) used a laboratory paradigm to compare Nazi-type authoritarian leadership with democratic and laissez-faire leadership. Personality theorists such as Erich Fromm (1936, 1941), Wilhelm Reich (1945), and Erik Erikson (1942) studied the reasons for people's susceptibility to the Nazi appeal.

At about this time, several investigators came together in Berkeley, California to carry out a series of studies that would have great impact on our understanding of prejudice and authoritarianism. These studies were reported by Adorno, Frenkel-Brunswik, Levinson, and Sanford in *The Authoritarian Personality*, a book that would become one of the most important of all social science works. The studies began with a focus on anti-Semitism, were conducted within a psychoanalytic framework, and led the researchers to the conclusion that prejudice is not an isolated aspect of an individual's functioning, but rather an integrated component of personality.

15

Personality may be conceived of as a consistent manner of thinking, feeling, and behaving. The authors of *The Authoritarian Personality* present what is essentially a personality theory. Our concern in this book, however, is the cognitive, or thinking, aspects of personality. The combination of clinical and empirical methods used by the Berkeley researchers led to the delineation of a personality type that was the starting point of later research on cognitive style. During the course of the studies, two important behavioral correlates of authoritarianism were isolated: rigidity and intolerance of ambiguity. Our focus in this chapter is on these two variables. We show how these types of behaviors, which are manifestations of an underlying cognitive style, emerged from the study of the authoritarian personality.

HISTORICAL BACKGROUND

The best historical summaries of the research effort that culminated in *The Authoritarian Personality* were written by Sanford (1954, 1956).

In 1943, R. Nevitt Sanford and some colleagues were engaged in studies relating "war morale" to personality factors. Sanford's approach was to employ a wide range of techniques, including clinical interviews, projective tests, and objective measurement, all from a psychoanalytic viewpoint. At this time an anonymous donation was made for research on anti-Semitism. There was a coming together of interests and staff, and by 1944–1945 the first papers on anti-Semitism were prepared.

The research effort began to make greater progress with financial support from the American Jewish Committee for research on anti-Semitism to be conducted with empirical procedures. Else Frenkel-Brunswik and Daniel J. Levinson had already begun work on the project when the last member, T. W. Adorno, joined the group. Else Frenkel-Brunswik and her psychologist husband, Egon Brunswik, had studied and taught at the University of Vienna during Hitler's rise to power. As a Jew, Frenkel-Brunswik's exposure to the anti-Semitism in this environment no doubt influenced her interest in this area. The Berkeley group was loosely organized, but a common theme was evident: the development of scales for the objective measurement of prejudice and the clinical analysis of individuals high and low on these scales. Sanford noted that the results reported in *The Authoritarian*

Personality are drawn from related but independent studies and that the book was never intended to provide a complete picture of the authoritarian individual.

Given the concerns about Fascism at the time of World War II, the major focus of the Berkeley investigators was the potentially Fascist individual, the individual susceptible to antidemocratic propaganda:

If a potentially Fascistic individual exists, what, precisely, is he like? What goes to make up anti-democratic thought? What are the organizing forces within the person? If such a person exists, how commonly does he exist in our society? And if such a person exists, what have been the determinants and what the course of his development? (Adorno et al., 1950, p. 2)

One type of antidemocratic thought is prejudice, and anti-Semitism was the specific type of prejudice to be researched. The first of the objective instruments developed as part of the project was the Anti-Semitism (A-S) Scale developed by Levinson and Sanford (1944).

The A-S Scale contained 52 items under five headings: offensive (Jews are dirty, conceited), threatening (Jews are ruthless, competitive), attitude items, which reflected behavioral tendencies (recommending various types of discrimination against Jews), seclusive (Jews are clannish), and intrusive (Jews want to move where they are not wanted). The scale was of the Likert type, in which the subject indicates his degree of agreement or disagreement with each of the items on a six-point scale. Since all items were written in an anti-Semitic direction, a high score (agreement with many items) indicated high anti-Semitism. Research with the A-S Scale has shown it to have a split-half reliability above .95 (Levinson & Sanford, 1944; O'Reilly & O'Reilly, 1954). The validity of the instrument was demonstrated in studies by Weatherley (1961, 1963) and Pulos and Spilka (1961).

In work with the A-S Scale it was found that individuals who were prejudiced toward Jews were also prejudiced toward other minority groups. Earlier, Sumner (1906) had introduced the term *ethnocentrism* to define the tendency to rigidly accept the culturally alike and reject the culturally different. This more generalized approach to the study of prejudice led to the development of the Ethnocentrism (E) Scale (Levinson, 1949).

Aside from the conceptual interest in developing the E Scale, there were some practical considerations that reinforced interest in such a scale. As the authors recognized (Sanford, 1956), the A-S Scale brought prejudice "painfully" into the open, especially when administered to groups containing Jews. A local chapter of the Anti-Defamation League complained that the A-S Scale helped to spread anti-Semitism. On the other hand, the dean of the graduate school objected to the "pro-Semitic bias" in the research. The E Scale was developed in an attempt to avoid these problems.

The E Scale contained three subscales to measure attitudes toward Negroes, minorities, and patriotism. A number of versions of the scale were developed. A 20-item scale was recommended by the original researchers. In format, the E Scale is similar to the A-S Scale. Some items are dated by references to "zootsuiters" and the "secret of the atom bomb." Shaw and Wright (1967) estimate the reliability of the 20-item form of the E Scale to be above .80. Studies of the validity of the instrument include those by Adorno et al. (1950), Siegel and Siegel (1957), and McGinnies and Altman (1959). The E Scale has provided a satisfactory measure of ethnocentrism in a large number of studies.

The next step was to relate ethnocentrism to political and economic factors. The Politico-Economic Conservatism (PEC) Scale was developed to measure right–left, or conservative–liberal, attitudes. The instrument was similar in format to its A-S and E antecedents. It was intended to measure allegiance to the status quo and resistance to social change. Several versions of the instrument were developed, including the initial 16-item form and a 5-item form. As expected, people who are high in political and economic conservatism tend to be high on ethnocentrism and anti-Semitism. Reliability estimates, based on various PEC forms, are in the .70–.75 range (Adorno et al., 1950).

The final and most important step in instrumentation was the development of a Fascism (F) Scale. The F Scale was developed to provide ". . . a valid estimate of antidemocratic tendencies at the personality level" (Adorno et al., 1950). As such, the F Scale is conceived of as a measure of personality, not attitudes. This instrument is considered in some detail in the next section.

The data obtained from the A-S, E, PEC, and F scales were complemented by data from interviews, clinical histories, and projective testing across a variety of samples. The investigators concluded that the authoritarian individual's impression of himself is more favorable than the impressions that unprejudiced people have of themselves.

The authoritarian individual is proper and concerned with status and success, probably stemming from his parents' insecurities with status. This parental concern and anxiety results in strict training practices. This strictness leads in turn to a repression of faults and shortcomings. Aggressive impulses that cannot be expressed against parents are displaced to weaker minority group members. The faults and shortcomings that were repressed are projected onto the minority group members, thus providing rationalizations for aggressive behavior. As Wrightsman (1974) noted, after a hiatus in the 1960s, concern about authoritarianism is again on the rise.

The focus of this chapter is the investigations relating authoritarianism to cognitive style. Specifically, interest in two types of behavior reflecting cognitive style—rigidity and intolerance of ambiguity— emerged during the investigations. The Berkeley group's examination of interview material revealed authoritarian subjects to be more intolerant of ambiguity and more rigid than nonauthoritarian subjects. The intolerance was felt to be a generalization of the individual's intolerance of emotional ambivalence. A person who is intolerant of ambiguity is likely to make infrequent use of limiting and qualifying language. The concept of rigidity refers to thought and behavior that is exceptionally resistant to modification. Rigidity was evident when the authoritarian individual refused to relinquish ethnic stereotypes when faced with information contradicting the stereotype. Another characteristic of rigidity is that the individual's cognitions are compartmentalized and walled-off from each other, resulting in an apparent lack of consistency. For example, the authoritarian individual can simultaneously hold the beliefs that Jews are clannish and that Jews are intrusive.

The distinctions between intolerance of ambiguity and rigidity are not always maintained in *The Authoritarian Personality* and subsequent research. Occasionally these constructs are treated as equivalent and synonymous with the terms *concrete* and *stimulus bound*. Several studies illustrating the use of the two concepts appear in the section on research. A similar problem occurs in the distinction between authoritarianism and ethnocentrism, and research findings based on the F and E scales are often intermingled.

In the next section we examine the F Scale, the major instrument developed in the course of the investigations on the authoritarian personality.

MEASUREMENT

A variety of objective and clinical instruments were used throughout the research project that culminated in *The Authoritarian Personality.* Three of the objective instruments, the A-S, E, and PEC scales, were discussed briefly in the previous section. The most important instrument, the F Scale, is discussed in this section. Although this instrument is not a direct measure of cognitive style, the importance of the research relating the F Scale to rigidity and intolerance of ambiguity and the importance of the F Scale as a forerunner of other instruments warrant its inclusion in this book.

The Berkeley investigators believed that the attitudes measured by the A-S and E scales did not exist in isolation; rather, these attitudes were expressions of "deep-lying personality needs." This position reflects the authors' psychoanalytic orientation, as seen in the section on development. The most direct approach to assessment would have been the direct measurement of these personality needs. The authors believed they could accomplish such direct measurement using individually administered clinical instruments and interviews, but that this clinical approach was not suitable for the study of large groups. A measure of personality needs, suitable for use for groups, was required. Therefore, the authors devised an attitude-type instrument with the assumption that responses to the attitude items would correlate with underlying personality. Because this new scale was designed to reflect the personality characteristics of the prejudiced person, scores on it should correlate with scores on the A-S and E scales. The major advantage would be that such an instrument could measure prejudice without reference to minorities and current issues. Because the instrument would not mention minority groups, the usual social desirability constraints to appear nonprejudiced would be avoided and a presumably undistorted expression of personality dynamics would emerge.

The development of the F Scale, then, centered around interest in an instrument suitable for group administration that would measure prejudice without appearing to have this measurement as its aim. From their analysis of clinical and interview material and objective test data, the authors concluded that their subjects were expressing fears, anxieties, values, and impulses. To create a scale that would measure these psychological dispositions, a variety of items were devised. Many of these items were suggested by fascist writings, speeches of anti-Semitic agitators, and the persistent themes in the interview and TAT material from high-E subjects.

The original F Scale (Form 78) contained 38 items. The final version (Form 40/45) contained 30 items. Unlike many scales, which originate with a large pool of diverse items, a limited number of F-Scale items were written, each to measure a supposed dimension of prejudice derived from the authors' studies and beliefs. In reviewing *The Authoritarian Personality*, it is difficult to determine whether the delineation of all nine dimensions reflected by the F Scale preceded or followed the writing of specific items. The fact that many items are included in more than one of the nine dimensions suggests that the dimensions were, at least in part, developed after the items were written.

RELIABILITY

The authors of *The Authoritarian Personality* reported a mean split-half reliability for the F Scale of .90. As pointed out by Christie and Cook (1958), reliability coefficients for the F Scale were generally not reported in subsequent research. Where reliability estimates were reported, Christie and Cook found them to vary from one sample to another and to be lower than the initially reported .90. However, since abbreviated versions of the F Scale were used in many studies, lower reliabilities are to be expected on psychometric bases alone. For example, using a 10-item F Scale, Christie, Havel, and Seidenberg (1958) reported reliabilities ranging from .34 to .78 in various samples. However, applying a Spearman-Brown formula to estimate reliabilities for the full test, the reliability estimates would range from .70 to .94. Thus the original F Scale appears to have acceptable reliability.

Messick and Jackson (1956) raised the question, could the reliability of the F Scale be attributed to the presumed measurement of authoritarianism or to the response set of acquiescence? The role of the acquiescence response set in responses to the F Scale is discussed later.

VALIDITY

The major purpose of the F Scale was to provide a measure of anti-Semitism and ethnocentrism by assessing underlying personality traits.

The central question concerning the validity of the F Scale is the success with which it accomplishes this task. Adorno et al. (1950) reported correlations of about .75 between the E and F scales. They noted that the correlations between scores on the F Scale and generalized ethnocentrism items of the E Scale were higher than those between scores on the F Scale and anti-Semitism items of the E Scale. The authors of *The Authoritarian Personality* pointed out that the F Scale was not designed to correlate perfectly with the A-S and E scales, since the F Scale provides what is essentially a personality measure, whereas A-S and E provide what are essentially attitude measures. Therefore, the authors were quite satisfied that their measure was valid. In a later review, Christie (1954) found that, although the correlations among A-S-, E-, and F-Scale scores fluctuated from one sample to another, they were always positive. Later, for example, Rule and Hewitt (1970) reported significant correlations between a 28-item F Scale and a 10-item short form of the A-S scale for a sample of 91 male undergraduates ($r = .49$) and for a sample of 113 female undergraduates ($r = .36$). Brown (1965) and McCandless (1961) noted that correlations between the F Scale and A-S and E scales may be artificially high because all three scales have an acquiescence component, and acquiescence contributes to the shared variance.

The nine dimensions used to categorize items on Form 40/45 of the F Scale are conventionalism, authoritarian submission, authoritarian aggression, antiintraception, superstition and stereotypy, power and "toughness," destructiveness and cynicism, projectivity, and sex. However, as seen in the next section, factor analytic studies have failed to replicate these nine dimensions.

Conventionalism is measured by four items reflecting an individual's subscription to middle-class values. Authoritarian submission is measured by seven items that supposedly reflect submission to middle-class moral authority. However, inspection of the seven items reveals them to be quite diverse, with little face validity for the measurement of the construction of authoritarian submission. The longest scale, consisting of eight items, is authoritarian aggression. The content of the items consistently reflects the tendency to be hostile toward people who violate middle-class norms. The fourth scale, antiintraception, is comprised of four items reflecting toughmindedness. The superstition and stereotypy scale is composed of six items that probably have some relationship to belief in external control. The sixth scale, power and "toughness," consists of seven items that reflect behavioral tendencies toward power and dominance. The destructiveness and cynicism scale is made up of only three items that do not appear on any other scale. The authors require two phrases, "generalized hostility, vilification of the human," to describe this scale. The eighth scale is projectivity. The five items on this scale supposedly reflect the projection of unconscious impulses. The final scale, sex, consists of three diverse items with sexual content.

At face value, none of these dimensions directly reflects cognitive style. However, themes of rigidity and stereotype run through many of the dimensions. Consider item 19 from the power and "toughness" scale: "An insult to our honor should always be punished." Strong agreement with this item is an indication not only of the authoritarian power trait, but also of a rigid, inflexible cognitive style.

Since the F Scale was constructed to measure nine dimensions of personality dynamics that presumably underly prejudice, the question arises whether these dimensions are highly interrelated or relatively independent of each other. This issue of the dimensionality of the F Scale is not trivial. If the F Scale is unidimensional, the use of a total F score is justifiable. However, if the F Scale is comprised of a number of independent dimensions, the interpretation of a total score is difficult.

Melvin (1955), in a dissertation cited by Eysenck (1954), factor analyzed the original Adorno data and obtained a strong general factor, arguing against the existence of the nine distinct dimensions proposed in that work. Christie (1956a, b) suggested that Melvin's finding may have resulted from questionable methodology. Kerlinger and Rokeach (1966) felt that other studies (Christie & Garcia, 1951; O'Neil & Levinson, 1954; Prothro & Keehn, 1956) had methodological problems; similarly, Crutchfield (1954) criticized Hofstaetter's (1952) factor analysis of the F Scale on methodological grounds.

Bendig (1959, 1960) found several factors accounting for only a small proportion of the interitem variance among F-Scale items. In an analysis by Krug (1961), several of the originally posited dimensions were validated. A similar validation was made by Rubenowitz (1963) using a 25-item Swedish translation of the F Scale. He found 10 factors, four of which were similar to those originally posited. Kerlinger and

Rokeach (1966) also found evidence for the existence of a number of the original dimensions.

Based on the original nine clusters of items, Gough and Lazzari (1974) developed a 15-item version of the F Scale. In studies involving several hundred undergraduates, this short form was shown to correlate .95 with the 30-item F Scale and to have satisfactory reliability.

We agree with the Christie and Cook (1958) review indicating that the F Scale is indeed made up of a number of dimensions. The results of studies are not always in agreement about the precise dimensions of the F Scale. The empirical work, however, often provides evidence for the existence of some of the originally postulated dimensions.

Another issue in assessing the validity of the F Scale is the extent to which scores on the instrument relate to measures of political conservatism. A number of studies have indicated that individuals high in authoritarianism have a rightist political orientation (cf. Hanson, 1975a). For example, Thompson and Michel (1972) found authoritarianism related to political conservatism and Christian traditionalism. Wilson, Dennis, and Wadsworth (1976), in a study of 115 undergraduates, showed that F Scale-measured authoritarianism correlated more highly with right-wing political orientation (e.g., liking the U.S. military, disliking militant students) than with left-wing political orientation.

Milton (1952) showed that subjects who scored high on the F Scale preferred conservative president candidates. Leventhal, Jacobs, and Kudirka (1964) showed, on the basis of abbreviated F scales, that high-authoritarian undergraduates preferred conservative over liberal candidates; the reverse was true for low-authoritarian undergraduates. Higgins (1965), as well as Kerpelman (1968), found that high authoritarian students favored the conservative candidate (Goldwater) over the liberal candidate (Johnson) in the 1964 presidential election. Higgins and Kuhlman (1967) reported similar results with regard to a gubernatorial election in California (Reagan vs. Brown). Luck and Gruner (1970) obtained similar results with regard to undergraduates' preferred candidates in the 1972 presidential election, as did Schwendiman, Larsen, and Cope (1970) with regard to the 1968 presidential election. Hanson and White (1973), in a study of 34 undergraduates, found that the 15 Nixon supporters had significantly higher scores on the F Scale than the 19 McGovern supporters. A similar finding was reported by Shikiar

(1975). In a departure from these results, Zippel and Norman (1966) found no differences in F-Scale scores between Johnson and Goldwater supporters.

In a related context, Chapko and Lewis (1975) presented an eight-item F Scale to a sample of 367 adults in Portland, Maine. Mailed responses were received from 233 individuals. Subjects low in authoritarianism were found to like the television character Archie Bunker (a character expressing authoritarian, conservative attitudes) less, and disagree with him more, than subjects of moderate and high levels of authoritarianism. Young, Beier, Beier, and Barton (1975) showed that undergraduate males expressing anti-Women's Liberation attitudes had significantly higher F-Scale scores than did undergraduates whose attitudes were pro-Women's Liberation.

With regard to predictive validity in general, Christie and Cook (1958), reviewing the initial flood of studies that followed the publication of *The Authoritarian Personality*, concluded that the data generally supported the expected relationships between F-Scale scores and other measures, especially when the hypotheses were properly derived from the original document. However, on the basis of the failure of high scorers on the F Scale to be perceived by their peers as authoritarian, Titus (1968) questioned the validity of the instrument.

The F Scale was designed to measure the underlying personality of the individual. However, some investigators have shown that F relates to intelligence, education, and socioeconomic status (e.g., Christie, 1952; Christie, Havel, & Seidenberg, 1958; Eysenck & Coulter, 1972; Frenkel-Brunswik, 1954; Jacobson & Rettig, 1959; Kornhauser, Sheppard, & Mayer, 1956; MacKinnon & Centers, 1956; Thompson & Michel, 1972; Vannoy, 1965). Marlowe and Gergen (1969) believe that, in light of these findings, F-Scale scores may reflect sociocultural norms rather than underlying personality dimensions.

Other investigators have criticized the F Scale along similar lines. Hollander (1954) maintains that high F-Scale scorers may lack social intelligence or social perception. Kelman and Barclay (1963) believe that the F Scale is a measure of the extent to which an individual has wide or limited experiences and that high scorers on the F Scale are relatively unsophisticated. Stagner (1965) noted that the negative correlations between scores on the F Scale and on measures of intelligence that are reported in the literature may occur not because individuals scoring low on the F Scale are nonauthoritarian, but because they see through the cliches that comprise the F Scale. Messick and Jackson (1956) questioned whether the F Scale is subject to social desirability bias.

Because of its correlations with intelligence, education, and socio-economic status, it has been argued that the F Scale is defective as a measure of personality. It seems to us that this type of distinction reifies the concept of personality and implies that personality is something other than what is influenced by the sociocultural environment. Our point of view is that the F Scale reveals differences across social classes because it reflects the differences in norms across the classes and in characteristic modes of behavior. These differences are personality differences. We feel that personality cannot be understood except as a relatively enduring set of behaviors developed and maintained by a wide variety of genetic and sociocultural influences.

Acquiescence Response Set.   The wording of each item of the F Scale is such that agreement with the item contributes to a higher authoritarianism score. This confounds the subject's tendency to respond to the content of the items with his tendency to respond in an acquiescent, or agreeing manner, regardless of content. That is, a high score on the F Scale might represent an authoritarian personality style, a tendency to agree with items regardless of their content, or some combination of personality and response style. This problem also occurs with the A-S and E scales, but not with the PEC Scale.

Cohn (1953, 1956) was the first investigator to call attention to the problem of the acquiescence response set with the F Scale. He suggested that the F Scale measures authoritarianism by virtue of acquiescence rather than content. He found a significant correlation of .41 between scores on the F Scale and scores on an MMPI-derived measure of acquiescence for a sample of 59 undergraduates. The problem of acquiescence was subsequently reviewed by a number of investigators, including Campbell, Siegman, and Rees (1967), Chapman and Campbell (1957), Couch and Keniston (1960), Gage, Leavitt, and Stone (1957), Jackson and Messick (1957, 1958), Jackson, Messick, and Solley (1957), Messick and Jackson (1956), Peabody (1961, 1966), Rokeach (1963), Rorer (1965), Shelley (1956), and Zuckerman, Norton, and Sprague (1958).

Bass (1955) compared responses to the original and a reversed-item form of the F Scale. He argued that if individuals were responding solely on the basis of content, one would expect high correlations between the original and the reversed forms. Bass obtained a correlation of −.20, indicating that response style contributed substantially to F-Scale scores. Bass performed a factor analysis on the correlations between items from the F Scale and his reversed F Scale. He found that a large portion of the F-Scale variance was attributable to a factor he labeled acquiescence. This conclusion was supported by Chapman and Bock (1958), who found that content accounted for 30–40% of reliable F-Scale variance and that the remainder of the variance was due to acquiescence and acquiescence-content covariation. Zuckerman, Norton, and Sprague (1958) concluded that acquiescence contributed about half of the variance of authoritarianism scores.

Couch and Keniston (1960), on the other hand, offered evidence that only about 14% of the variance of the F-Scale scores could be attributed to acquiescence. Clayton and Jackson (1961) also found little relationship between authoritarian attitudes and acquiescence. Brown and Datta (1959) concluded that acquiescence is relatively unimportant. Chapman and Campbell (1959) found evidence of an acquiescence bias, although the F Scale appeared to them to retain its validity.

Christie, Havel, and Seidenberg (1958) criticized studies using reversed items as a method for assessing the effects of acquiescence on the measurement of authoritarianism. One problem is that the grammatical reversal of an item does not imply psychological reversal. Another is that undergraduates, given the psychological demand characteristics of an experiment, may be more prone to acquiesce than other populations. Related to this point is the finding that the F Scale is subject to faking by college students (Cohn, 1952; Sundberg & Bachelis, 1956) and naval cadets (Hollander, 1954). Christie et al. (1958) also maintained that reversed items were often worded in the extreme. In this connection, Clayton and Jackson (1961), comparing an F Scale with absolute wording to one with probabilistic wording, found that acquiescence was more strongly and consistently evoked by the items with absolute wording. Christie and his associates conducted several studies and concluded that the identification of authoritarianism with acquiescence is not supported by the data. They developed a 30-item reversed form of the F Scale that they believe avoids the usual problems of reversed F Scales. In a factor analytic study, however, Klein (1965) found the Christie scale not to be a valid control for acquiescence for college students.

Rokeach (1963) hypothesized that subjects could agree to an item and its reversal because they were lying, they did not perceive the contradiction, or they were acquiescing. Samelson and Yates (1967) made the point that acquiescence on reversed-item forms of the F Scale may be produced not by the acquiescence response set, but because the original item and its reversal are not, in fact, contradictory. This contention has been challenged by Bernhardson (1971). Miklich (1970) tested the idea that the response set on the F Scale is related to item ambiguity. Although the author's data were not relevant to this issue, it is noteworthy that he computed 56,400 t tests in the process!

Other approaches to the study of the acquiescence response set and the F Scale have been taken. Campbell, Siegman, and Rees (1967) constructed positively worded and negatively worded versions of the Taylor Manifest Anxiety Scale (Taylor, 1953) that correlated .98 with each other. If F-Scale scores were not contaminated by acquiescence, they would correlate equally well with both forms of the Taylor MAS. However, Campbell, Siegman, and Rees found a significantly higher correlation (.41) between scores on the F Scale and on the positively worded version of the MAS, compared to the correlation of .27 between F and the negatively worded MAS. These results suggest that acquiescence does play a part in F-Scale scores. Webster (1956) corrected F-Scale scores for acquiescence by using an independent measure of acquiescence. As Zuckerman, Norton, and Sprague (1958) suggested, separate measures of authoritarianism and acquiescence might lead to the useful differentiation of authoritarian leaders (high authoritarianism, low acquiescence) from authoritarian followers (high authoritarianism, high acquiescence).

Berkowitz and Wolkon (1964) developed a 25-item forced-choice F Scale. Each item consisted of an originally worded F-Scale item and a reversal, either from Bass (1955) or from Christie, Havel, and Seidenberg (1958). The respondent is required to indicate the extent of his agreement with either the positively or negatively worded statement. Scores from the Berkowitz and Wolkon forced-choice instrument correlate well (.69–.83) with the original F Scale. This study confirms the results of other investigations; that is, although the F Scale confounds content and the acquiescence response set, the bias caused by acquiescence does not seriously affect the validity of the instrument, since acquiescence and authoritarianism are positively correlated. The authors recommend an abbreviated, 12-item version of their forced-choice instrument that correlates .77 with the original F Scale and may be useful to investigators requiring a shorter instrument free of the acquiescence response set. Leavitt, Hax, and Roche (1955) reversed half the items of the F Scale. Based on the scores of their subjects on the originally worded items, they found acquiescence associated with high F scores, but not with low F scores. Thus, to the extent that acquiescence was confounding authoritarianism, it was confounding it in the right direction.

Based on our review of the many studies concerning acquiescence and the F Scale, two conclusions emerge. One is that the relationship between F-Scale scores and acquiescence has not been demonstrated in studies using reversed items. This conclusion is justified by arguments that the relationships between the F Scale and reversed F may be attributable to the absence of logical contradiction among items. Agreement to both an F-Scale item and its supposed reversal may therefore be due to the content of the items, and not to an acquiescence set. The second conclusion is that some small portion of the F-Scale score variance is due to acquiescence (cf. Zuckerman and Eisen, 1962). However, individuals who acquiesce are also likely to be authoritarian; thus the response set may not adversely bias the instrument (Messick and Frederiksen, 1958). Neither of these two conclusions invalidates the use of the F Scale.

OTHER VERSIONS OF THE F SCALE

In addition to the modifications of the F Scale discussed above, other attempts have been made to balance the F Scale (e.g., Athanasiou, 1968; Kohn, 1972; Ray, 1972a). Lee and Warr (1969) reported the development of a 30-item balanced F Scale with satisfactory psychometric properties. However, the items for the new scale were developed independently of the original F Scale; thus the relationship between the two scales is unclear.

In the next section, the Children's Antidemocratic Scale (Gough,

Harris, Martin, & Edwards, 1950), a measure of children's authoritarianism is introduced. Adelson (1953) presented a measure of authoritarianism intended for use with Jewish students. Webster, Sanford, and Freedman (1955) used a 123-item test that parallels the F Scale, but is more personality and less ideology oriented. Cohn and Carsch (1954) translated the F Scale into German, Melikian (1956) translated some items into Arabic, Rubenowitz (1963) used a Swedish version, Bhusan (1971) used a Hindi version, Perry and Cunningham (1975) developed a Hebrew version, Gough and Lazzari (1974) developed a short form in Italian, and Niyekawa (1960) used a Japanese translation of Christie's reversed form. A review of a number of instruments designed to measure authoritarianism is contained in Robinson and Shaver (1973).

DEVELOPMENT

Because of the importance of a developmental perspective for psychoanalytic theory, it is not surprising that the authors of *The Authoritarian Personality* were interested in how authoritarianism developed in the family setting. Their conclusions were based on material from interviews conducted with 80 high and low scorers on the A-S and E scales and from the data of studies of 120 extremely prejudiced and unprejudiced 11–16-year-olds and their parents conducted by Frenkel-Brunswik (1948, 1951). The picture that emerged of the childhood of the subjects studied was as follows:

The parents of the authoritarian/ethnocentric subjects were concerned with achieving conventional goals. Many were socially and economically marginal, anxious about their positions in the social structure, and defined goodness in terms of that which helps one climb the social ladder. To achieve their conventional goals, these anxious parents resorted to harsh, threatening, and rigid child-rearing procedures. This parental discipline was viewed by the children as arbitrarily imposed, the parents being, in Frenkel-Brunswik's (1948) words, "capricious arbiters of punishment." The family atmosphere was one of dominance by the parents and submission by the children. The children submitted fearfully to the parental demands and were required to suppress "unacceptable" impulses, especially those connected with sex and aggression. The child reacts to these practices with feelings of hostility toward the parents. Since this hostility cannot be expressed directly, two things happen. One is a "rigid glorification and idealization of the parents." The other is a displacement of the repressed hostility onto minority group members, who are perceived as weaker than the parents.

These dynamics are similar to those involved in a frustration–aggression paradigm of prejudice. One presentation of this hypothesis, as summarized by Himelhock (1947), is that the child is frustrated by parents and others against whom he cannot aggress. To maintain "psychic eqilibrium," he displaces his aggression onto culturally sanctioned scapegoats. At the same time his own aggression is projected onto the scapegoat groups, and it becomes those groups that hate him and his group.

A number of studies of the development of authoritarianism are presented below. To ease interpretation of the results of these studies, they may be grouped into five categories.

AUTHORITARIANISM AND CHILDREN'S PERCEPTIONS OF CHILD-REARING PATTERNS OF PARENTS

Lyle and Levitt (1955), studying two groups of fifth-grade children (*N*s of 58 and 157), administered an incomplete sentences test to provide a measure of the child's perception of parental punitiveness and the Children's Antidemocratic Scale (Gough, Harris, Martin, & Edwards, 1950), designed to be similar to the F Scale. The data from both groups indicated that authoritarianism in the children was associated with perceptions of parental punitiveness (correlation coefficients of .28 and .32 for the two samples, respectively). In a study involving seventy 13–18-year-old delinquent girls, Mosher and Mosher (1965) examined the relationship between authoritarianism and perceptions of the child-rearing attitudes of the mothers. Using items from the original F Scale and the scale by Gough et al. (1950) cited previously, and measuring child-rearing attitudes with Shoben's (1949) Parent Attitude Survey and the Parent Questionnaire by Harris, Gough, and Martin (1950), they obtained a significant correlation of .30 between the daughters' authoritarianism and the daughters' perceptions of their mothers' authoritarian child-rearing attitudes.

Thus the results of the two studies are in agreement and indicate a small, positive relationship between authoritarianism and perceptions of controlling child-rearing attitudes of parents.

AUTHORITARIANISM AND PARENT CHILD-REARING ATTITUDES

In the Mosher and Mosher (1965) study, a nonsignificant correlation was obtained between a measure of daughters' authoritarianism and mothers' authoritarian child-rearing attitudes. Byrne (1965) studied 108 college students and their mothers and fathers. His measure of authoritarianism consisted of 32 items, 27 of which were selected from versions of the F Scale and 5 of which were reversed items from Christie, Havel, and Seidenberg (1958). Byrne's measure of child-rearing attitudes was a 35-item Traditional Family Ideology (TFI) scale (Levinson & Huffman, 1955). The TFI, developed in part by one of the authors of *The Authoritarian Personality,* is designed to measure the family orientation believed conducive to the development of authoritarianism (e.g., moralistic rejection of impulse life, extreme emphasis on discipline, and conventionalism). Byrne analyzed his data separately by sex of offspring and sex of parent. His only significant finding was a correlation of .33 between the authoritarianism of sons and the authoritarian family ideology of fathers.

These studies, using direct measures of parental attitudes, provide only marginal evidence of a relationship between authoritarianism and parental child-rearing attitudes.

INTRAINDIVIDUAL AUTHORITARIANISM AND CHILD-REARING ATTITUDES

In the first section, studies summarizing the relationship between the offspring's authoritarianism and his *perception* of parental child rearing were presented. In the next section, *direct* measures of parental child-rearing attitudes were related to authoritarianism in the offspring. In this section we are concerned with studies that measure authoritarianism and child-rearing attitudes directly in the same subject.

As part of a study of 100 military officers, Block (1955) administered a 20-item inventory designed to measure the restrictive–permissive dimension of child-rearing attitudes. The 20 highest scoring and 20 lowest scoring fathers were contrasted on the F and E scales. The restrictive group scored significantly higher on both measures. Hart (1957) interviewed 126 mothers whose children were between $2^1/2$ and $5^1/2$ years old. The interview schedule contained 38 items of children's behavior, each of which called for a controlling response on the part of the parent. The mothers' responses to each item were coded for (1) love orientation, (2) nonlove orientation, or (3) ambiguous orientation, according to a system of classification developed by Whiting and Child (1953). Hart found that authoritarian mothers made more nonlove-oriented responses and fewer love-oriented responses than nonauthoritarian mothers. Mothers in the midrange of authoritarianism were in the midrange of love-oriented and nonlove-oriented responses, indicating a monotonic relationship. Although some areas of child behavior tended to elicit more love-oriented responses than other areas, there was no interaction between authoritarianism and type of behavior.

Mosher and Scodel (1960) related the ethnocentrism of parents of 161 sixth and seventh graders to a version of the Harris, Gough, and Martin (1950) Parent Questionnaire designed to measure parental authoritarian child-rearing attitudes. They obtained a significant correlation of .48 between the two variables. Mosher and Mosher (1965) found a significant correlation of .58 between measures of mothers' authoritarianism and their authoritarian child-rearing attitudes. Byrne (1965) reported significant correlations between F-Scale scores and TFI scores for mothers (.61) and fathers (.61).

In their study of two groups of fifth graders cited earlier, Lyle and Levitt (1955) obtained significant correlations of .50 and .28 between a measure of antidemocratic tendency in children and the child's tendency to choose the punitive alternative in a test involving responses to various situations. Kates and Diab (1955) administered the F Scale and Shoben's (1949) Parent Attitude Survey to 172 undergraduates. For males, authoritarianism was significantly related (.29) to the ignoring scale of the Parent Attitude Survey, and ethnocentrism was significantly related (.29) to total score. For females, authoritarianism was significantly related to the scales of dominance (.34), possessiveness (.28), and total score (.34); ethnocentrism was also correlated with dominance (.30), possessiveness (.28), and total score (.30).

Levinson and Huffman (1955), using a 40-item version of the TFI, found a significant correlation of .65 with the E Scale and .73 with the F Scale for a sample of 109 evening psychology students. Using a 12-item form of the TFI, Levinson and Huffman obtained similar correlations with similar samples. Zuckerman and Oltean (1959) studied the relationship between F-Scale scores and scores on the authoritarian-control, hostility-rejection, and democratic attitude factors of the Parent Attitude Research Inventory (PARI) (Schaefer & Bell, 1958). Statistically significant correlations were obtained between F-Scale scores and authoritarian-control scores for a sample of 32 female psychiatric patients (.51) and 88 unmarried student nurses (.61). The correlations between F-Scale scores and the two remaining PARI factors were not statistically significant. When the relationship between the authoritarian-control factor and F-Scale scores was calculated with acquiescence partialed out, the correlation of .61 in the nurses group was reduced, but remained a significant .44 (Zuckerman, Norton, & Sprague, 1958). Byrne (1965), in the study cited above, found a significant correlation of .62 between F-Scale and TFI scores for his sample of college students.

In the single study with negative results that we have located, Gallagher (1957) found no relationship between F-Scale scores and scores on a 21-item Children's Attitude Scale designed to measure attitudes of harshness toward children. The subjects of the study were 59 students in child psychology courses at Michigan State College.

Thus the preponderance of evidence indicates a moderate relationship between authoritarianism and controlling and cold child-rearing attitudes for a variety of samples.

AUTHORITARIANISM IN THE PARENT AND OFFSPRING

Cooper and Blair (1959) found that undergraduates perceived themselves as similar to their mothers and fathers in authoritarianism when the parents were positively evaluated. In this study a 150-item Parent Evaluation scale and Gough's (1951) 30-item authoritarianism scale were administered to 179 undergraduates. These findings were replicated with high school students in a study by Cooper and Lewis (1962).

In their study of 161 sixth and seventh graders and the children's mothers, Mosher and Scodel (1960) found a significant correlation of .32 between the prejudice of the children, measured by a social distance scale, and their mothers' E-Scale scores. Williams and Williams (1963) found a significant correlation of .28 between the F-Scale scores of sons and their mothers and a significant correlation of .24 for daughters and their fathers. In this study the investigators began with a sample of 614 undergraduates, but obtained only a 44% return from mailed questionnaires to parents. Overall, the students were significantly less authoritarian than their parents. Mosher and Mosher (1965) obtained a significant correlation of .25 between the authoritarian attitudes of daughters and their mothers. They obtained a statistically significant correlation of .61 between daughters' authoritarian attitudes and the daughters' *perceptions* of their mothers' authoritarian attitudes. Byrne (1965) found significant correlations between the F-Scale scores of sons and their mothers (.30) and fathers (.38) and between the scores of daughters' and their mothers (.32). Byrne reported other data indicating that low authoritarianism in the offspring is likely to occur when at least one person is low in authoritarianism, regardless of the sex of that parent.

The results of these studies indicate that authoritarianism of children shows a low, positive correlation with that of their parents. Several of the investigators sought to determine whether similarities were greater for like-sex than for opposite-sex parents and their children. The findings in this regard have been inconsistent.

OTHER FACTORS CONTRIBUTING TO AUTHORITARIANISM

A number of influences outside the family contribute to the development and maintenance of authoritarianism. Although this aspect of the development of authoritarianism has not been studied as extensively as child rearing styles, a number of factors have been isolated. For example, Levitt (1955) showed that children's authoritarianism can be influenced by teachers. Greenberg, Guerino, Lashen, Mayer, and Piskowski (1963) classified 264 undergraduates in terms of ordinal position in the family. He found no significant differences in authoritarianism among groups categorized along this dimension. Plant (1965a) showed significant decreases in authoritarianism over a four-year period among groups of college-aspiring and college-attending youths. Webster (1956) showed that college seniors had significantly lower scores on the F Scale than college freshmen in both cross-sectional and longitudinal studies. A report by Greenberg and Fare (1959) supported the latter conclusions. College seniors were less authoritarian than freshmen, and college students were less authoritarian than high school students. On the other hand, in a study of 379 undergraduate sociology students, Thompson and Michel (1972) failed to find significant differences in authoritarianism among undergraduates differing in year of college.

Some investigators have argued that authoritarian child-rearing styles are conducive to the establishment of authoritarian governments that, in turn, help perpetuate an authoritarian nationalistic style (cf. Erikson, 1942; Fromm, 1936, 1941; Reich, 1945). Brown (1965) noted that authoritarianism is characteristic of low-socioeconomic, less-educated individuals. For example, Stewart and Hoult (1959) postulated that authoritarianism is negatively correlated with the number of social roles an individual is able to play. They reviewed a number of studies showing that high authoritarianism is found among the less educated, older people, rural residents, the disadvantaged, members of more dogmatic religious organizations, members of lower socioeconomic groups, and social isolates, as well as among people reared in authoritarian families. In each case, the potential for mastering a variety of roles is limited. Stewart and Hoult postulated that individuals with limited role experience cannot take the roles of others outside their reference group, that they cannot understand or sympathize with such outsiders, and that they feel hostile toward, and reject, members of such outgroups.

In a similar vein, Christie and Garcia (1951) found regional differences among undergraduates in E- and F-Scale scores. The authors hypothesized that the differences were due to the exposure of members of the more highly prejudiced group to ". . . an environment characterized by a narrower range of expressed ideology which was fairly conservative in nature." The authors expressed doubt as to whether the obtained differences could be due to differences in child-rearing practices. Greenberg and Fare (1959), summarizing data on almost 3500 subjects, also noted regional differences in authoritarianism; easterners were less authoritarian than southwesterners. Although the authors also believe that exposure to authoritarian environments is a causal factor, they add that authoritarian family structure may contribute to differences in authoritarianism.

Kelman and Barclay (1963), in an analysis of the F-Scale scores of 282 Negro college freshmen, found females to be more authoritarian than males, younger students to be more authoritarian than older students, and Southerners to be more authoritarian than subjects from border states. There were no statistically significant differences based on a breakdown by father's occupation. In the previously cited report, Greenberg and Fare (1959) found Blacks to be more authoritarian than Whites; across all subjects, there were no sex differences. Zippel and Norman (1966) also failed to obtain sex differences in authoritarianism.

These studies indicate that a complete picture of the development of authoritarianism must take into account other factors in addition to parent-child interaction.

RESEARCH

Adorno et al. were interested in studying the relationship between personality, antidemocratic attitudes, and behavior. In the course of their work, they found evidence that high authoritarians were rigid and intolerant of ambiguity. The studies reviewed in this section focus on the relationship between authoritarianism and these two variables. Many investigators have been interested in other correlates of authoritarianism, and many studies have been done on rigidity and intolerance of ambiguity. However, we are concerned with studies relating authoritarianism to measures reflecting cognitive style. In succeeding chapters, the focus is cognitive style itself. For the authors of *The Authoritarian Personality,* interest in cognitive style was tangential to the main thrust of the work, and the F Scale must not be considered a measure of cognitive style (Scott, 1963).

The central thesis of *The Authoritarian Personality* is that the expression of social attitudes is a function of underlying personality needs. These needs are reflected not only in social attitudes but also in perceptual, cognitive, and behavioral styles. Two of the coding categories used to score the interviews with high- and low-ethnocentric subjects were rigidity versus flexibility and intolerance versus tolerance of ambiguity. The scoring of the interview protocols resulted in significantly more ratings of rigidity and intolerance of ambiguity for high-ethnocentric individuals. It was also found that tolerant individuals made use of limiting and qualifying language forms, whereas intolerant subjects used more absolute language.

ANTECEDENTS OF RIGIDITY AND INTOLERANCE OF AMBIGUITY

Frenkel-Brunswik (1948) considered intolerance of ambiguity a generalization of the intolerance of emotional ambivalence of the prejudiced person, and that intolerance of ambiguity is motivated by status anxiety and the ban on aggression toward authority. She noted that some children tolerated emotional ambivalence better than others (Frenkel-Brunswik, 1949). This led to the question of whether this intolerance extended beyond the social and emotional areas to perceptual and cognitive aspects of functioning. She felt that the existence of such emotional ambivalence and the individual's ability to face such ambivalence was an important personality variable.

The child learns to reduce conflict and anxiety by keeping some experiences out of awareness. Once attitudes are developed, they are rigidly maintained regardless of new evidence. Frenkel-Brunswik (1949) also reported that discipline in the homes producing authoritarian children is often based on the expectation that the child quickly learn externally provided, rigid rules. Whether the diffuse, concrete behavior of the young child, fostered by this training regimen, progresses to higher developmental stages depends on the atmosphere of the home.

An excellent restatement of this orientation was made by McCandless (1961). According to McCandless, when toilet training is too severe or initiated too early, the preverbal child learns to be continent *and* to dread situations that are unclear or ambiguous. The rewards and punishments surrounding the training present contingencies about which the child is unclear, and he comes to expect unknown and possibly unpleasant things to happen when he is in unclear situations. The child becomes intolerant of anxiety and, to reduce this anxiety, he attempts to force things into rigid molds and clear classifications. McCandless cited the Sears, Maccoby, and Levin (1957) study showing several child-rearing variables to be associated with severe toilet-training practices. He noted that these practices, which he likened to rearing for a police state, reduce the need for conscience, or inner controls, because of the presence of external controlling forces. Under these conditions of rearing, children learn to fear insecurity and unclarity and to be rigid.

DISTINCTION BETWEEN RIGIDITY AND INTOLERANCE OF AMBIGUITY

The distinction between rigidity and intolerance of ambiguity was not carefully maintained in either the original Berkeley investigations or in much of the subsequent research. Indeed, the two terms have sometimes been used interchangeably. In the analysis of the interview material itself, the two categories were probably not coded independently. Frenkel-Brunswik reported in *The Authoritarian Personality* that "most subjects received the same ratings on the two variables." Brown (1965) suspected that the two categories may have been coded whenever protocols revealed more obvious signs of authoritarianism.

Some evidence of the looseness with which the two terms are used is found in Frenkel-Brunswik's (1949) paper on intolerance of ambiguity. At one point, writing about attempts to control aggression toward too powerful parents, she noted ". . . the tendency rigidly to avoid ambiguity of any sort" (p. 117). She commented on the multitude of definitions of rigidity and wrote that ". . . the term 'rigid' refers in this paper to the various kinds of intolerance of ambiguity discussed" (p. 117). This imprecision is also found among later researchers: "Rigidity is defined in this study as the relative inability to shift set or tolerate ambiguity . . ." (Blum, 1959). French (1955), describing her version of a dog-to-cat test, referred to it as a "measure of intolerance for ambiguity" and, later in the same paragraph, wrote that ". . . a high score indicates rigidity." Jones (1955) wrote that "In a . . . more perceptual sense, rigidity may mean intolerance of ambiguity."

Although studies on rigidity and intolerance of ambiguity differ in their definitions of the concepts, central themes can be identified for each. Rigidity is best defined as a continuation of former behavior patterns when a change in the situation requires a change in behavior for more efficient functioning. Intolerance of ambiguity is best defined as the unwarranted imposition of structure when the situation is unstructured. In the next section we review studies on the relationship between authoritarianism and rigidity. In a later section we review studies on the relationship between authoritarianism and intolerance of ambiguity. In presenting this material we do not attempt to maintain a distinction between authoritarianism and ethnocentrism since this distinction was not maintained by the early researchers.

RIGIDITY

One of the most frequently cited studies on rigidity and ethnocentrism was that undertaken by Rokeach (1948). He presented subjects with a modification of a task used earlier by Luchins (1942). Luchin's *Einstellung* problem requires the subject to determine how to measure out a specific quantity of water. Consider the following problem. Three jugs with capacities of (A) 31 quarts, (B) 61 quarts, and (C) 4 quarts, are available, as is an unlimited supply of water. The task is to measure precisely 22 quarts of water. The solution to the problem is to fill the 61-quart jug, pour off 31 quarts, and pour off 4 quarts twice. This solution is of the form B-A-C-C. After some preliminary examples, Rokeach's subjects were presented with two "set" problems that could be solved only with this B-A-C-C formula. The next five problems, called "critical" problems, could be solved using the indirect B-A-C-C formula, or they could be solved more directly. The first critical problem presented jugs of 23, 49, and 3 quarts. The problem was to measure off precisely 20 quarts. Although the B-A-C-C formula works, the problem may be solved more directly by A-C. Subjects who persevered in the original, indirect solution were considered rigid.

In one of Rokeach's studies, 70 college sophomores were divided at the median on the basis of 10 E-Scale items. Rokeach compared the total number of rigid solutions by members of the two groups and found high-ethnocentric subjects to be more rigid. He reported similar results in four earlier studies involving college students. In another experiment, with seventh- and eighth-grade children, Rokeach used a 50-item scale to measure ethnocentrism and increased the number of

Einstellung problems. He found that 118 of his 193 children had to be eliminated from the study for such reasons as not understanding the instructions or inability to do the required arithmetic. The remaining 75 subjects were divided into high- and low-ethnocentric groups. For all 10 of the critical problems in the series, the high-ethnocentric group gave a greater proportion of rigid solutions than did the low-ethnocentric subjects. For four of the problems the difference was statistically significant.

Frenkel-Brunswik (1949) reported that the Einstellung rigidity scores obtained by the children in the Rokeach study "tend to correlate" with rigidity scores obtained from her clinical interview study of attitudes toward parents, sex roles, and moral issues. Einstellung rigidity was also correlated with scores on a personality inventory designed to measure "dichotomizing" in social-emotional attitudes.

Shortly after the publication of Rokeach's study, the findings were attacked by Luchins (1949) and defended by Rokeach (1949). Luchins began his attack by questioning the reliability and validity of the E Scale and California Attitude Scale I for children. Rokeach responded by citing satisfactory reliability coefficients for both scales and stating that his data provided validity for the measures. Since Rokeach divided his subjects into high- and low-ethnocentric groups on the basis of the scores falling above or below the median, Luchins argued that there was no way of knowing whether the two groups were high and low in ethnocentrism in a normative (vs. ipsative) sense; Rokeach did not answer this criticism. In another argument to which Rokeach failed to respond, Luchins criticized Rokeach's discussion of the average ethnocentric or nonethnocentric person, since such an average may not be representative of any real person.

Rokeach hypothesized that individuals who were rigid in solving social problems would also be rigid in solving nonsocial problems. This implied that the E Scale is a measure of social rigidity, an implication that Luchins challenged. Rokeach's answer was that his phrase, "The rigidity inherent in ethnocentric person's solution of social problems . . ." is an experientially derived premise. Thus Rokeach's response was not directed at the criticism of the E Scale as a measure of social rigidity.

Luchins next argued that Einstellung is not a nonsocial situation, since social factors, for example, emotional attitudes toward arithmetic (cf. Luchins, 1951), influence performance on the task. In response, Rokeach ventured that ". . . purely 'nonsocial' problems do not exist." He wrote that the Einstellung task is as nearly nonsocial as can be found.

One of Luchins' most serious criticisms was that, since the A-C solution may not be more efficient than the indirect solution, the task does not satisfy Rokeach's definition of rigidity. Rokeach's answer was that the conditions of the experiment *demanded* that the subject change his set. As one example of this, he pointed out that if the indirect solution were as efficient as the simpler, direct solution, the subjects who used the indirect solution in response to the first critical problem should continue to use it. However, his data indicated progressive decreases in the frequency of indirect solutions on later problems.

Luchins also pointed out that the magnitude of the differences, although statistically significant at times, was small, and that some ethnocentric subjects performed like the nonethnocentric subjects and vice versa. Rokeach's response was that the results were based on data from a large number of subjects and that a statistically significant result is a significant result.

As a final criticism of the water jug study, Luchins pointed out that, based on the results of one investigation, Rokeach hypothesized the existence of a general rigidity factor that would manifest itself in any social or nonsocial problem. Luchins' argument was that rigidity is not a personality factor, but a function of situational conditions. Rokeach wrote that he cited eight studies indicating the generality of a behavioral rigidity factor, and, in fact, Luchins had also written about rigidity as a personality structure.

In an attempt to replicate Rokeach's findings, Brown (1953) failed to obtain a significant relationship between ethnocentrism and Einstellung rigidity among hundreds of undergraduates enrolled in a laboratory course at the University of Michigan. Brown felt that Rokeach's experimental situation was more stressful than the experimental environment at the University of Michigan. Rokeach had presented the Einstellung problem as an arithmetic test in a formal lecture situation. At the University of Michigan, the experiments were performed in small laboratory sections, where the experiments were young and the atmosphere relaxed. Based on these differences, Brown hypothesized that the relationship of ethnocentrism and rigidity was dependent on the atmosphere in which the tasks were carried out. Specifically, he hypothesized that ethnocentric subjects would manifest rigidity under "ego-involving" instructions. The issue raised here regarding the effects on behavior of the interaction between the person and environment was more fully explored in the work on integrative complexity, which is considered in a later chapter.

To test his hypothesis, Brown administered Einstellung problems and the F Scale to 162 freshmen drawn at random from a second-semester English course. For one group of 82 subjects Brown was aloof, serious, and formal during the administration of the tests. For the second group Brown dressed informally and related to the subjects in a casual, relaxed manner. For the second group, the correlation between F and Einstellung scores was .00. For the first group, the correlation of .40 was statistically significant. Thus authoritarian and nonauthoritarian subjects perform similarly under relaxed conditions. When threatened, the subjects with high scores on the F Scale performed more rigidly than the subjects scoring low on the F Scale. Brown concluded that the authoritarian's rigidity is a defensive mechanism to ward off failure.

In a similar vein, Applezweig (1954) studied the effects of real-life stress on the relationships between ethnocentrism and a variety of measures of rigidity, including a set of Einstellung problems. Her subjects were 79 candidates for submarine school. In the stress situation, the candidate was required to withstand 50 pounds of atmospheric pressure and, if successful, to escape from a tank of water 100 feet deep. One group of subjects was tested the day before this task, a second the day after the task, and a third a week after the task. Correlations between subjects' scores on the E Scale and the Einstellung rigidity test did not support Rokeach's findings. The correlations between the two measures were not statistically significant for the groups tested the day before and the week after the stress situation. For the group tested the day after the stress situation, a statistically significant correlation of −.34 indicated that high Es were less rigid. This finding is the opposite of what Rokeach found. However, the two testing situations were different.

When the subjects in each of the three groups were divided at the median into high- and low-ethnocentric groups, the group tested the day before the stress situation yielded results similar to those of Rokeach. That is, high-ethnocentric subjects produced more rigid responses than low-ethnocentric subjects. The finding that rigidity and ethnocentrism are related in a stress situation corroborates Brown's findings. There was no significant difference between high and low Es in the week-after group. In the day-after group, however, high Es produced significantly fewer rigid responses. This finding is similar to that found in the correlational analysis and is again the reverse of what Rokeach found. Although one may spin elaborate webs to account for these various findings, it is clear that the relationship between rigidity and ethnocentrism/authoritarianism is dependent on the testing situation.

In a study involving University of Iowa undergraduates, Levitt and Zelen (1953) showed that there was a statistically significant relationship between ethnocentrism and Einstellung performance under "free conditions of administration," but not under conditions involving incentives for fast task completion. Again, we have findings that indicate that when situations differ, the relationship between ethnocentrism and Einstellung performance differs. The parameters along which the situations vary are not clear. For example, it is unclear whether the "free conditions" of the Levitt and Zelen study approximate the test-like conditions of Rokeach, the informal atmosphere of Brown, or are markedly dissimilar from both.

French (1955) attempted a direct investigation of the effects of ego-involving and relaxed conditions of administration on the relationship between F-Scale scores and Einstellung rigidity. The subjects were 100 airmen in basic training. Under the ego-involving condition, the tests were described as measures of intelligence and all-around ability, and the results were described as important in future assignments. Under the relaxed condition, the tests were described as new and in the process of development and were taken "anonymously." The correlation between authoritarianism and rigidity was not statistically significant under either the ego-involving or the relaxed condition. In another context, Sales and Friend (1973) showed that subjects experiencing stress due to failure tended to increase slightly in authoritarianism, whereas subjects experiencing success tended to decrease slightly in authoritarianism.

In reviewing earlier research, Jackson, Messick, and Solley (1957) hypothesized that the relationship between authoritarianism and Einstellung rigidity might be due to a tendency on the part of subjects to conform and acquiesce, an observation similar to that made by Levitt and Zelen (1953) and Pitcher and Stacey (1954). To test this hypothesis, Jackson, Messick, and Solley administered an F Scale, a reversed-item F Scale (Jackson & Messick, 1957), and a set of Einstellung problems to a group of 77 students from a midwestern municipal university. After eliminating some subjects, they were left with 32 who always used the indirect solution, and 22 who always used the direct solution on the critical problems. The investigators found that subjects who used indirect (rigid) solutions for the Einstellung problems had significantly higher F-Scale scores than those who solved the problems directly. However, subjects who used indirect solutions also scored significantly higher on the reversed-item F Scale. The authors interpreted these data as indicating that acquiescence was the determinant of the relationship between authoritarianism and Einstellung rigidity.

It must be noted, however, that the statistical significance reported by Jackson and his associates was based on one-tailed tests of significance, an approach that many statisticians (e.g., Cohen, 1965) feel to be inappropriate. If two-tailed tests had been used, the differences in both F-Scale and reversed-item F-Scale scores would not have been statistically significant. Therefore, the Jackson, Messick, and Solley findings must be interpreted cautiously.

Levitt (1956) reviewed the results of nine studies involving tests of the relationship between Einstellung rigidity and E- or F-Scale scores. Five of the 18 analyses involved in these studies were statistically significant. However, when the author calculated a mean correlation, he obtained a nonsignificant .04. Levitt also presented data to challenge Brown's hypothesis that the relationships between rigidity and authoritarianism are higher under stressful or ego-involving conditions.

In trying to compare the results of the various studies, two problems become apparent. The first is that the investigators used slightly different instruments and different operational definitions of stress and relaxation. Second, the absolute level of authoritarianism/ethnocentrism or rigidity may have differed in the various samples. It is possible that scores falling above the median for a sample in one study might fall below the median for a sample in a different study. This would create problems if the relationship between rigidity and authoritarianism occurred only when the absolute level of authoritarianism were, for example, high.

The validity of the Einstellung test as a measure of rigidity was, as noted earlier, questioned by Luchins (1949, 1951). This criticism was also raised by Levitt and Zelen (1953, 1955). A person is rigid if he would behave more effectively by changing his behavior and does not make that change. Failure to use a direct solution for the critical problems in the Einstellung task is the measure of rigidity. This implies that using the direct method is more effective, and Levitt and Zelen (1953) suggested using the time necessary to complete the Einstellung task as a measure of efficiency. They presented data showing that use of the direct solution was not associated with increased speed in completing the task. Therefore, they argued, the Einstellung task, as used by Rokeach, is not a test of rigidity.

Levitt (1956) also attacked the Einstellung rigidity test on other grounds. He offered three criticisms: (1) Because of the novelty-insight factor, no reliability estimate can be made for the test. (2) A large proportion of subjects must be eliminated from the final analyses because they cannot complete the task for a variety of reasons. (3) The distribution of scores violates the assumption of normality necessary for the use of parametric statistics. The first two of these criticisms, together with the previously mentioned idea that the direct solution is no more efficient than the indirect solution, cast doubt on the validity of the Einstellung test as a measure of rigidity. Levitt and Zuckerman (1959) reviewed additional studies on the validity of the water jug problem as a measure of rigidity. They concluded that it is a measure of intelligence rather than rigidity.

Given these criticisms and the data from the studies reviewed, it must be concluded that a consistent relationship between authoritarianism and Einstellung rigidity has yet to be demonstrated. Second, the appropriateness of the Einstellung problems as a measure of rigidity is highly questionable.

To this point, we have been concerned with the Einstellung measure of rigidity in relation to authoritarianism. Although this has been the most frequently used measure of rigidity in studies of authoritarianism, it is by no means the only one. For example, Schroder and Streufert (1962) reported a significant correlation of .41 between F Scale scores and scores on the Gough and Sanford (1952) Rigidity Scale for a sample of 147 male high school students.

In the course of her study, Applezweig (1954) administered a total of five tests of rigidity. In addition to the Einstellung problems, these included the Angyal Perceptual Test (Angyal, 1948), the Luchins Hidden Words Test (Luchins, 1942), a group-administered Rorschach scored for rigidity (Fisher, 1950), and a Hidden Objects Test (Cattell & Tiner, 1949). Of 30 correlations among the tests across three testing periods, only one correlation was found to be statistically significant. Thus the measures of rigidity used in Applezweig's study were independent of one another. Similar failures to obtain significant correlations among measures of rigidity were reported by Fisher (1950), Forster, Vinacke, and Digman (1955), and Chown (1959). In factor analytic studies, Cattell and Tiner (1949) and Baer (1964) failed to isolate single rigidity factors. Because of the lack of statistically significant relationships between measures of rigidity, it is difficult to draw conclusions regarding the relationship between rigidity and authoritarianism.

Several studies on the relationship between authoritarianism and rigidity in children made use of another approach to the measurement of rigidity. The initial investigations of ethnocentric children were conducted by Frenkel-Brunswik (1948). The author reported that the children were rated on the basis of the clinical material, without knowledge of their prejudice score, for intolerance of ambiguity and rigidity "defined in a general manner." The extremely prejudiced children were reported to have received high ratings on these traits. She also reported that these children tended to subscribe to personality inventory statements revealing "a dichotomizing attitude, a rejection of the different, or an avoidance of ambiguities in general."

Frenkel-Brunswik also reported the results of a number of experiments, the most important of which was a "tentative" study that Brown (1965) felt could serve to distinguish intolerance of ambiguity and rigidity. Lower-middle-class groups of highly prejudiced and unprejudiced children were shown a series of pictures, the first clearly identifiable as a dog, the last as a cat. Intermediate pictures presented a transition from dog to cat. As each card was shown, the subject was asked to identify the object pictured. Frenkel-Brunswik reported that the prejudiced children held on longer to the perception of the ambiguous intermediate figures as dogs. In addition, they often haphazardly guessed at the identity of the ambiguous object rather than admit not knowing what was pictured. Brown (1965) interpreted the former behavior as rigidity and believed that by not reporting the intermediate pictures as indistinct, the children were manifesting intolerance of ambiguity.

In a related study by Livson and Livson cited by Frenkel-Brunswik (1949), ethnocentric children were slow to recognize numbers emerging from indistinctness and slow to recognize numbers changing from other numbers; the prejudiced children evidenced prolonged clinging to the first impression, even when it was faulty.

Blum (1959) studied 17 nursery school children and their parents on a task similar to that used in the original Frenkel-Brunswik investigation. The children were presented with a Child Transition Test, involving a five-step transition from cat to dog. The Adult Transition Test involved a seven-step transition. The children were asked to identify each figure; the parents were requested to sort the pictures into sequence and to explain the basis of their sorts. The children and their parents were ranked separately as to rigidity. The multiple correlation of these rankings of rigidity was a reportedly significant .46 for the relationship of the scores of both parents with the child's score. The children's scores did not correlate significantly with those of either parent taken alone.

However, Asher (1961) correctly pointed out that a multiple correlation based on three variables and 17 subjects must exceed .59 for statistical significance at the .05 level, and that the correlation of .46, reported as statistically significant, is in fact not significant. Asher's conclusion, however, is puzzling:

It would appear that the small number of observations would almost invariably lead to indeterminant results unless significant findings ensue. The results must be accepted for the moment. (p. 608)

Although it is true that the small sample size limits the power of the statistical test, making it less likely to uncover a relationship when one exists, Asher's conclusion must be rejected. Furthermore, a multiple R is artificially inflated because of capitalization on chance factors. This is especially true when the sample size is small. Correcting the multiple R for this type of bias (shrinkage), Blum's coefficient of multiple correlation reduces to .32. Thus it must be concluded that Blum did not demonstrate a statistically significant relationship between rigidity in the child and rigidity in the parents.

In reviewing studies of rigidity, it was shown that the condition of administration was important for the relationship between rigidity and authoritarianism. In the study by French (1955) cited previously, 100 male airmen in basic training were also tested with the dog-to-cat picture transition test in relaxed and ego-involving conditions. As with the Einstellung measure of rigidity, there were no significant relationships under either condition between performance on the transition test and authoritarianism.

In a pair of studies, Kidd and Kidd (1971, 1972) used a measure of rigidity similar to the one used originally by Frenkel-Brunswik. They developed 10 sets of pictures, each set involving a 10-step transition between the first and last picture. In one set, for example, they began with a bird and ended with a jet plane. In the first study, three personality measures were also administered: the Sanford–Gough Rigidity Test (cf. Rokeach, 1960), the Taylor Manifest Anxiety Scale (Taylor, 1953), and the Holtzman Inkblot Test (Holtzman, Thorpe, Swartz, & Herron, 1961). The subjects were 116 coeds ranging in age from 18 to 21 years. The sample was divided into two subsets for cross-validation purposes.

The position of the card in the 10-card sequence on which subjects reported a perceived change was averaged across all 10 sets of cards. This average rigidity score was significantly correlated in both subsets of subjects with rigidity as measured by the Sanford-Gough test and with the following Holtzman scores: location, anatomy, hostility, color, and movement. These significant relationships persisted when data were analyzed for subjects whose average perceptual rigidity scores were high, but the relationships were nonsignificant for subjects low in perceptual rigidity. The Holtzman data were interpreted as indicating that rigidity was related to authoritarian personality, including low affective responsivity and high hostility.

The results of this study suggested a more direct examination of the relationship between rigidity and authoritarianism. Kidd and Kidd (1972) related scores on a 29-item F Scale to their measure of average perceptual rigidity. They obtained a correlation of .76 for their sample of 100 college females, indicating a highly significant relationship between rigidity and authoritarianism.

Studies using picture transition tests seem to offer promise in investigating the relationship between authoritarianism and rigidity. This approach makes reliability estimates possible, does not require the deletion of many subjects, and seems to satisfy the definition of rigidity. Studies using this procedure suggest the existence of a relationship between authoritarianism and rigidity.

INTOLERANCE OF AMBIGUITY

The second of the two variables studied as a correlate of authoritarianism was the intolerance of ambiguity. Frenkel-Brunswik (1954) defined intolerance of ambiguity, in part, as ". . . undue preference for symmetry, familiarity, definiteness, and regularity; tendency toward black-white solutions, oversimplified dichotomizing, unqualified either-or solutions, premature closure, perseveration and stereotypy . . ." (p. 247).

A frequently cited study of intolerance of ambiguity among ethnocentric college students is Block and Block's (1951) investigation involving the autokinetic phenomenon. The autokinetic phenomenon is the perception of movement of a physically stationary pinpoint of light in a totally dark room (Sherif, 1936). In the Blocks' study, 65 male college students were required to press a button when they "saw" the light move. Five seconds later the light was shut off, and each subject recorded his estimate of the distance the light traveled. The procedure was repeated 100 times for each subject. A general finding in connection with the autokinetic phenomenon is that subjects tend to stabilize their estimates of the distance the light moves, a process known as reaching an "individual norm." Block and Block reasoned that subjects who establish an individual norm quickly are more intolerant of ambiguity. Their data indicated that subjects who established norms of movement during the 100 trials of the experiment had significantly higher E-Scale scores than subjects who did not establish individual norms. Similar findings were reported by Taft (1956), who used social distance as a measure of ethnocentrism, and by Zacker (1973), who used the F Scale as a measure of authoritarianism.

Montgomery, Hinkle, and Enzie (1976) studied the persistence of conformity to confederates' arbitrary norms in the autokinetic situation. Fifty-eight high F scorers and 58 low F scorers were selected from a pool of 300 undergraduates. The situation was one in which participants in four-person groups were gradually replaced. It was found that high-authoritarian subjects initially conformed to confederates' judgments to a greater extent than low-authoritarian subjects. When subjects were replaced and confederates phased out, high-authoritarian subjects persisted longer than low-authoritarian subjects in maintaining the original arbitrary norms.

Another study employing the autokinetic procedure was reported by Millon (1957). Millon presented data from 60 of 69 students in an introductory psychology course who established a norm in the autokinetic situation. The F Scale had been previously administered to these subjects. Approximately half the subjects were instructed that performance on the perceptual task reflected ability and intelligence (ego-involving condition); the other subjects were told that the equipment was being considered for a later study on vision (task-involving orientation). Millon found that high authoritarian subjects formed a norm more quickly. There were no statistically significant differences in the relationships between intolerance of ambiguity and authoritarianism under the ego- and task-involving conditions.

Millon also used the autokinetic phenomenon to provide an index of rigidity. He demonstrated that, when a second light is introduced into the standard single-light autokinetic situation, subjects generally reported a curtailment of movement. He reasoned that the resistance to shift from the previously established norm under this changed condition is a measure of rigidity. It seems to us, however, that what is being measured is a tendency to perseverate; rigidity refers to the tendency to maintain a previously established pattern of behavior when a shift in behavior would lead to more effective behavior (Rokeach, 1948).

Millon found significantly less shifting under the ego-involving conditions than under the task-involving conditions, indicating a relationship between his index of rigidity and test conditions. He also found a near significant relationship between authoritarianism and rigidity; the more authoritarian subjects evidenced greater rigidity. In his summary of results, Millon reported that the relationship between authoritarianism and rigidity was "clearly significant" under ego-involving conditions but not under task-involving conditions. However welcome, this conclusion is not warranted, since Millon reported a nonsignificant interaction between authoritarianism and testing conditions.

Davids (1955, 1956) also provided some data on the relationship between authoritarianism and intolerance of ambiguity under relaxed
and stressful conditions. In the first study, conducted with 20 undergraduates under relaxed conditions, he failed to obtain significant relationships between authoritarianism and two measures of intolerance
of ambiguity. Intolerance of visual ambiguity was measured by counting the number of experimenter-provided concepts on the Rorschach
test that were rejected by the subject. Intolerance of auditory ambiguity was measured by counting the number of ideas recalled when a
passage containing contradictory ideas was read to the subject. In the
second study Davids created a stress situation by testing 22 undergraduates in an employment interview. Again, there were no significant relationships between F-Scale scores and the intolerance of ambiguity
measures. Thus Davids failed to extend Brown's findings of a relationship between rigidity and authoritarianism under stress to the relationship between intolerance of ambiguity and authoritarianism under
stress. This may be due to the different stress situations, the absence of
a relationship between intolerance of ambiguity and authoritarianism, or the inappropriateness of Davids' measures of intolerance of
ambiguity.

The relationship between intolerance of ambiguity and authoritarianism was also studied by Jones (1955). Jones used frequency of fluctuation of the Necker Cube as his measure of intolerance of ambiguity.
In viewing this cube it is unclear which side is near and which is far,
and subjects report a fluctuation in which side is perceived as near or
far. Jones reasoned that authoritarian subjects would perceive less fluctuation, because fluctuation implies tolerance of ambiguity. Using two
separate groups of naval aviation cadets, Jones found significant but
low correlations in the expected direction.

Other measures have been developed to assess intolerance of ambiguity. Levitt (1953) used two measures of intolerance of ambiguity in
his study of the relationship of intolerance and ethnocentrism. The
Decision-Location Test is made up of a series of pictures that increase
in detail. The subject's task is to identify the final picture as early in the
series as possible. The more the subject is willing to indicate that he
cannot identify the picture, the more tolerant of ambiguity he is. The
second test presents the subject with 42 popular misconceptions, each
of which may be answered true, false, or do not know. The more items

the subject checks true, the greater is his intolerance of ambiguity. It is unclear to us why responses of false should not also indicate intolerance of ambiguity. The Gough et al. (1950) scale was used to measure ethnocentrism. The average age of the 47 subjects was 10 years. The Decision-Location Test correlated significantly (.39) with ethnocentrism, but the correlation of the misconceptions test with ethnocentrism was not statistically significant.

The studies in this section relating authoritarianism to *perceptual* measures of intolerance of ambiguity generally indicate that subjects who are authoritarian tend to be less tolerant of ambiguity than nonauthoritarian subjects.

Johnson and Bommarito (1971) cited a study by Muuss (1959) indicating a relationship between a measure of intolerance of ambiguity and the Children's Antidemocratic Attitude Scale. Muuss administered his 12-item instrument to 232 sixth-grade public-school children and obtained a statistically significant correlation of .41 between the scores on the two measures.

Siegel (1954) measured authoritarianism with 30 F-Scale and E-Scale items and developed his own Tolerance-Intolerance of Cognitive Ambiguity (TICA) test. Sixteen pictures of the faces of unknown people were randomly selected from popular magazines at least five years old. Sixteen statements (e.g., "We hear about such incidents right away," "I knew a streetcar conductor once that had six toes on his foot") were randomly selected from different magazines. In the TICA test, the pictures were placed on one page, the statements on another. Subjects were required to write the number of the picture next to the statement if they felt the person pictured made that statement.

Siegel assumed that subjects who were intolerant of ambiguity would match a greater number of pictures and statements than subjects low in intolerance of ambiguity. His subjects were 99 freshmen coeds at Stanford University. Subjects who were above the median in intolerance of ambiguity had significantly higher authoritarianism scores than subjects who had scored lower on the TICA test. Siegel obtained a contingency coefficient (derived from a three-by-three table) of .40 between authoritarianism and TICA scores.

MacDonald (1970) expanded a 16-item true-false test of intolerance of ambiguity developed by Rydell and Rosen (1966) into a 20-item format. As part of his investigation, MacDonald found a significant correlation of .30 between his measure of intolerance of ambiguity and a 29-item version of the F Scale for 90 male physical-education majors at Ithaca College. Hampton (1968) used two measures of intolerance of ambiguity and found that the measures did not correlate significantly with each other or with a modified F Scale. His subjects were 322 students ranging in age from 10 to 22 years. It is unclear whether the negative results of this study were due to inadequacies in measures of intolerance of ambiguity, the modified F Scale employed in the study, or the lack of a relationship between the two variables. Hogan (1975) suggested that his nonverbal measure of authoritarianism, earlier reported to be a measure of intolerance of ambiguity, is a valid substitute for the F Scale. It does not appear to us that Hogan's scale is a valid measure of intolerance of ambiguity, nor are Hogan's nonverbal measure and the F-Scale equivalent.

Other studies have also shown scores on Walk's A Scale to correlate with authoritarianism. O'Connor (1952), in a study of 77 Harvard undergraduates, obtained a significant correlation of .55 between an 18-item E Scale and the A Scale. Kates and Diab (1955) found significant correlations between scores on the A Scale and the F Scale (.21) and E Scale (.15) in their study of 172 university students. Pilisuk (1963) combined Walk's A Scale with a nine-item scale developed by Webster, Sanford, and Freedman (1955) to provide a measure of intolerance of ambiguity. With a sample of 154 male college students, Pilisuk obtained a significant correlation of .58 between this measure and 23-item F Scale. Kelman and Barclay (1963) obtained a statistically significant correlation of .43 between A-Scale and F-Scale scores for a sample of 282 Negro college freshmen.

These findings are surprising in light of Ehrlich's (1965) criticism that the A Scale has poor internal consistency. Child (1965) reported similar difficulty with his own scale. In general, as was found with measures of rigidity, one of the difficulties with measures of intolerance of ambiguity is the construct validity of the measuring instruments. Kenny and Ginsberg (1958) administered 12 measures of intolerance of ambiguity to 76 volunteer female adults. Of 66 correlations among the measures, only seven were statistically significant, and, of these seven, two were in the wrong direction. Two of the 12 correlations between measures of intolerance of ambiguity, one of which was Walk's (1950) A Scale, were significantly correlated with a measure of authoritarian-submission derived from the work of O'Neil and Levinson (1954).

The MacDonald (1970) scale cited earlier, Walk's A Scale, and a scale developed by Budner (1962), seem to be promising pencil-and-paper measures of intolerance of ambiguity. Budner's 16-item carefully developed scale was shown to be free of acquiescence and social desirability bias and to correlate significantly with F-Scale scores in six of nine samples involving college, nursing, and medical students. The mean correlation of .32 across the nine samples indicates some shared variance between the two measures. In a study of 113 male undergraduates, Vannoy (1965) obtained a significant correlation of .28 between scores on a modified F Scale and scores on Budner's measure.

As was true of studies involving perceptual measures of intolerance of ambiguity, subjects high in authoritarianism tend to score high on paper-and-pencil measures of intolerance of ambiguity. The relationship exists despite evidence that the paper-and-pencil measures of intolerance of ambiguity are not highly interrelated and may be substandard psychometrically.

Harvey and Beverly (1961) showed that high authoritarian subjects were more likely to change their attitudes toward the use of alcohol when they were asked to write arguments contrary to their beliefs. This finding would appear to be consistent with the general finding of intolerance of ambiguity by authoritarian subjects. This and other related studies were discussed by Harvey (1963a).

In research on tolerance of ambiguity, Steiner (1954) studied the degree to which inconsistent traits would be viewed as occurring together in the same individual. From a pool of 52 undergraduates, Steiner selected the 13 subjects with the highest E-Scale scores and the 13 with the lowest E-Scale scores. He found that subjects high in ethnocentrism were less apt to accept the possibility that disparate traits could occur in an individual than subjects low in ethnocentrism. In a later study, Steiner and Johnson (1963) found that subjects high in authoritarianism were less tolerant of trait inconsistency than subjects low in authoritarianism. Similarly, Warr and Sims (1965) found a positive correlation between scores on the F scale and the tendency to view similarly evaluated traits as coexisting in an individual.

Nye (1973) also studied the relationship between authoritarianism and intolerance of ambiguity in the interpersonal realm. On the basis of scores on a modified F Scale, undergraduate subjects were divided into groups of 48 authoritarian and 48 nonauthoritarian individuals. Nye used an impression formation task in which the subjects were presented with information about the social behavior of three men. Early information was supplemented by either incongruous or congruous information, the former presenting an ambiguous situation. The authoritarian subjects tended to form strong initial impressions, changed their impressions drastically when presented with incongruous information, were less indecisive in their impressions, and were more likely to perceive the inconsistencies between the stimulus material. Nye interpreted these findings as evidence that authoritarian individuals are intolerant of ambiguity.

Thus several studies indicate that authoritarian subjects tend to be intolerant of ambiguity, as reflected in their performances on impression formation tasks. This finding is consistent with that reported for other measures of intolerance of ambiguity.

AUTHORITARIANISM AND OTHER MEASURES OF COGNITIVE STYLE

In presenting research on cognitive functioning associated with authoritarianism, we have focused primarily on rigidity and intolerance of ambiguity. However, other behavior reflecting cognitive style has been related to authoritarianism, and we briefly summarize the results of some studies dealing with these variables.

The relationship between concreteness and ethnocentrism was the subject of a study by Rokeach (1951b). Rokeach's interest in concreteness originated in his concern with problems in the definition of rigidity. As we have seen, rigidity is defined as the perseveration of an inefficient solution to a problem. It is often difficult to judge which of two alternatives is the inefficient solution to a complex problem. Rokeach reasoned that previous research showed a relationship between rigidity and concreteness and maintained that concreteness is more readily definable. He argued that an attempt should be made to relate ethnocentrism to concreteness. The subjects of his study were 144 undergraduates who were asked to define five religious concepts (Buddhism, Catholiscism, Christianity, Judaism, Protestantism) and five political–economic concepts (capitalism, communism, democracy, fascism, and socialism). Ethnocentrism was measured with a 10-item E Scale. Rokeach hypothesized that high-ethnocentric subjects would base definitions on the concrete aspects of the concept, whereas low-ethnocentric subjects would define the concepts more abstractly.

Each subject's definitions were categorized as abstract, concrete, reification, or miscellaneous. Subjects were divided into four groups on the basis of their ethnocentrism scores. Rokeach interpreted his data as indicating that the least ethnocentric subjects were the most likely to use abstract definitions. However, the conclusion does not appear to be warranted. The significant results were achieved only by comparing the lowest quartile with a combination of the other three, and two of the three reportedly significant comparisons required one-tailed tests to achieve significance at the 5 and 10% levels, respectively.

In the previously cited study by O'Connor (1952), the relationship between ethnocentrism and abstract reasoning was also examined. The latter was measured by a series of 15 syllogisms. Ethnocentrism was found to relate to poor abstract reasoning ability.

The Authoritarian Personality was the impetus for an interesting study of the cognitive functioning of prejudiced children by Kutner (1958) and a follow-up by Kutner and Gordon (1964). In the original publication, Kutner hypothesized that prejudiced children would establish "inefficient mental sets" and would attempt to break these sets inappropriately.

Kutner's sample consisted of 60 seven-year-old children, most of whom were of middle and upper-middle socioeconomic status and 80% of whom were Jewish. Prejudice was assessed with the author's projective Ethnic Attitude Test, requiring responses to prejudicial statements about various ethnic groups. Kutner classified 42 of the children as very unprejudiced or somewhat unprejudiced, and these comprised the unprejudiced group; 18 children were classified as somewhat prejudiced or prejudiced and comprised the prejudiced group.

To study rigidity, Kutner used three pillboxes. In each task, the child hid his eyes while the experimenter moved the three boxes. The child was then required to "guess" the correct box of the three. For example, test 1 presented the child with the three boxes in an oblique, vertical, and horizontal orientation, respectively. The correct box was the one on the left-hand side. On later trials the boxes were reoriented randomly, but the correct box was always the one in the left position. The child was allowed 25 trials to solve the problem; five correct consecutive solutions and a correct verbalization were the criteria of success. In test 2, the obliquely oriented box, regardless of its left-middle-right position, was the correct box. Four such tests were used.

The measure of rigidity was the establishment of perseverative mental sets leading to failure on successive problems. The errors were analyzed for evidence of a perseverative set, but the data revealed few differences between the two groups. Additional analyses, however, indicated that the two groups approached the problems differently. On the basis of the rigidity tasks and the other problems, Kutner summarized the cognitive functioning of the prejudiced child as characterized by rigidity, overgeneralization, categorizing and dichotomizing, concretization, simplification, furcation, dogmatism, and intolerance of ambiguity.

Nine years after the first testing, 33 of the original sample were available for follow-up (Kutner & Gordon, 1964). The subjects' prejudice was reevaluated with nine items from the E Scale. Several tests of cognitive ability were also administered. The data indicated that when the child was initially prejudiced and remained prejudiced, his cognitive functioning was poor; when the child was initially unprejudiced and remained unprejudiced, his cognitive functioning was better. The child who was initially prejudiced and who became unprejudiced improved to an intermediate level of cognitive functioning; the child who was initially unprejudiced and who became prejudiced fell to an intermediate level of cognitive functioning.

CRITIQUE

It should not be surprising that a work as monumental as *The Authoritarian Personality* generated much research and much criticism. Some of this subsequent research was reviewed by Titus and Hollander (1957), Christie and Cook (1958), and Kirscht and Dillehay (1967). Hanson (1975a) compiled a list of over 500 doctoral dissertations concerned with authoritarianism or dogmatism, completed from 1950 through 1974, as well as a list of master's theses in these areas (Hanson, 1974). The most detailed collection of critical papers is *Studies in the Scope and Method of "The Authoritarian Personality,"* edited by Christie and Jahoda (1954).

A number of methodological criticisms have been directed toward the series of studies reported as *The Authoritarian Personality,* the most telling of which were made by Hyman and Sheatsley (1954). As is true of virtually all studies in the social sciences, the sample studied was not representative of the population of the country as a whole. This would not be so serious an error if the authors had limited their conclusions and generalizations to the relatively young, well-educated, middle-class volunteers who were the subjects of the study. Another biasing factor was that the subjects were often active members of formal groups. Many of the conclusions were based on the study of extreme groups and then generalized to a continuum.

Hyman and Sheatsley were also critical of the measuring instruments used. Although the authors of *The Authoritarian Personality* used both clinical procedures and standardized questionnaires, the former were often given greater weight. As Hyman and Sheatsley noted, "In the marriage of the two methodologies, the quantitative statistical method is all too often cast in the role of the stodgy husband who just answers, 'Yes, dear' to all the bright suggestions made by the wife." The interviews were not standardized, and the interviewers, having knowledge of questionnaire data on the authoritarianism of the subjects, may have conducted biased interviews. Since interview material was used to "validate" the authoritarianism scores, with the implication that the two were independently collected, this represents a serious flaw in the study. Similarly, there is some question as to whether the 90 interview categories could possibly be coded independently, as we have noted in regard to the coding categories of rigidity and intolerance of ambiguity. Hyman and Sheatsley cited the danger of a "halo effect," in which coders, having access to all the interview material, may have sought out expected differences.

From our own presentation on measurement, it is obvious that there are some specific difficulties with the F Scale. We discussed the confounding of authoritarianism with acquiescence and the attempts that were subsequently made to develop an instrument that would avoid this difficulty. However, as we have seen, this response bias might not affect the validity of the F Scale because of the tendency of authoritarians to acquiesce. Another problem concerned the factorial purity of the F Scale. Several investigators have presented data indicating that the F Scale is comprised of several independent factors. Although this does not necessarily imply that a single, total score is meaningless, unless the factors measure different aspects of a more broadly conceived construct of authoritarianism, the use of such a total score could present difficulties.

Another problem relating to measurement is that different investigators often use modified versions of the E and F scales. This makes it difficult to arrive at generalizations across the results of several studies. Even when it is claimed that the same instrument is used, puzzling discrepancies arise. For example, Bendig (1959) reported using Form 40/45 of the F Scale, which he claimed to be a 28-item scale. Krug (1961) also used Form 40/45, which he found had 29 items. Faced with this discrepancy, we counted the number of items reported by Adorno et al. as constituting Form 40/45 and independently verified the claim of Adorno et al. that the form contains 30 items.

Many investigators seem to use the E and F scales interchangeably. For example, Rokeach's (1948) frequently cited study on the relationship between authoritarianism and Einstellung rigidity actually employed the E Scale. In his follow-up of Rokeach's findings, Brown (1953) used the F Scale rather than the E Scale.

In another vein, Hyman and Sheatsley pointed out that differences between high- and low-ethnocentric subjects could be due to some uncontrolled variable. The authors of *The Authoritarian Personality* attempted to control for age, sex, political and religious affiliation, and national and regional background. However, level of education was neglected, and Hyman and Sheatsley showed that subjects varying in level of education respond differently to several F-Scale items. As we have seen, this is related to the argument presented by several investigators that authoritarianism reflects a subcultural norm rather than a personality dynamic.

A disturbing element, particularly characteristic of Frenkel-Brunswik's writing, is the reporting of tentative and incomplete studies and the reporting of significant differences without the presentation of tables summarizing the data. For example, in using a dog-to-cat transition to study rigidity/intolerance of ambiguity, Blum (1959) was unable to determine how similar his instrument was to that developed by Frenkel-Brunswik. Although Frenkel-Brunswik's work citing her use of this instrument had been published a decade earlier, Blum reported that Frenkel-Brunswik indicated an unwillingness to distribute her instrument since the work was exploratory and only indicative of trends.

In studying the relationship between authoritarianism and child-rearing practices, the authors of *The Authoritarian Personality* relied heavily on retrospective reporting by the subjects. A number of studies have pointed out discrepancies between retrospectively reported events and the events observed in the present (Robbins, 1963; Yarrow, 1963). Just as the memory of events is taken as fact, so a small amount of data is used to bear the weight of an elaborate edifice of theorizing. For example, one interviewee stated, "Well, the Jews are a ticklish problem." As Hyman and Sheatsley noted, Frenkel-Brunswik wrote that the key to interpreting the statement was the word "problem," which was used to give the impression of careful consideration and scientific detachment and to provide a rationalization for prejudice. Although this may be true, it is an unwarranted inference from this bit of data.

Hyman and Sheatsley wrote, "Our major criticisms lead us inevitably to conclude that the authors' theory has not been proved by the data they cite. . . ." We, along with Jahoda (1954) and Smith (1950), have not found a clear statement of the authoritarian personality theory or the conclusions of the research. It is therefore difficult to judge whether research does or does not support the theory, theories, or premises underlying the authoritarian personality study. What is important is that the welter of hypotheses and clinical and statistical studies generated much subsequent research on a crucial social issue. One aspect of that research, of special concern here, was the impetus given to later investigators of cognitive style.

Although intolerance of ambiguity and rigidity had been of academic interest before *The Authoritarian Personality,* the investigations of Frenkel-Brunswik and her associates, which attempted to place the constructs within a unified personality theory, provided an important social context for subsequent research. Based on a review of the subsequent research, we believe that identifiable cognitive styles are associated with differences in authoritarianism. However, these relationships vary in different situations and depend on the specific measuring instruments used. Although stress appears to be implicated as a situational variable, no systematic research has been undertaken to dimensionalize the environment and relate authoritarianism to these dimensions.

CHAPTER THREE
Dogmatism

As indicated in the previous chapter, many studies were generated by *The Authoritarian Personality*. Although the F Scale often yielded the predicted results, a number of criticisms were raised regarding its use. One of the criticisms that opened a new area of research in cognitive style concerned the limited view of authoritarianism presented in the original work. Specifically, it was argued that the F Scale, because of its evolution from an interest in anti-Semitism and fascism, was adequate only as a measure of authoritarianism of the right.

Shils (1954) was the first to present this argument in detail. He pointed out that, by the end of the nineteenth century, a radical-conservative dimension was being used to describe political institutions and activities. Because of the events surrounding World War II, the Berkeley group was concerned with conservative, or rightist, authoritarianism. These investigators have been criticized for neglecting leftist authoritarianism. From one point of view, this is an unreasonable criticism, since the researchers deliberately limited their research at the outset of the project to a study of authoritarianism of the right (Sanford, 1956). However, the authors of *The Authoritarian Personality* were aware of authoritarianism of the left and attempted to develop a typology to take this into consideration.

Milton Rokeach (1956) pointed out that the treatment of authoritarianism produced by Adorno, Frenkel-Brunswik, Levinson, and Sanford was not adequate for the broad-ranging phenomenon of authoritarianism as it varies along a conservative-radical dimension. He argued that authoritarianism was independent of political ideology or prejudice. In an early study of similarities in cognitive style of adherents of the extreme left and right, Taylor (1960) combined the F Scale and a social distance scale and showed that members of both left and right groups performed similarly on a perceptual closure measure of cognitive style.

Rokeach was interested in developing a measure of cognitive style that would be independent of the content of thought. His research began in 1951 with the observation that individuals were dogmatic, or closed, about various things (Rokeach, 1951a, 1960). He theorized that, as a cognitive style, dogmatism mediates between external stimuli and the individual's responses to those stimuli. Because of this cognitive mediation, the individual who is dogmatic in one area is likely to be dogmatic in another. Rokeach posited a continuum of dogmatism ranging from open to closed and used the term *closed-minded* interchangeably with *dogmatic*. As presented in Chapter 1, consistency across situations is one postulated characteristic of cognitive approaches to personality theories (Brody, 1972).

Rokeach's analysis of the nature of cognitive systems began with a discussion of ideological dogmatism, which he defined as "(a) a relatively closed cognitive organization of beliefs and disbeliefs about reality, (b) organized around a central set of beliefs about absolute authority which, in turn, (c) provides a framework for patterns of intolerance and qualified tolerance toward others" (Rokeach, 1954). This definition is expanded in the later discussion of the Dogmatism Scale.

The first component of this definition is the structural aspect of dogmatism. As Rokeach (1954) pointed out, an individual with a closed belief system may be pro-Freudian or anti-Freudian. Common to both positions, however, are similar cognitive characteristics, which are detailed later. Rokeach was concerned with dogmatically held beliefs, regardless of the content of these beliefs. In this connection, Rokeach acknowledged his indebtedness to Eric Hoffer's (1951) *The True Believer,* a book in which the similarities in background and ideas of rabid Nazis and rabid communists were noted.

The second component of Rokeach's definition of ideological dogmatism involves an authoritarian outlook on life. Regardless of the content of the belief-disbelief system, Rokeach postulated that the dogmatic person glorifies authorities who support his belief system. The dogmatic person is also hypothesized to support an elite class.

The final component of Rokeach's definition involves intolerance toward those with opposing beliefs. Rokeach postulated that the dogmatic individual polarizes his beliefs and rejects individuals whose beliefs fall at the other pole.

A central notion of Rokeach's conceptualization of dogmatism is that the individual's cognitive system is organized into belief and disbelief systems. The belief system is made up of the ideas an individual accepts as true. The disbelief system is comprised of a number of subsystems of ideas the individual rejects as false. To illustrate this point, Rokeach (1956) wrote that an individual holding the belief system of *Catholicism* can be best understood if his attitudes toward Catholicism are studied along with his disbelief systems of Lutheranism, Calvinism, Judaism, and so on.

MEASUREMENT

The principles of organization of the belief system and disbelief subsystems are the basis of Rokeach's Dogmatism Scale, which was revised four times. The initial scale had 89 items; the final scale, Form E, contains 40 items. Like the F Scale, the Dogmatism Scale is a Likert type instrument requiring a response to each item along a six-point scale from "I agree very much" to "I disagree very much." For each item, agreement is scored as closed-minded (dogmatic) and disagreement as open-minded. A copy of the Dogmatism Scale may be found in Rokeach (1960).

The organization of the Dogmatism Scale is complex. The multifaceted theory was examined and items were written to assess a number of the elements of the theory. An effort was made to develop items that would reflect structure rather than content.

The first four items were written to measure aspects of the belief-disbelief system previously discussed. To the extent that the individual is dogmatic, Rokeach hypothesized greater isolation between disbelief systems. Items 5–36 measure aspects of a central-peripheral system, comprised of three levels. Primitive beliefs concern adequacy of the self, certainty regarding the future, and judgments of the friendliness of the world. The more closed or dogmatic the individual, the more helpless, isolated, alone, and uncertain he is. Items 5–17 reflect these primitive beliefs. Items 18–33 reflect the second, intermediate region, beliefs that involve authoritarianism and intolerance. The more closed the individual, the more he sees authority as absolute and the more he is intolerant of disagreement with his beliefs. The final region of the central-peripheral system is the peripheral region, having to do with the content-oriented beliefs, and disbeliefs emanating from positive and negative authority. The more closed the individual, the more the content of his beliefs will emanate from authority figures. Items 34–36 are concerned with how peripheral beliefs change to correspond to information derived from authority.

It is worth noting that no items directly assess the peripheral region, because this region is the content of beliefs. Rokeach posits the absence of a relationship between the content of beliefs and the extent to which they are dogmatically maintained. An individual may be a dogmatic Republican or a dogmatic communist, but this should reveal nothing about his level of dogmatism.

The final items of the Dogmatism Scale, 37–40, assess the time-perspective dimension. The more closed the individual, the more his belief-disbelief system will be future or past oriented; the present will be rejected as unimportant.

RELIABILITY

Rokeach (1960) reported reliability coefficients for Form E of the Dogmatism Scale for 10 samples. Two reliability estimates, .71 and .84, were based on test-retest data. In eight other samples, the reliability estimates for internal consistency varied from .68 to .93. We computed the average correlation using Fisher's z transformation and found it to be .79.

In their major review of research on dogmatism, Vacchiano, Strauss, and Hochman (1969) cited studies indicating generally high reliability for adult and high school samples. Zagona and Zurcher (1965) reported a 15-week test-retest reliability of .70 for a sample of 517 undergraduates. However, they found the reliability for subjects in the middle third of the dogmatism range to be extremely low ($r = .19$) because of the restricted range of scores.

VALIDITY

The major reason for the construction of the Dogmatism Scale was to provide an instrument that would be sensitive to authoritarianism of the left as well as authoritarianism of the right. Several research tactics have been used to find whether this aim was attained. One tactic was to study the relationship between dogmatism and measures of conservatism. Another was to study dogmatism scores of groups of subjects differing in political preference or political group membership. Still other researchers examined the relationship between dogmatism and attitudes toward the Viet Nam War.

Several studies have shown that scores on the Dogmatism Scale are independent of scores on scales that measure conservatism. Steininger and Lesser (1974) did not find a statistically significant relationship between dogmatism and scores on a scale of liberalism–conservatism. Stimpson and D'Alo (1974) failed to find differences in dogmatism scores among subjects differing in conservatism on issues of women's liberation, beards on young men, socialized medicine, and the United States' relations with Russia. Klyman and Kruckenberg (1974), in a study of about 100 subjects, found no differences in the evaluation of police by groups differing in level of dogmatism.

On the other hand, several investigators found a positive relationship between dogmatism and measures of conservatism (Hanson, 1973; Kirtley & Harkless, 1969; Thompson & Michel, 1972). Steffensmeier (1974) showed that highly dogmatic adults scored higher than low-dogmatic adults on a scale measuring law-and-order attitudes.

If the F and E scales are considered measures of conservatism, studies relating scores on the Dogmatism and F or E scales are also relevant to the issue. For a sample of 147 male high-school students, Schroder and Streufert (1962) found a statistically significant correlation of .56 between scores on the Dogmatism Scale and the F Scale. Zippel and Norman (1966) reported a significant correlation of .67 between the two measures for a sample of 381 undergraduates and other young adults. Sheikh (1968) found a significant correlation of .65 between scores on the Dogmatism and E Scales for a sample of 25 undergraduates. Rule and Hewitt (1970) reported a significant correlation between a 28-item F Scale and the Dogmatism Scale for a sample of 91 male undergraduates ($r = .45$) and for a sample of 113 female undergraduates ($r =$

.56). Thompson and Michel (1972) obtained a correlation of .64 between scores on the F Scale and a modified Dogmatism Scale for a sample of 379 undergraduates, and Kahoe (1974) reported a significant correlation of .66 between Dogmatism- and F-Scale scores for a sample of 188 undergraduates. Hession and McCarthy (1975) found a statistically significant correlation of .54 between scores on the F Scale and Form D of the Dogmatism Scale for a sample of 28 Irish graduate business students.

Plant (1960) reasoned that if scores on the Dogmatism Scale correlated more highly with scores on the F Scale than with scores on the E Scale, this would provide evidence that the Dogmatism Scale was relatively free of ethnocentric-rightist attitudes, since the F Scale is presumably less a measure of rightist orientation than the E Scale. Using data from two samples of English workers and undergraduates reported by Rokeach (1956) and two San Jose State College undergraduate samples each in excess of 1000, Plant showed that the Dogmatism–F-scale correlations were higher than the Dogmatism—E-Scale correlations. Although Plant did not report using tests of significance, we found the reported differences for all four samples to be statistically significant.

Plant also hypothesized that the correlation between *dogmatism* and *ethnocentrism* would be lower than the correlation between *authoritarianism* and *ethnocentrism,* since dogmatism should be freer of rightist orientation than authoritarianism. Reviewing Plant's data, we found statistical support for this hypothesis in two of the four samples. However, we are uncomfortable with these indirect tests of the sensitivity of the Dogmatism Scale as a measure of authoritarianism of the left and right. We are also troubled by the conclusions of a study reported by Hanson (1968), who writes, "While there was no significant difference in dogmatism between Authoritarians (*As*) and Non-Authoritarians (*Ns*), authoritarian responses were more highly correlated with dogmatism than were nonauthoritarian. . . ." It was difficult for us to follow the logic of Hanson's methods and to understand his conclusion.

Thus studies relating performance on the Dogmatism Scale to performance on scales of conservatism have yielded mixed results, except with regard to the consistent positive relationship between scores on the Dogmatism and F scales. One factor that probably contributes to the latter finding is the shared method variance of the two instruments.

The second group of studies is concerned with the relationship between political preference or group membership and dogmatism. In the major report of his work, Rokeach (1960) presented only limited data on this issue. He showed that rightist groups (Catholics from Michigan and New York) and leftist groups (nonbelievers and English communists) all scored high on the Dogmatism Scale. As expected, the rightist groups were higher on the F Scale than were the leftist groups. Eysenck and Coulter (1972) also found that fascists were more authoritarian than communists.

Unfortunately, there are a number of problems with Rokeach's research. For example, there were only six subjects in the nonbeliever group and 13 in the communist group, and many of the conclusions were based on inferences across two studies without statistical tests. For these reasons, data supporting the Dogmatism Scale as a measure of authoritarianism of the right and left must be sought elsewhere.

In one of his studies, Barker (1963) compared the Dogmatism Scale and F Scale scores of three student groups differing in political orientation. He studied 26 students active in rightist causes, 29 active in leftist causes, and 61 "nonorganized" students of presumed intermediate political persuasion. There were highly significant differences among all three groups on F-Scale scores, as might be expected. However, contrary to theoretical expectations, there were also differences on the Dogmatism Scale. Members of the rightist group were significantly more dogmatic than members of either of the other groups.

A number of investigators have studied the relationship between presidential candidate preference and dogmatism. Based on Rokeach's theory, it might be expected that supporters of Republican and Democratic candidates are equally dogmatic. The data do not bear this out. DiRenzo (1968) studied differences in political party preference and presidential candidate preference between high- and low-dogmatic undergraduates. DiRenzo's analysis concerned the 1964 election, in which Johnson opposed Goldwater. In both analyses, DiRenzo obtained statistically significant chi squares and attributed this to a concentration of nondogmatic scorers preferring Democrats and endorsing Johnson. Our reexamination of DiRenzo's data indicates that his interpretation is incorrect. The significant chi squares are produced by an overrepresentation of dogmatic subjects with preferences for Republicans and Goldwater. Regarding the same election, Zippel and Norman (1966) found no differences in presidential preference as a function of Dogmatism-Scale scores. For the 1968 election, DiRenzo (1971) found a greater preference for the conservative candidate, Wallace, by undergraduate and graduate students who were high in dogmatism.

Later, Steininger, Durso, and Pasquariello (1972) obtained more favorable ratings of Nixon and Agnew from higher dogmatic undergraduates than from lower dogmatic undergraduates ($N = 177$). Jones (1973) studied 120 undergraduates eligible to vote in the 1972 presidential election and found that students with dogmatism scores above the mean were more likely to choose Nixon, whereas those scoring below the mean were more likely to favor McGovern. In contrast, Steininger and Lesser (1974) found no differences in dogmatism between Nixon and McGovern supporters for samples of undergraduates and their parents.

The third set of studies relates dogmatism to support of the Viet Nam War. Karabenick and Wilson (1969) found, contrary to expectations based on Rokeach's theory, that students with negative attitudes toward the Viet Nam War were less dogmatic than subjects with moderate or positive attitudes. Overall, they obtained a significant correlation of .23 between attitudes toward Viet Nam and an abbreviated 20-item Dogmatism Scale for their sample of 678 undergraduates. The authors cited a similar finding by Bailes and Guller (1968; cf. Bailes & Guller, 1970) of a correlation of .25 between dogmatism and a different measure of attitudes toward the Viet Nam War. Findings in the same general direction were reported by Larsen (1969) and Steininger, Durso, and Pasquariello (1972). Granberg and Corrigan (1972) found a small relationship between dogmatism and orientations toward the Viet Nam War, but a somewhat stronger relationship between authoritarianism and such attitudes. These studies, then, also suggest that high dogmatism is associated with rightist attitudes.

In a direct study of the content of Dogmatism-Scale items, Parrott and Brown (1972) instructed 48 undergraduates to classify each item as implying a left/liberal orientation, a right/conservative orientation, an indeterminate political orientation, or an apolitical orientation. Their data indicated that 10 items were rated apolitical, and 14 items were of unclear orientation; 14 items were classified politically rightist, and two were classified politically leftist. These results suggest that, to the extent that subjects identify Dogmatism-Scale items as politically left or right, they respond to the content of the instrument, and that the Dogmatism-Scale scores are not entirely free of content bias.

Thus the studies reviewed in this section indicate that individuals who score high on the Dogmatism Scale are likely to be rightist in political orientation. Rokeach's attempt to develop an instrument that would be equally sensitive to dogmatism of the right and left was not successful.

Acquiescence Response Set.   Since the Dogmatism Scale, like the F Scale, is worded so that agreement with each statement contributes to a high score, it is to be expected that the same concern about acquiescence response tendencies would hold for the measurement of dogmatism. In the preceding chapter, we saw that Couch and Keniston (1960) developed an independent measure of acquiescence response set and showed that it correlated significantly (.37) with the F Scale. Using the same group of 61 paid Harvard undergraduates, they obtained a significant correlation of .40 between their measure of acquiescence and the Dogmatism Scale, indicating some influence of acquiescence on the measurement of dogmatism.

Peabody (1961), using a reversed-item approach, found some evidence for acquiescence in both American and English student samples. Rokeach (1967) challenged Peabody's (1961, 1966) citation of a substantial acquiescence response set by referring to the many successful predictions involving the Dogmatism Scale and pointing out difficulties with the reversed-item approach as a measure of acquiescence.

There have been several other attempts to develop balanced forms of the Dogmatism Scale (Haiman, 1964; Haiman & Duns, 1964; Ray, 1970, 1974; Stanley & Martin, 1964). Rather than simply reversing items, Ray (1970) wrote negative items and combined these with 18 of the original Dogmatism Scale items to produce a 36-item balanced scale. The correlation between the 18 original (positive) items and the new 36-item (positive and negative) scale was .88 for a sample of 120 Australians who were members of church study groups. Additional work on the Dogmatism Scale led to the development of a 40-item balanced scale (Ray, 1974).

Lichtenstein, Quinn, and Hover (1961) used two independently derived measures of acquiescence to study response bias in the Dogmatism and F scales. One of these was based on a reversed-item ap-proach; the second was the number of "true" responses on the MMPI. Using a sample of 40 adult male psychiatric inpatients, the authors ob-tained significant correlations ranging from .38 to .51 for the two meas-ures of acquiescence and the Dogmatism and F Scales. The use of the MMPI index, however, is questionable, since the number of "true" scores is also an index of psychopathology.

Roberts (1962) used a measure of intratest variability to study re-sponse set. He found a significant correlation of .21 between his meas-ure of response set and Dogmatism-Scale scores in a study of 100 undergraduates. He also showed that the correlation between F-Scale and Dogmatism-Scale scores is not significantly affected by response set as he measured it. Roberts' approach to the study of response set by way of intraitem variability is provocative, but it has a number of limi-tations discussed by the author.

The results of these studies are similar to those from the larger body of research on acquiescence bias in the F Scale. Again, a small portion of the variance of Dogmatism-Scale scores is attributable to acquies-cence response set. It may be recalled that research on the F Scale showed that acquiescence was more characteristic of high F-Scale scorers than low F-Scale scorers. It seems reasonable to assume that a similar relationship exists between acquiescence and dogmatism; thus the acquiescence effect may not reduce the validity of the Dogmatism Scale.

Social Desirability and Faking. Stanley and Martin (1964) adminis-tered the Martin Social Desirability Scale, the lie scale of the Maudsley Personality Inventory (Gibson, 1962), and the Dogmatism Scale to 127 Australian undergraduates. The correlation between social desirability and dogmatism was a significant $-.23$, indicating that subjects low on dogmatism had a slight tendency to respond in a socially desirable way. The correlation between the lie scale and dogmatism scores was not statistically significant. However, Ray and Martin (1974), with a sample of 51 Australian undergraduates, failed to find a significant rela-tionship between scores on the Dogmatism Scale and the Martin Social Desirability Scale.

In an analysis using the Marlowe–Crowne Social Desirability Scale (Crowne & Marlowe, 1964), Becker and Dileo (1967) found no social desirability differences among 216 undergraduates grouped as high-, middle-, and low-dogmatic. In another study using the Marlowe–Crowne Social Desirability Scale, however, a significant correlation of −.20 was obtained between social desirability and dogmatism scores for a sample of 97 Canadian undergraduates (Bernhardson, 1967). Mac-Donald (1970) reported a significant correlation of .23 between the same two variables for a sample of 341 undergraduates. Thus the evidence indicates that there is at most a slight contamination of Dogmatism-Scale scores by social desirability response set.

Wolfer (1967) showed that Dogmatism-Scale scores could be manipulated by instructing undergraduates to respond in an open-minded or closed-minded way. In another study, he found that informing subjects about what was measured by Dogmatism Scale did not affect performance.

Factor Structure.   The first investigation of the factorial structure of the Dogmatism Scale was reported by Rokeach and Fruchter (1956). Their major concern was the relationship of the Dogmatism Scale to a variety of other measures, including the F Scale, E Scale, PEC Scale, and the Gough–Sanford Rigidity Scale. The latter is included as the flexibility scale of the California Psychological Inventory. The investigators used a 43-item version of the Dogmatism Scale and subjectively derived three scores from it: a dogmatism score (30 items), a self-rejection score (five items), and a paranoia score (eight items). Rokeach and Fruchter hypothesized that these subscales would be discriminable from authoritarianism, ethnocentrism, and rigidity.

The factor analysis was performed on scores from the three subscales and seven other instruments including those cited above. Data were collected from 207 college students in the New York metropolitan area. Rokeach and Fruchter interpreted their findings as supporting their hypotheses. The F Scale and the dogmatism subscale correlated .64. The two scales had their primary loadings on the same factor (rigidity–authoritarianism). However, the dogmatism subscale had a secondary loading on factor I (anxiety), and the F Scale had a secondary loading on factor II (liberalism–conservatism). Thus, although there was considerable overlap between the two scales, there was also evidence that the scales are discriminable. These results were replicated by Fruchter, Rokeach, and Novak (1958) for a sample of Michigan State University undergraduates.

Rokeach and Fruchter also reported that the intercorrelations between the three subscales of the Dogmatism Scale ranged from .30 to .52. The paranoia and self-rejection subscales had their primary loadings on factor I; the dogmatism subscale had a secondary loading on this factor. The dogmatism subscale had its primary loading on factor III, and the self-rejection subscale had a secondary loading on this factor. Thus it appears that some differences exist among the three subscales.

A more direct comparison of differences in factor structure between the F Scale and the Dogmatism Scale was made by Kerlinger and Rokeach (1966). Their subjects were 1239 students at three colleges. The subjects were given a protocol that contained randomly mixed F-Scale and Dogmatism-Scale items. The investigators obtained correlations ranging from .65 to .77 between total scores on the two scales. The factor analysis was performed on the items from both scales combined. On the basis of items with factor loadings greater than .25, five of the 10 extracted factors were identified as dogmatism factors, three were authoritarian factors, and two were mixed. Independent factor analyses of the Dogmatism Scale and the F Scale yielded similar factors. The results indicated that, despite the high correlation between the two scales, the Dogmatism and F scales are factorially discriminable. The results of a second-order factor analysis of the 10 obliquely rotated factors that emerged from the analysis of the combined F and Dogmatism scales also supported the conclusion that the two scales are factorially discriminable. Kerlinger and Rokeach interpreted the five dogmatism factors as somewhat consistent with Rokeach's hypothesized dimensions of dogmatism.

Warr, Lee, and Jöreskog (1969) reanalyzed the Kerlinger and Rokeach (1966) data using a different method of factor analysis and obtained essentially the same results. In a second analysis with 421 Princeton graduate and undergraduate students, Warr, Lee, and Jöreskog used a balanced F Scale (Lee & Warr, 1969) along with the Dogmatism Scale and again replicated the Kerlinger and Rokeach finding that the F Scale and the Dogmatism Scale are factorially discriminable. In a factor analysis using selected items from the Dogmatism and F scales, as well as from other instruments, Poley (1974) also noted the factorial complexity of the two instruments.

Vacchiano, Schiffman, and Strauss (1967) factor analyzed the responses to Dogmatism-Scale items for a sample of 175 undergraduates. Their nine significant factors accounted for 50% of the total variance and were interpreted as supporting Rokeach's dimensions. Separate factor analyses were performed for the 87 males and 88 females and indicated different factorial structures for the two groups. However, the small N relative to the number of items in the test raises doubt as to the reliability of these sex differences.

Pedhazur (1971) also computed separate factor analyses of the Dogmatism Scale for a sample of 526 female and 309 male teachers and graduate students in the New York metropolitan area. The results of the two analyses were similar. Five factors were extracted, and oblique rotations of these factors indicated that the factors were relatively independent of one another. Pedhazur also interpreted his factors to be similar to Rokeach's originally proposed constructs.

Parrott (1971) was concerned with the distinction between the Dogmatism Scale and the Gough–Sanford Rigidity Scale. He administered the two scales, with responses scored agree-disagree, to 1074 Michigan State University general psychology students. A two-factor solution of the matrix of intercorrelations among the items showed that 36 Dogmatism-Scale items had significant loadings ($> .30$) on factor I, whereas 17 of the 22 rigidity items loaded significantly on factor II. Parrott reported the results of an 11-factor solution for the combined items as supporting the factorial discriminability of the two scales; we do not share this interpretation of his reported findings.

Parrott also factor analyzed the Dogmatism-Scale items separately for the total sample and for two subgroups of 300 subjects each. All three analyses yielded nine or 10 factors, but the sets of factors were not similar to one another.

Another factor analysis of the Dogmatism Scale was performed by Gulo and Lynch (1973). Their subjects were 376 undergraduates. The first 14 factors accounted for 58% of the total variance. The investigators compared their factors with those obtained by Pedhazur (1971) and concluded that the factors were different.

The results of some of these studies indicate that the factorial structure of the Dogmatism Scale is similar to that postulated by Rokeach. The Dogmatism Scale, although correlated with the F Scale, is nevertheless discriminable from it.

OTHER VERSIONS OF THE DOGMATISM SCALE

In the course of developing the Dogmatism Scale, Rokeach made four revisions of the instrument. Most of the items were written by him. The original pool consisted of 89 items; the final version, Form E, contains 40 items.

Several investigators have been interested in reducing the length of the Dogmatism Scale. Schulze (1962) developed a 10-item form based on a Guttman scalogram analysis. For two samples, the 10-item Dogmatism Scale correlated .76 and .73 with Form E. Troldahl and Powell (1965), in a carefully done study of 227 Boston suburbanites and a cross-validation sample of 84 Lansing, Michigan adults, reported items that can be reliably used in both interview and self-administration formats to comprise short forms of the Dogmatism Scale. Steininger and Lesser (1974) selected 15 items based on previous factor analyses of the Dogmatism Scale and found that scores based on these 15 items correlated about .90 with scores based on the entire scale for four samples of undergraduates and their parents.

DiRenzo (1967) used an Italian version of this scale in his study of Italian politicians; Gaensslen, May, and Wolpert (1973) used a German translation of the Dogmatism Scale in their study of anxiety.

An elementary school version of the Dogmatism Scale was developed by Figert (1968). Felker and Treffinger (1970), however, have questioned the validity of this instrument. These authors generated five hypotheses regarding expected relationships between dogmatism and other variables. In a study of 120 fourth, fifth, and sixth graders and in separate analyses of data from boys and girls, Felker and Treffinger were generally unable to demonstrate the expected relationships. In fairness to Figert's instrument, some of the hypotheses tested by Felker and Treffinger were somewhat removed from a direct test of dogmatism theory. Murray (1974) presented a 20-item version of the 50-item Figert scale that correlated .78 with the original for a sample of almost 1300 children. Kemp and Kohler (1965) reported that Form E of the Dogmatism Scale is suitable for use with eighth and ninth graders. Teachers' ratings of dogmatism correlated .74 with Dogmatism-Scale scores for a sample of 20 extremely high- and 20 extremely low-dogmatic children.

SCORING. METHODS

Several investigators have been interested in whether the Dogmatism Scale could be scored on a two-point disagree-agree scale, rather than on the six-point scale originally proposed by Rokeach. Peabody (1962) and Korn and Giddan (1964) obtained significant correlations of .93 and .94 for sample sizes of 88 and 195, respectively, between scores based on the original system of scoring and a simple count of the number of "agree" responses. Shupe and Wolfer (1966) showed that two-point and six-point scoring of the Dogmatism Scale yielded comparable test-retest reliability data. These studies, then, suggest that a Dogmatism-Scale score based on the number of "agree" responses yields scores that are similar to scores based on the more complex, standard scoring.

NORMS

Most of the studies involving the Dogmatism Scale delineate high-dogmatic subjects in terms of high scores for the sample under investigation. Alter and White (1966) provided a valuable service by reporting the means and standard deviations of Dogmatism-Scale scores for 37 samples ranging in size from 1436 to 20 with a total of 12,977 subjects. The authors reported an overall mean of 159.21 and standard deviation of 31.38. The wide range in means from one sample to another suggested subcultural differences in dogmatism. Alter and White also found the scores of males to be consistently higher than those of females. However, in a paper by Anderson (1962) that was not cited by Alter and White, an analysis of dogmatism scores of 768 eighth, tenth, eleventh, and twelfth graders revealed no sex differences.

DEVELOPMENT

The only developmental data presented in *The Open and Closed Mind* are contained in a study reported by Rokeach and Kemp (1960). The subjects of the study were 104 "religious-minded persons" enrolled in a denominational college (Kemp, 1960). Students whose dogmatism scores were in the upper quartile were labeled "open," those in the lower quartile were labeled "closed," and the remaining half of the subjects were placed in a "middle" group. Based on responses to open-ended questions, relationships with parents were described as "ambivalent," "mildly ambivalent," or "glorification of parent." Data were analyzed separately for mother and father. About 65% of the "open" group were ambivalent toward their parents, whereas about 58% of the "closed" group were mildly ambivalent toward their parents.

These results were interpreted by Rokeach and Kemp as consistent with those obtained with regard to the F Scale in *The Authoritarian Personality*. However, 72% of the subjects in Rokeach and Kemp's "middle" group were categorized as making statements that reflected a glorification of parents. Rokeach and Kemp were at a loss to explain this finding and pointed out that the research in *The Authoritarian Personality* was done with extreme groups. This unexpected finding with a group in the middle range highlights the danger of generalizing across a continuum from data collected from extremes of that continuum.

In addition to these findings, Rokeach and Kemp presented some data suggesting that open subjects are more likely to report that they were influenced by a wider number of individuals outside the family than were more closed subjects.

As postulated in *The Authoritarian Personality*, Rokeach hypothesized that the inability to express ambivalence toward the parents results in the repression of hostility and is anxiety provoking. Rokeach and Kemp therefore expected symptoms of anxiety in childhood to coexist with the inability to express ambivalent feelings, which in turn is related to dogmatism. They showed that the middle and closed groups reported more childhood symptoms of anxiety (e.g., nightmares) than the open group.

A more direct test of these relationships was reported by Hanson and Clune (1973). The authors administered an unpublished children's Dogmatism Scale (Dommert, 1967) to 73 seventh- and eighth-grade children. Children scoring one standard deviation or more above the mean were labeled high dogmatics, and those scoring one standard deviation or more below the mean were labeled low dogmatics. As in the Rokeach and Kemp study, Hanson and Clune found that the high-dogmatic children reported more childhood symptoms of anxiety.

However, they failed to substantiate the Rokeach and Kemp findings that high dogmatics have a narrower circle of people who influence them.

Rebhun (1967) is one of the few investigators who offered direct evidence on the relationship of dogmatism to child-rearing practices. He administered eight scales of Schaefer and Bell's (1960) father form of the Parent Attitude Research Instrument (PARI) to three samples of undergraduates totaling 311 subjects. Rebhun found significant positive correlations between dogmatism and the PARI scales, indicating that high-dogmatic subjects were expressing controlling child-rearing attitudes. He interpreted this as an attempt by dogmatic subjects to protect their closed belief systems.

In a study by Lesser and Steininger (1975), the Dogmatism Scale was administered to 78 male and 89 female college students, who in turn administered the scale to 108 of their fathers and 138 of their mothers. The correlations between the dogmatism scores of children and their parents and between husbands and wives were statistically significant, ranging from .20 to .40. There was also an indication that parents were more dogmatic than their children.

EDUCATION

A number of investigators have been interested in the relationship between the level of dogmatism and education. Anderson (1962) judged 26 items of the Dogmatism Scale to be suited to the level of maturity of eighth-, tenth-, eleventh-, and twelfth-grade students. He administered these 26 items to such a sample of students and found the twelfth graders to be significantly less dogmatic than children in the other three groups. The eleventh graders were found to be significantly less dogmatic than the eighth graders. Pannes (1963) studied the relationship between scores on a 25-item reworded Dogmatism Scale and grade level among 675 seventh to twelfth graders. She obtained a significant correlation of $-.13$, indicating a slight decrease in dogmatism with increasing school grade.

The results of several studies indicate that students who are in the later stages of their college careers are less dogmatic than college freshmen. Lehmann (1963) tested 1051 Michigan State University students in their freshman year and again in their senior year. He found a significant decrease in dogmatism for both males and females. On the basis of data from a subsample, he found that much of the change for both males and females was accounted for by the end of the sophomore year. Lehmann reported a significant decrease in the variance of dogmatism scores for his male subjects between the freshmen and senior testings; the change in variance for female subjects was not statistically significant. The test-retest correlations between dogmatism scores over the college years were statistically significant for both males ($r = .53$) and females ($r = .50$). Turck (1969) found a significant decrease in dogmatism for a group of 396 education majors tested as freshmen and again as seniors. In a later cross-sectional study with similar subjects, Ayers and Turck (1976) provided data that we find indicative of a significantly lower level of dogmatism for seniors than for freshmen.

Berdie (1974) found significant decreases in levels of dogmatism after only one-quarter of the freshman year for a total of 379 students. There were no special reductions in dogmatism that could be attributed to a human relations course. McLeish and Park (1973) found that Dogmatism-Scale scores were not influenced by participation in any of several human relations training groups, and Heikkinen and German (1975) found that dogmatism scores were not influenced by a one-month counseling practicum. Davis, Frye, and Joure (1975) demonstrated that low-dogmatic individuals were more open and less negative in their behavior in T-groups than high-dogmatic individuals. The investigators did not report data on changes in levels of dogmatism as a function of the experience. Foulds, Guinan, and Warehime (1974) reported a significant decrease in Dogmatism-Scale scores for a group of 15 undergraduates who had participated in a 24-hour marathon growth group. The post-test was administered seven days following the group experience. A control group of 15 subjects selected from a waiting list showed no such change.

In a series of studies (Plant, 1965a, b; Plant & Telford, 1966) the Dogmatism Scale was administered to applicants to a number of California colleges. Later, subjects were retested; some had attended college, and some had not. Significant decreases in dogmatism scores were found for subjects who had attended college for one to eight semesters, as well as for the subjects who had not attended college. These results paralleled those obtained with the authoritarianism and ethnocentrism scales. As Plant pointed out, the finding of significant decreases in dogmatism scores among subjects who did not attend college challenges the interpretation that the college experience is responsible for decreases in dogmatism. The interpretation of the findings is complicated, however, because of several methodological problems. One problem is that of extensive missing data (return rates for retesting ranging from 67 to 46%), raising the question of subject selectivity. Another problem is that the first administration of the testing instruments was part of a preenrollment testing situation, whereas follow-up testing was by mail.

Marcus (1964) found a significant difference in dogmatism scores between first- and fourth-year medical students; fourth-year students were less dogmatic. Marcus also reported that freshmen college students had significantly higher dogmatism scores than the medical students. Again, these results must be interpreted with caution. The college and first-year medical students were administered the Dogmatism Scale in large groups; the fourth-year medical students responded to mailed questionnaires. The college students are likely to have differed from the medical students on a number of personal-social dimensions. Finally, Marcus did not test subjects of similar age who did not attend college.

Available research on developmental issues indicates family relationships similar to those found in the more extensive work on the development of authoritarianism. Highly dogmatic individuals seem to be ambivalent toward their controlling parents. Studies also indicate a decrease in dogmatism with increasing age. However, there is some question whether education leads to decreasing dogmatism.

RESEARCH

The information-processing ability of subjects varying in level of dogmatism has been studied with regard to a variety of experimental issues, including the relationship of dogmatism to openness to information, independence of judgment, creativity, and decision making. As shown in the preceding chapter, the two major cognitive style variables of concern in the study of authoritarianism were rigidity and intolerance of ambiguity. Because interest in dogmatism was rooted in the study of authoritarianism, our survey of relevant research begins with a consideration of the relationship of dogmatism to rigidity and intolerance of ambiguity.

INTOLERANCE OF AMBIGUITY

There have been relatively few studies of the relationship between dogmatism and intolerance of ambiguity. In a study reported by Barker (1963), data were gathered from 160 graduate students in the New York City area. Among a battery of tests that was administered were the Dogmatism Scale and Siegel's (1954) Test for Tolerance-Intolerance of Cognitive Ambiguity. The high-dogmatic subjects were significantly more intolerant of ambiguity than the low-dogmatic subjects.

The measure of intolerance of ambiguity developed by Budner (1962) was used in several studies. Day (1966) gathered data from 26 female nursing students and obtained a nonsignificant correlation between scores on the Dogmatism Scale and the Budner measure. However, Feather (1969b) found that Dogmatism-Scale scores were significantly correlated with scores on Budner's measure of intolerance of ambiguity. For a sample of 77 male undergraduates, $r = .50$; for a sample of 81 female undergraduates, $r = .30$. In a later study, Feather (1971) obtained statistically significant correlations of .20 and .21 between dogmatism and Budner's test for two samples of Australian undergraduates. Norton (1975), in a study of 79 undergraduates, failed to find a statistically significant correlation between the Budner test and Troldahl and Powell's (1965) short-form Dogmatism Scale. Neither Norton's own measure of intolerance of ambiguity nor a measure developed by Martin and Westie (1959) correlated significantly with the Trodahl and Powell test.

In the preceding chapter it was reported that authoritarianism was significantly related to MacDonald's (1970) Intolerance of Ambiguity Scale (AT-20). MacDonald also reported a statistically significant correlation of .42 between dogmatism and intolerance of ambiguity for his sample of 698 male and female undergraduates. Chabassol and Thomas (1975) administered the AT-20 and the Dogmatism Scale to a sample of 400 eighth to eleventh graders and obtained a statistically significant correlation of .37 for the total sample.

Jones (1955) had reported that authoritarianism was releated to intolerance of ambiguity as measured by perceptions of Necker Cube reversals. Sanders (1977) hypothesized that individuals high in dogmatism would also be less likely to see reversals on a Necker Cube, and would be more likely to see alternation (rather than fusion) on a binocular retinal rivalry task. For a sample of 84 undergraduates, significant correlations of .35 and .49 were found in the two conditions, supporting the hypothesis that high-dogmatic subjects tend to be intolerant of ambiguity.

The weight of the evidence suggests that high-dogmatic subjects are less tolerant of ambiguity than low-dogmatic subjects, a finding paralleling that for authoritarianism.

RIGIDITY

Beginning with the first publication of his theory of dogmatism, Rokeach (1954) sought to distinguish dogmatism from rigidity. Although both dogmatism and rigidity imply resistance to change, Rokeach (1954) views dogmatism ". . . as a higher-order and more complexly organized form of resistance to change." Rokeach (1960) noted correlations ranging from .37 to .55 between the Dogmatism Scale and the Gough and Sanford (1952) Rigidity Scale for various samples. In a study of 195 male college freshmen by Korn and Giddan (1964), a statistically significant correlation of .36 was found between Dogmatism-Scale scores and rigidity as measured by the flexibility subtest of the California Psychological Inventory. The flexibility subtest was originally the Gough and Sanford Rigidity Scale. For a sample of 147 male high-school students, Schroder and Streufert (1962) found a significant correlation of .37 between the Dogmatism Scale and the Gough and Sanford Rigidity Scale; for a sample of 787 undergraduates, MacDonald (1970) reported a significant correlation of .36 between the two measures, and Hession and McCarthy (1975) obtained a significant correlation of .39 for a sample of 28 Irish graduate students. Riley and Armlin (1965) showed a relationship between dogmatism and inflexibility in performance on the Porteus Mazes, a pencil-and-paper test requiring the subjects to trace paths out of mazes.

White and Alter (1965) found evidence of rigidity among high-dogmatic subjects in a psychophysical task. The performance of undergraduate students who had scored in the top 15% of a class of 410 students in dogmatism and authoritarianism was compared with that of students in the lower 15% in dogmatism and authoritarianism. In a task in which the subjects were asked to make comparisons among five weights and an anchor, the high-dogmatic/authoritarian subjects were less influenced by the introduction of the anchor and continued to make judgments closer to their preanchor judgments, exhibiting greater rigidity. White and Alter failed to find a hypothesized difference between high- and low-dogmatic/authoritarian subjects in the number of categories used to judge weights or the range of categories used.

Although the interpretation of the White and Alter study is difficult because of the confounding of authoritarianism and dogmatism, there generally is an indication that high-dogmatic subjects are rigid.

ANALYTIC AND SYNTHESIZING ABILITY

To differentiate rigidity from dogmatism, a distinction was made between *analytic* aspects of thinking and *synthesizing* phases of problem solution (Rokeach, McGovney, & Denny, 1955, 1960). The former refers to the replacement of old beliefs with new beliefs. The latter refers to the integration of the new beliefs into a belief system. Rokeach predicted that high- and low-rigid subjects could be distinguished with regard to analytic thinking; that is, subjects high in rigidity would have difficulty changing old beliefs. Rokeach maintained that high- and low-dogmatic subjects could be differentiated with regard to their ability to synthesize; that is, subjects high in dogmatism would have difficulty integrating new beliefs into belief systems. The hypothesized inability of high-dogmatic subjects to synthesize new beliefs into a belief system follows from their tendency to maintain isolation among beliefs. However, this relationship between synthesizing and isolation is not explicit in Rokeach's writings.

To distinguish operationally between rigidity and dogmatism, it was necessary to employ a research task that would permit the separation of analytic and synthesizing aspects of problem solution. The task used by Rokeach, called the Denny Doodlebug Problem, was originally devised in 1945 by M. Ray Denny and modified by Rokeach and Denny for this application. The problem was presented originally by Rokeach, McGovney, and Denny (1955). The subject is informed about Joe Doodlebug, an imaginary bug that can jump only north, south, east, or west. There are a number of other constraints on Joe's movement. Within these constraints, the subject is asked to solve a problem having to do with Joe's movement to a dish of food. There is only one correct solution to the problem. This solution requires the subject to break several implicit sets.

In Rokeach's studies, subjects were allowed 30–45 minutes to attempt a solution. At various intervals, hints were given. Each hint was designed to overcome a set (belief) that presumably blocks the solution of the problem. The time taken to incorporate the new beliefs, as well as the number of beliefs overcome without outside help, are indices of the facility with which the subject accomplishes the analytic phase. The second stage of solution of the problem is the integration of these new beliefs into a belief system. The speed with which the subject achieves solution once he has passed through the analytic phase is an index of his synthesizing ability.

In the first study reported by Rokeach and his colleagues (Rokeach, McGovney, & Denny, 1955), four groups of 15 subjects each were formed: high dogmatism–high rigidity, high dogmatism–low rigidity, low dogmatism–high rigidity, and low dogmatism–low rigidity. These groups were formed on the basis of scores obtained on an early version of the Dogmatism Scale, and on the Gough and Sanford Rigidity Scale. Using the number of sets overcome in the first 10 and first 15 minutes as indices of the effectiveness of analytic thinking, Rokeach found that the high-rigid subjects were less likely to overcome any of the three sets than were the low-rigid subjects; there were no statistically significant differences in analytic thinking between high- and low-dogmatic subjects.

A measure of synthesizing ability is the time necessary to solve the problem once the new beliefs have been learned. There were no statistically significant differences between high- and low-dogmatic subjects, nor between high- and low-rigid subjects, when time was measured beginning from the point at which the three beliefs were overcome. However, high-dogmatic subjects took significantly longer than low-dogmatic subjects to solve the problem when time was measured from the point at which two of the beliefs were overcome.

Although this result is in the hypothesized direction, the data regarding synthesizing ability are not as consistent as the data regarding analytic ability.

In a subsequent study by Rokeach and Vidulich (1960), it was shown that high- and low-dogmatic subjects were consistently different with regard to their synthesizing ability but not their analytic ability. The use of subjects with more extreme scores on the Dogmatism Scale may have accounted for these results. In *The Open and Closed Mind*, Rokeach presented additional data from studies involving variations of the Denny Doodlebug Problem that confirm other aspects of dogmatism theory.

Studies by Fillenbaum and Jackman (1961) and Lyda and Fillenbaum (1964) demonstrated that the final Doodlebug hint is extremely important for the solution of the problem. The hint they provided their subjects, however, differed slightly from the hint provided in the Rokeach studies.

The hypothesis that dogmatic subjects vary in their synthesizing ability, originally explored by the use of the Doodlebug problems, was also explored in the perceptual area. Levy and Rokeach (1960) used an embedded figures test adapted from Witkin (1950) and the block design subscale of the Wechsler Adult Intelligence Scale to study differences in analytic and synthesizing perceptual ability. The Embedded Figures Test, another measure of cognitive style about which we have more to say in Chapter 6, requires the subject to recognize a simple design embedded in a complex configuration. This task was viewed as tapping analytic cognitive ability, and Levy and Rokeach (1960) hypothesized that high- and low-dogmatic subjects would not differ in their performances. The block design scale requires the subject to use blocks to reconstruct a geometric design pictured on a card. This task was used as a measure of synthesizing ability. It was hypothesized that high-dogmatic subjects would not perform as well on this task as low-dogmatic subjects.

Seventeen extremely high-dogmatic subjects and 16 extremely low-dogmatic subjects, equated for intelligence, were selected from a pool of about 400 students. There were no differences in performance by the open and closed subjects on any of the 12 embedded figures. For the first three block-design problems there were no significant differences between the two groups; for the remaining three the differences were interpreted as "nearly significant" on the basis of one-tailed tests of significance at the .06 and .09 levels of significance.

An interesting experiment in the study of the synthesizing ability of high- and low-dogmatic subjects in the perceptual area was made by Iverson and Schwab (1967). Subjects viewed two different pictures through a stereoscope. It was possible for a subject to report fusion (i.e., seeing a composite of the two pictures) or bifurcation (i.e., seeing one or the other of the two pictures). The investigators reasoned that low-dogmatic subjects, because of their superior synthesizing ability, would tend to make more fusion responses than would high-dogmatic subjects. The results generally supported this hypothesis. However, Iverson and Schwab contrasted subjects high in both dogmatism and ethnocentrism with those low in both dogmatism and ethnocentrism; thus their results are limited to comparisons of high-dogmatics of the right with low-dogmatics of the left. Because of this design, it is difficult to disentangle effects due to attitude from those due to cognitive style.

Another aspect of analyzing ability is the individual's ability to discriminate sensory information. Kaplan and Singer (1963) contrasted the sensory acuity of high- and low-dogmatic subjects across five sensory modalities. From a pool of 40 subjects they selected the 13 highest and 13 lowest scorers on dogmatism. The authors showed that low-dogmatic subjects performed significantly better on acuity tasks for four of the five modalities (smell, taste, touch, and hearing); there were no significant differences in visual acuity. Dogmatism was significantly and negatively correlated (−.61) with a total sensory acuity score.

In another investigation, Mouw (1969) compared the analyzing and synthesizing ability of subjects varying in level of dogmatism. Mouw used five scales from an instrument developed by Kropp and Stoker (1966). Four of these scales measured analytic ability; the fifth measured synthesizing ability. Mouw reasoned that low-dogmatic subjects would perform similarly on the synthesizing and analytic scales, whereas the high-dogmatic subjects would perform better on the analytic than the synthesizing scale. The subjects in the study were 84 undergraduates. The performance of these subjects did not support the hypothesis. However, it is not clear that Mouw's experimental paradigm provided an appropriate test of Rokeach's contention that subjects varying in rigidity would differ in analyzing ability, whereas those varying in dogmatism would differ in synthesizing ability.

Thus Rokeach's hypothesis seems to have found its major support when performance on the Doodlebug problem was used to assess analyzing and synthesizing ability. Studies involving other tasks have yielded equivocal results. However, the tasks used to measure analytic and synthesizing ability often differed in many important respects from Rokeach's definition of these variables; thus some of the studies are not valid tests of the hypothesis.

INFLUENCE BY AUTHORITY

Another aspect of the definition of dogmatism deals with ". . . the extent to which the person can receive, evaluate, and act on relevant information received from the outside on its own intrinsic merits, unencumbered by irrelevant factors in the situation arising from within the person or from the outside" (Rokeach, 1960). The influence of the source of the message on a person's judgment of the content of the message is one area in which the effect of irrelevant information on high-dogmatic subjects has been studied. Rokeach wrote that the essence of the differentiation between an open-minded and a closed-minded subject is ". . . the capacity to distinguish information from source of information and to evaluate each on its own merit."

Powell (1962) showed that the evaluations of political statements by high-dogmatic subjects were less independent of their evaluations of the political candidates making the statements than were evaluations made by low-dogmatic subjects. Powell's 76 subjects were drawn from the population of Lansing, Michigan, and the surrounding township, on the basis of modified quota sampling. The subjects made semantic differential ratings of Kennedy and Nixon, the two major presidential candidates in 1960, and of statements dealing with domestic policy, foreign policy, and racial integration. One-half of the subjects first rated the candidates and then the statements attributed to them; the remaining one-half first rated the statements (without attribution to the candidates) and then rated the candidates after being told who had made the statements. In both situations the high-dogmatic subjects rated the candidates and their statements more similarly than the low-dogmatic subjects, indicating that high-dogmatic subjects were more influenced in their judgments of the message by their evaluation of its source than were low-dogmatic subjects. It was also shown that the evaluation of the source was similarly influenced by prior evaluation of the message.

Becker (1967) obtained different results. His 150 undergraduate subjects made judgments about the humor of each of six jokes attributed to different comedians. He found that subjects scoring in the middle range of dogmatism rated the humor of the jokes independently of the popularity of the comedian to whom the joke was attributed. However, both low- and high-dogmatic subjects were influenced by the popularity of the comedian. Unfortunately, since Becker did not provide the range of the dogmatism scores of his subjects, it is impossible to compare the level of dogmatism of his subjects with those in other studies. It may well be, for example, that Becker's middle group was similar in dogmatism to the low-dogmatic subjects in the previous study.

Vidulich and Kaiman (1961) studied the effect of high- and low-status confederates on subjects' judgments in the autokinetic situation. They hypothesized that high-dogmatic subjects would conform with the judgments of a high-status confederate but would reject the judgments of a low-status confederate. Low-dogmatic subjects should show little difference in their reactions to the two types of confederates. From a pool of 307 undergraduates, the authors selected 30 females who were high in dogmatism and 30 who were low in dogmatism. The high-status confederate was presented as a college professor; the low-status confederate was presented as a high-school student.

First each subject made 30 judgments in the autokinetic situation of the perceived right–left movement of the light source. The next 30 judgments were made after judgments by the confederate. The confederate made 80% of his judgments in the direction initially least favored by the subject. Vidulich and Kaiman's data indicated that high-dogmatic subjects rejected the judgments of the low-status confederate, but shifted toward the judgments of the high-status confederate.

In the study by Mouw (1969) previously cited no differences were found in the analytic and synthesizing abilities of high- and low-dogmatic subjects. The series of tasks used in the study varied in the degree to which the solutions were dependent on authority. For example, at one extreme, performance required remembering material; at the other extreme the scale required the putting together of parts to form a whole. The former was dependent on authority (i.e., repeating authoritative information); the latter was independent of authority (i.e., requiring reliance on one's own problem-solving ability). Mouw's data indicated that low-dogmatic subjects improved their performances as the tasks required more autonomy, whereas high-dogmatic subjects did not perform as well on tasks requiring autonomy.

Another study with implications for the effects of authority on the synthesizing ability of high- and low-dogmatic subjects is that by Bettinghaus, Miller, and Steinfatt (1970). The authors presented valid and invalid syllogisms to 60 high-dogmatic and 60 low-dogmatic subjects, selected mostly from a population of undergraduates. Four of the syllogisms were on neutral topics, such as baseball; the remaining 16 concerned escalation of the war in Viet Nam. In one presentation, the syllogisms were attributed to positively evaluated sources (Dwight Eisenhower, Billy Graham, Eugene McCarthy, and Earl Warren); in another they were attributed to negatively evaluated sources (H. Rapp Brown, George Wallace, Stokely Carmichael, and Ralph Shelton). Bettinghaus and his colleagues found some evidence that dogmatic subjects were more responsive to the source to whom the syllogistic argument was attributed. When high-dogmatic subjects viewed the source as positive, and the argument was valid, they tended to be correct more frequently than low-dogmatic subjects. When the high-dogmatic subjects viewed the source as negative, and the argument was invalid, they were more often correct than were the low-dogmatic subjects.

Schultz and DiVesta (1972) examined the effects of expert endorsement of Doodlebug beliefs on the solution of the Doodlebug problem. The investigators presented their subjects with pairs of hints, one of the pair being a useful hint ("new belief") and one being a hindrance ("old belief"). For some subjects, the new beliefs were presented as endorsed by experts; for others the old beliefs were presented as endorsed by experts. Schultz and DiVesta argued that expert endorsement of new beliefs would facilitate the performance of high-dogmatic subjects relative to low-dogmatic subjects, whereas expert endorsement of old beliefs would have the opposite effect. They reasoned that, since high-dogmatic subjects are more likely to accept authority-backed statements uncritically, their performances would be facilitated when the advice was correct. Low-dogmatic subjects, on the other hand, would not accept authority and therefore would not be helped as much when experts provided correct clues, nor would they be hindered as much when experts endorsed incorrect hints. The data obtained from 90 undergraduates supported the hypotheses.

Harvey and Hays (1972) studied whether high- and low-dogmatic subjects were differentially influenced by expert opinion. A four-page typescript of a speech on air pollution control was attributed to either a research physiologist or a high school senior. Using 80 female undergraduates as subjects, Harvey and Hays found that high-dogmatic subjects were more influenced by the high-authority position.

Rosenman (1967) predicted that low-dogmatic subjects would more positively evaluate the movie *Dr. Strangelove* on the basis of the movie being a satire of authority figures in the United States. The author found that extremely high-dogmatic subjects rated the movie less favorably than extremely low-dogmatic subjects. However, one would not necessarily be led to this prediction from dogmatism theory. One would expect, for example, that high-dogmatics of the left would rate the film quite favorably. The result obtained is probably because of the inclusion of a high proportion of dogmatics of the right in the sample or bias in the instrument.

Taken collectively, there is evidence in these studies that high-dogmatics are more influenced by authority than are low-dogmatics.

CONSISTENCY

A number of other investigators have been interested in the openness of dogmatic subjects to new information. Based on Rokeach's (1960) writings, Kleck and Wheaton (1967) reasoned that high-dogmatic subjects would prefer information consistent with their opinions. Using 72 high-school students as subjects, the researchers failed to confirm this hypothesis. The issue studied was the age at which driver's licenses should be issued. The students were given a choice of reading one of two fictitious newspaper articles, one favoring the status quo (licenses at age 16), the other favoring raising the age to 18. Both the high- and low-dogmatic subjects tended to choose the article consistent with their beliefs, a finding consistent with cognitive dissonance theory.

In a second stage of the experiment, all students were presented with both articles. Kleck and Wheaton found that high-dogmatic subjects were less able to recall information from the article that was inconsistent with their beliefs than were low-dogmatic subjects. There was also evidence that high-dogmatic subjects evaluated the article that was consistent with their beliefs more positively than low-dogmatic subjects. The difference with regard to the article that was inconsistent with the subjects' beliefs was not statistically significant. Gormly and Clore (1969), in their study of 96 undergraduates, found no evidence that high dogmatics recalled fewer attitude statements that contradicted their opinions.

A study similar to the first part of the Kleck and Wheaton (1967) study was conducted by Rosnow, Gitter, and Holz (1969) as part of a larger investigation of factors related to information preference. The subjects were 106 undergraduates. Each subject was presented with either a favorable or unfavorable evaluation of a Peace Corps candidate and asked to rate the candidate's suitability for the Peace Corps. Following this, the subjects were given an opportunity to listen to an evaluation of the Peace Corps candidate by a psychologist. The evaluation was either consistent or inconsistent with the subjects' ratings. The subjects were divided at the median on the basis of their Dogmatism-Scale scores. There was no significant difference between high- and low-dogmatic subjects in their preferences for information consistent or inconsistent with the ratings they had made. This failure to find differences between the high- and low-dogmatic subjects is similar to the findings of Kleck and Wheaton (1967). In the Kleck and Wheaton study, both groups preferred information consistent with their beliefs; in the Rosnow, Gitter, and Holz study, both groups preferred information inconsistent with their beliefs. This difference in information preference found in the two studies illustrates the complexity of the determinants of information preference.

Clarke and James (1967) gave their 79 undergraduates an opportunity to request additional information in three experimental conditions: in preparation for a debate, in preparation for public discussion, and for private use. They obtained a statistically significant correlation of .40 between dogmatism and requests for information supporting the individual's point of view under the private use conditions. Dogmatism was not related to requests for information under either of the public conditions. Clarke and James reasoned that, under private conditions, high dogmatics seek supportive information to maintain cognitive consistency, whereas under public conditions ". . . dogmatism is not a correlate of information preferences, because situational factors evoke other personality needs." However, we find nothing in Rokeach's theory that would lead to these differential predictions. We believe that the relationship between dogmatism and information preference should have been predicted across all three conditions.

Durand and Lambert (1975) provided evidence that high-dogmatic subjects are unlikely to seek out information that contradicts their own political beliefs. In their study of 181 undergraduate and graduate students, they found that high-dogmatic subjects indicated a greater unwillingness to attend talks by political candidates in the 1972 presidential primary with whom they disagreed than did low-dogmatic subjects.

Hunt and Miller (1968) showed that high-dogmatic undergraduates became more opposed to disarmament when asked to write arguments against disarmament. There was no such shift for low-dogmatic subjects. This study provides further support for the finding that high-dogmatic subjects have less tolerance for inconsistency than low-dogmatic subjects. In this situation, when the high-dogmatic subjects were required to prepare material that was discrepant from their original attitudes, their attitudes shifted in the direction of the discrepant material. Osborn (1973) reported similar findings in a study of 104 undergraduates. He observed that low-dogmatic subjects changed more when dealing with congruent information and that high-dogmatic subjects changed more when dealing with incongruent information.

In related research, Smith (1968) found that high-dogmatic subjects, when highly interested in a topic (federal aid to parochial schools), were more likely to be familiar with arguments contradictory to their own beliefs than were low-dogmatic subjects. Among subjects with little interest in the issue, the reverse was true. Smith hypothesized that highly interested, low-dogmatic subjects are more likely to change their beliefs in the direction of their knowledge, whereas high-dogmatic subjects retain both the knowledge and the contradictory beliefs, rigidly compartmentalizing between the two. Since no tests of statistical significance were employed, the findings must be regarded with caution.

Feather (1969b) found that high-dogmatic undergraduates preferred arguments consistent with their points of view and arguments that were familiar, whereas low-dogmatic subjects showed preferences for novel arguments and arguments inconsistent with their points of view. In another study (Feather, 1969a) undergraduates were asked to write arguments consistent and inconsistent with their beliefs. No differences were found between high- and low-dogmatic subjects in the number of consistent versus inconsistent arguments they listed.

Franklin and Carr (1971) criticized the Feather (1969a) study on methodological grounds. They argued that a belief system is comprised of arguments both for and against one's opinion. That is, an individual who believes in the legalization of marijuana usage may agree with a number of arguments both for and against this position. Considering both belief and disbelief systems in this way, Franklin and Carr studied differences between high- and low-dogmatic subjects with regard to opinions about the withdrawal of United States troops from South Viet Nam. They found that high-dogmatic subjects had less differentiated disbelief systems than low-dogmatic subjects. They also found more isolation in both belief and disbelief systems among high-dogmatic subjects. The investigators accounted for the difference between their results and those of Feather in terms of the conceptualization of belief and disbelief systems. In a rejoinder, Feather (1973) applied Franklin and Carr's method to data from three of his previous studies. Generally, he found no differences in performance by high- and low-dogmatic subjects, thus failing to replicate the Franklin and Carr results.

In an interesting variation of these studies, Snoek and Dobbs (1967) compared the GSR responses of high- and low-dogmatic subjects to arguments that varied in level of presumed similarity to the subjects' attitudes. They reasoned that since large GSR responses are an index of anxiety, high-dogmatic subjects would be more anxious in the presence of discrepant information and would exhibit larger GSRs than would low-dogmatic subjects. Although it was found that high-dogmatic subjects evidenced greater GSR responses overall, they did not differentially overreact to the discrepant information. In another study, Crano and Sigal (1968) showed that high-dogmatic subjects, when confronted with material discrepant from their attitudes, tended to accept or reject the source and message in a consistent manner.

Adams and Vidulich (1962) hypothesized that high-dogmatic subjects would have greater difficulty learning paired associates when the stimulus response pair was incongruent (e.g., Hobo-rich) than when it was congruent (e.g., Hobo-poor). Using 36 undergraduates as subjects in the study, Adams and Vidulich showed that all the subjects had more difficulty learning the incongruent pairs and that high-dog-matic subjects generally performed worse than low-dogmatic subjects. However, the hypothesized significant interaction between dogmatism and congruence-incongruence was not demonstrated in the analysis of variance.

The subjects in a study by Pyron and Kafer (1967) were required to supply the end of a sentence when the first part was presented as a stimulus. The two parts of each sentence were only remotely con-nected. Half the sentences were considered interesting (e.g., "She rubbed brandy into the eyes of: the piano.") and half uninteresting (e.g., "The shape of the building was: infrequent."). As the investiga-tors hypothesized, subjects higher in dogmatism had more difficulty performing the learning task for the interesting sentences than did subjects lower in dogmatism; there were no differences among the subjects differing in level of dogmatism for the uninteresting pairings. These findings also support the notion that high-dogmatic subjects have more difficulty with novel material.

Foulkes and Foulkes (1965) argued that since high-dogmatics would have difficulty synthesizing, they would react differently from low-dog-matics when presented with inconsistent trait information about hypo-thetical individuals. Sixty-two female undergraduates were presented with several descriptions of young women. In four of these descrip-tions, the first nine items included statements that presented a con-sistent trait description; the remaining six items included statements that contradicted the information previously presented. The authors found some evidence that high-dogmatic subjects shifted impressions either a great deal or very little, compared to the low-dogmatic sub-jects, who shifted moderately. The data in this study were analyzed by using four chi-square analyses, only one of which was statistically significant. The study is in need of replication. In a study containing data on the relationship between dogmatism and reaction to incon-sistent personality descriptions, Steininger and Eisenberg (1976) failed to obtain significant relationships between scores derived from the Dogmatism Scale and changes of ratings of personality based on the inconsistent information.

Thus the research reviewed in this section fails to provide a clear picture of the relationship between dogmatism and consistency.

OPENNESS

Mikol (1960) studied the reactions of high- and low-dogmatic subjects to a new musical system. Mikol wrote that there are new music systems that, like the Doodlebug problems, violate our usual belief systems. With regard to the latter, Mikol was interested in the violation of beliefs ". . . about what constitutes pleasing music."

Mikol hypothesized that high-dogmatic subjects would be more likely to reject a new musical system than would low-dogmatic subjects, but that there would be no difference in the preference of the two groups for conventional music. From a group of 133 subjects, Mikol selected the 20 highest and 20 lowest in dogmatism. The subjects listened to 2½-minute excerpts from string quartets by Brahms (conventional) and Schonberg (novel). As hypothesized, there were no differences between high- and low-dogmatic subjects in the number of positive adjectives used to rate Brahms or his music. However, the low-dogmatic subjects were more accepting of Schonberg and his music. A second experiment only partially corroborated these findings.

Zagona and Kelly (1966) extended Mikol's work to a study of the relationship of dogmatism to a novel audiovisual presentation. Their subjects were the 44 highest and 44 lowest scorers on the Dogmatism Scale selected from a pool of 515 introductory psychology students. The subjects viewed an eight-minute film showing lines and colors in motion, synchronized with a novel jazz score. High-dogmatic subjects rated the film significantly less enjoyable than did the low-dogmatic subjects. Zagona and Kelly used adjectives similar to those used by Mikol, but found no significant differences in the favorableness of the adjectives attributed to the creators of the film or the film itself. Zagona and Kelly interpreted their questionnaire data as indicating that the high-dogmatic subjects disliked the film ". . . because of its novelty, lack of structure, and synthesizing demands."

Other investigators have also been interested in the relationship between dogmatism and attention to novel stimuli. Day (1966), in his study of 38 female nursing students, presented slides of visual stimuli varying in level of complexity. Dogmatism-Scale scores were not significantly related to the time spent viewing the 60 slides. Leckart and Wagner (1967) presented 68 undergraduates with familiar and unfamiliar photographs taken from the covers of *Science*. Half the photographs were of objects familiar to the subjects, such as landscapes and cloud formations; the remaining photographs were of unfamiliar objects, such as unusual microscopic organisms and crystal structures. Although the students as a group spent more time viewing the novel photographs, there was no significant interaction for viewing time as a function of dogmatism and familiarity of the stimuli.

In another extension of this line of research, Miller and Bacon (1971) studied the ability of high- and low-dogmatic subjects to recognize humor in a picture. They hypothesized that when humor involves the introduction of information contrary to existing beliefs, high-dogmatic subjects require more time to recognize the humor than low-dogmatic subjects. The humorous stimulus was a *Harvard Lampoon* centerfold of a nude woman ". . . tanned where one would normally expect her to be untanned, and untanned where one would normally expect her to be tanned." Miller and Bacon found that their high-dogmatic undergraduates required a longer time to be able to verbalize the humor of the situation.

These studies offer only partial corroboration of the hypothesis that high-dogmatic subjects are closed to novel information.

ACCURACY OF JUDGMENT

Insofar as high-dogmatic subjects are influenced by irrelevant factors such as ". . . unrelated habits, beliefs, and perceptual cues . . ." (Rokeach, 1960), their judgments of others should be less accurate than those of low-dogmatic subjects. Burke (1966) showed that low-dogmatic subjects were able to judge more accurately the level of dogmatism of other people than were high-dogmatic subjects.

Jacoby (1971) argued that the findings of the Burke study are limited because Burke's subjects were asked to estimate the dogmatism of the "average" college student, rather than follow a procedure that was closer to the perception of people in real-life situations. Jacoby's own data were obtained from 46 graduate students organized into 13 small groups, the members of which interacted over a 10-week period for the purpose of preparing a term paper. At the end of this period, every subject was administered the Dogmatism Scale. One person in each group was designated a stimulus person, and each of the other group members was instructed to complete the Dogmatism Scale as they thought the stimulus person would complete it. In support of Rokeach's hypothesis, Jacoby showed that low-dogmatic subjects were more accurate in perceiving the level of dogmatism of others than were high-dogmatic subjects.

CREATIVITY

A number of investigators have studied the relationship between dogmatism and creativity. Since creativity seems to involve openness to new information, synthesizing ability, and flexibility, it is expected that individuals high in dogmatism would score low on measures of creativity.

Jacoby (1967), in a study of 24 undergraduate students, failed to find a significant correlation between Mednick's (1962) test of creativity and scores on the Dogmatism Scale. In a study of 316 high-school students, Uhes and Shaver (1970) found significant correlations between dogmatism and originality ($r = .29$), flexibility ($r = .20$), and a composite measure of divergent thinking ($r = .26$). It was also shown that the open-minded subjects obtained higher composite convergent thinking scores than the dogmatic subjects ($r = .18$). Thus, although high-dogmatic subjects performed worse on measures of creative thinking, they also performed worse on a measure of conventional thinking. Further, high-dogmatic subjects performed at a higher level on convergent compared to divergent tasks, whereas low-dogmatics performed equally well on the two types of task.

In a similar study, Williams, Harlow, and Borgen (1971) showed that for three measures of creativity (fluency, flexibility, and originality), the only significant correlation for a sample of 483 elementary school students was between Figert's (1968) measure of open-mindedness and originality ($r = .11$).

OTHER ASPECTS OF COGNITIVE FUNCTIONING

Long and Ziller (1965) demonstrated that dogmatism is related to tendencies to reserve judgment in decision-making tasks. The investigators presented 72 freshmen women with tasks involving the completion of words, the attainment of concepts, and judging the relative size of two lines, along with a 38-item attitude scale to measure the tendency to give a "don't know" response to opinion items. There were low but significant correlations of about .25 between dogmatism and each of the four measures of decision–delay, with low-dogmatic subjects delaying more than high-dogmatic subjects in making decisions. These findings are consistent with the previously cited studies showing that high-dogmatic subjects are responsive to authority-based information, whereas low-dogmatic subjects seem more willing to search their environments for information.

Taylor and Dunnette (1974) showed that high-dogmatic subjects made decisions faster and were more confident and accurate in their decisions than subjects low in dogmatism. The amount of information requested was unrelated to dogmatism. The subjects were 79 male industrial managers; the experimental task was a simulated management decision situation. In this study there was a statistically significant correlation of .29 between dogmatism and intelligence, which might account for the greater decision accuracy of high-dogmatic subjects.

Another study on the receptivity of dogmatic subjects to information was conducted by Robbins (1975). Sixty-six undergraduates were divided into high-, medium-, and low-dogmatic groups on the basis of their scores on Form D of the Dogmatism Scale. The subjects were asked to form impressions of a person on the basis of positive and negative statements about the person. The data indicated that the low-dogmatic subjects utilized more information before rendering a judgment. These subjects also made more extreme judgments about the person.

In a study of information processing, Brightman and Urban (1974) compared the performance of 17 undergraduates high in dogmatism with that of 17 undergraduates low in dogmatism on a task involving probability estimates. The data were only marginally supportive of the hypothesis that high-dogmatic subjects process information differently from low-dogmatic subjects. Specifically, there was some evidence that dogmatism relates to simple strategies for information processing and to the need to reduce uncertainty.

One of the findings of the previously cited study by Long and Ziller (1965) was that low-dogmatic subjects took longer to attain concepts than did high-dogmatic subjects, although in this study it was advantageous to have taken more time on the task. White, Alter, and Rardin (1965) studied another aspect of concept formation. These investigators were interested in the relationship between dogmatism and the number of categories used in sorting items. They hypothesized that high-dogmatic subjects would utilize fewer categories when sorting items on a dimension relevant to them than would low-dogmatic subjects. Further, when sorting items that were neutral, the investigators expected the two groups to perform similarly.

White, Alter, and Rardin selected 24 subjects from a pool of 410 undergraduates on the basis of extreme scores on both the Dogmatism and F scales—12 subjects in each of two groups. The dimension relevant to the subjects was made up of items dealing with undesirable social acts, ranging from such minor statements as "fishing without a license," to major acts such as "having incestuous relations with your parent." The less central dimension dealt with items describing occupations. In sorting the 149 items of each dimension into categories on the basis of undesirability, subjects were instructed to form as many categories as necessary. As hypothesized, high-dogmatic subjects used fewer categories for the relevant dimension, but they did not differ from low-dogmatic subjects in the number of categories used to sort the items dealing with occupations. Since the subjects who were high in dogmatism were also high in authoritarianism, the results of the study may not be applicable to dogmatics in general.

In a study utilizing the same subjects, White and Alter (1965) found no differences between high- and low-dogmatic subjects in the breadth or number of categories used in making judgments about lifted weights. Torcivia and Laughlin (1968) found that high-dogmatic high-school students were more likely than low-dogmatic students to use conservative strategies in solving concept formation tasks and were ". . . less able to organize new beliefs and integrate them into their already existing belief system in their problem-solving processes."

Larsen (1971) hypothesized that high-dogmatic subjects would tend to place items into extreme categories (i.e., highly favorable and highly unfavorable) when asked to judge an item's favorableness on an 11-point scale. Two hundred and sixty-three Brigham Young University students judged 121 statements about three issues: communism, whether liquor should be served by the drink, and television. Larsen divided his subjects into three levels of dogmatism and concluded that his hypothesis was supported. The results indicated that dogmatic subjects, faced with an issue, take extreme viewpoints, favorable or unfavorable. However, the analysis of variance used by Larsen was not of the repeated measures design necessary to draw valid conclusions from the data.

In a study of 91 undergraduates, Stimpson and D'Alo (1974) found no statistically significant correlations between dogmatism and the intensity or extremity of attitudes held in four content areas.

In a series of studies relating the extremity of response to dogmatism, authoritarianism, and integrative complexity, Warr and Coffman (1970) found that the extremity of response was not related to cognitive style except under conditions of high involvement, in which simpler subjects tended to make extreme responses. In a later paper, Warr and Rogers (1974) showed that the tendency of authoritarian subjects to use extreme categories is related to the content of the stimulus items being judged and is not a purely stylistic phenomenon.

CRITIQUE

In intent and format, there are a number of parallels between the Dogmatism Scale and the F Scale. Although the latter was designed as a measure of rightist authoritarianism, Rokeach intended the Dogmatism Scale to provide a measure of closed-mindedness independent of the content of thought. To the degree that Rokeach succeeded, his instrument is closer to a measure of cognitive style than is the F Scale.

A question of the utmost importance, then, is the degree to which this effort to develop a content-free measure of cognitive style was successful. The studies reviewed in this chapter indicate that, although the Dogmatism Scale is less influenced by content than the F Scale, a conclusion also reached in a review by Hanson (1976), it too is biased to the right. That is, subjects with rightist positions tend to score higher on the Dogmatism Scale than subjects whose orientation is leftist. Thus, when used as a measure of cognitive style, some variance is attributable to the attitudinal position of the subject.

Because it is similar in format to the F Scale, the Dogmatism Scale is also open to criticism concerning response style bias. Like the F Scale, some portion of the variance of Dogmatism Scale scores appears attributable to acquiescence. Although research on this aspect of the Dogmatism Scale is much less extensive than similar research on the F Scale, it is likely that the acquiescence response bias contributes a relatively small amount of Dogmatism-Scale score variance. Further, it is likely that acquiescence is a characteristic of high-dogmatic subjects; thus the validity of the instrument is not damaged by the acquiescence response bias.

Factor-analytic studies of the Dogmatism Scale have replicated a number of the dimensions posited by Rokeach in the development of the instrument and have shown that the Dogmatism Scale differs in factor structure from the F Scale. However, this research raises some question about the meaning of the unidimensional score generally obtained for the Dogmatism Scale. The relationships between dogmatism and other variables might be clarified if factor scores were derived from the Dogmatism Scale and used in the research.

In many studies, the rationale underlying the use of the Dogmatism Scale is unclear. The instrument is often used without regard for the complex underlying theory. In a major review of the literature, Ehrlich and Lee (1969) concluded that high-dogmatic subjects are less able to learn new beliefs and modify old beliefs. The overall number of studies yielding significant results, although well beyond the chance level, were accompanied by a sufficient number of studies yielding negative results to lead the authors to conclude that a number of intervening variables were uncontrolled in the studies reviewed. Ehrlich and Lee suggested the need to control five variables: centrality, novelty, presentation of the belief by positive or negative authority, congruence with existing beliefs, and the mode of presentation of the material. Many of the studies reviewed did not differentiate the analytic and synthesizing aspects of cognition. Because of this, the studies may not have been appropriate tests of Rokeach's theory that high- and low-dogmatic subjects differ in synthesizing new beliefs into a new belief system, but do not differ in the analytic process of acquiring new beliefs. For example, in one of Ehrlich's (1961) own studies, the finding of superior test performance by low-dogmatic students on a true-false sociology test was not a direct test of Rokeach's theory, because such performance does not necessarily involve synthesizing ability.

As was true of studies employing the F Scale, studies in which the Dogmatism Scale was used often involved groups of extreme high and low dogmatics, eliminating the middle range of subjects. In discussing their findings, however, authors often made generalizations regarding the entire dogmatism continuum. The dangers of this approach were illustrated in the study by Rokeach and Kemp (1960). Data from subjects high and low in dogmatism supported the hypothesis that, although high dogmatics were highly ambivalent toward their parents, low dogmatics were mildly ambivalent. However, contrary to expectations, the group of moderately dogmatic subjects had the most favorable attitudes toward their parents.

An important shortcoming of research on dogmatism has been the very few studies concerned with the development of dogmatism. The available data suggest a dynamic similar to that demonstrated in studies of the development of the authoritarian personality. This seems to have dampened the ardor of investigators for a more thorough investigation of the development of dogmatism.

One disturbing aspect of research on dogmatism is the disjunctive nature of the research. In the preceding chapter, we saw that a number of lines of research were developed in the study of authoritarianism, with issues pursued through an interaction among researchers. Often, the study of one researcher served as a catalyst in leading others to perform more refined work. This was apparent through the cross-referencing of studies in the published material. One example of this systematic approach was the series of studies concerned with authoritarianism and Einstellung rigidity, in which the original work by Rokeach was criticized by Luchins and followed up by Brown and others. It is this approach to research that leads one to the feeling that cumulative knowledge is being developed; the work of one researcher is of use to the next. With dogmatism, we find virtually no such consistency to the research. Even researchers working on a similar aspect of dogmatism theory seem unaware of each other's work. It may be that this is due to the complexity of dogmatism theory, which posits a host of relationships that, by Rokeach's own admission, were not fully worked out by 1960, the date of publication of his book.

CHAPTER FOUR

Personal Constructs and Cognitive Complexity

In Chapter 1 we saw that cognitive style was explored as a correlate of rightist authoritarianism. The investigators were led to a concern with cognitive style through observations that authoritarian individuals displayed evidence of rigidity and intolerance of ambiguity. In the work on dogmatism an attempt was made to generalize authoritarian functioning to individuals of the political left as well as those of the political right. Some elements reflecting cognitive style were introduced directly into the major measuring instrument. It was hypothesized that similarities in cognitive style would be characteristic of individuals at both ends of the political continuum. In the work of George A. Kelly (1955), the role of cognitive style was brought into a central position.

Two decades before the publication of his major work, *The Psychology of Personal Constructs,* Kelly prepared a handbook of clinical procedures, intended to aid the clinician in understanding a client's behavior from the client's perspective. Over time, Kelly became dissatisfied with what he thought of as a cookbook approach to the treatment of patients. He decided that he would also have to present the theory underlying the clinical techniques he proposed. *The Psychology of Personal Constructs* was the product of this effort.

For Kelly, man was not simply a stimulus–response organism who reacted automatically to environmental stimuli. Rejecting the implied human quiescence of this model, in which man's natural state is one of inactivity until goaded by a stimulus, Kelly argued that man is actively involved in cognitively organizing the world around him; the essence of man's activity is his forecasting of events. The individual makes predictions about what will occur and modifies his ideas based on the outcome of these predictions. Kelly termed these ideas *constructs*. A basic notion of Kelly's formulation is that man is capable of *representing* the environment, not merely *responding* to it, and that differing representations lead to different behaviors.

To clarify his position, Kelly used the analogy of scientific endeavor, in which the scientist develops a hypothesis, tests the hypothesis, and modifies his hypothesis on the basis of the results of his tests. Kelly argued that men in general proceed in much the same way—developing constructs, testing their predictive efficiency, and modifying their constructs to fit events.

Even if the individual misrepresents his environment, his misrepresentations are real themselves. As Kelly wrote:

Man looks at his world through transparent patterns or templets which he creates and then attempts to fit over the realities of which the world is composed. (Kelly, 1955)

These patterns are Kelly's *constructs,* and it is the constructs that bring organization to behavior.

At the heart of Kelly's theory is a notion of *constructive alternativism:* the individual's present constructs are subject to revision or replacement. In Kelly's view, no one is a prisoner of his past. There are alternative ways of looking at the world, and man is free to choose among these alternative constructions.

This philosophical underpinning was presented by Kelly as a formal theory, with a fundamental postulate and 11 corollaries. It was elaborated at great length by Kelly (1955, 1970) and a number of others (e.g., Bannister & Fransella, 1971; Bannister & Mair, 1968; Hinkle, 1970). Since our concern here is cognitive style, we focus on only those aspects of the theory and the measurement techniques derived from the theory that have generated relevant research. In particular, we exclude from consideration a large body of research on the applications of Kelly's theory to clinical work.

MEASUREMENT

To provide a measure of the constructs that individuals use to structure their environments, Kelly developed the Role Construct Repertory Test (Rep Test). The Rep Test, designed to be used in a clinical setting, is a task in which a client rates people in terms of concepts, or constructs, of his own devising. There are several versions of the Rep Test, involving written or oral presentations and individual or group administrations. In *The Psychology of Personal Constructs,* Kelly presented eight variations of the test. For purposes of illustration, we discuss first Kelly's grid form of the Rep Test and later an important variation developed by Bieri, Atkins, Briar, Leaman, Miller, and Tripodi (1966).

In Kelly's grid version, the subject is presented with a figure list and asked to identify an individual known to him who fits each of a variety of roles. Then three of the individuals in the figure list are considered at one time, and the subject is asked to think of an important way in which any two of the individuals are similar to each other and different from the third. The word or phrase indicating how the two figures are similar is entered as the *construct;* the opposite of the construct is entered as the *contrast.* Next, the subject is asked to consider each of the other individuals in the figure list and indicate whether each individual belongs on the construct or contrast side of the dimension. It is important to note that, following the theory, constructs are bipolar and have no middle range.

The scoring of the Rep Test in this form is complex and well described in Kelly's original presentation. Basically, a matrix is developed in which each column represents a role figure and each row a construct. By comparing the pattern of responses from one row to another, it is possible to determine the simplicity or complexity of the pattern that emerges from the ratings of the role figures. To the extent that the pattern of responding for any two rows is similar, it is inferred that the two constructs used to sort the figures are similar, regardless of the labels used by the subject to identify the constructs. To the extent that all the rows (constructs) are similar to each other, the subject is presumed to have a simple cognitive system.

The response patterns may also be considered across columns. Insofar as similar patterns of response are found column by column, it may be said that the subject views the roles in an undifferentiated manner. A third, related, scoring approach involves an analysis of the similarity of the pattern of responses on the self column with the patterns of response on the other columns. This analysis is of greatest interest to clinicians.

The Rep Test has been used to measure a cognitive style variable, cognitive complexity. Cognitive complexity is measured on the Rep Test by the number of different constructs a subject uses in his protocol.

Another approach to scoring Rep-Test protocols has been through the application of factor analytic techniques. Levy and Dugan (1956) factor analyzed four different Rep-Test protocols and suggested that the number of factors might be related to cognitive complexity. In a study of 37 female English undergraduates, Honess (1976) found that the number of factors was not significantly related to a measure of cognitive complexity developed by Bieri et al. (1966). Jones (1961) proposed using the first factor as a measure of complexity (cf. Bonarius, 1965). The greater the proportion of the total variance accounted for by the first factor, the simpler the cognitive structure. J. V. Kelly (1964) developed a scoring method using a nonparametric factor analysis that has been used occasionally. Bonarius (1965) listed nine other Rep Test-derived measures of cognitive complexity. Bavelas, Chan, & Guthrie (1976) found "fair agreement" among the nine measures of cognitive complexity that they studied.

Over the years, a number of other techniques have been developed for scoring the Rep Test and its variants. Seaman and Koenig (1974), in a study of 146 undergraduates, derived seven measures of cognitive complexity from the Rep Test. They found that three factors were necessary to account for 78% of the total variance and concluded that cognitive complexity is multidimensional. Guertin (1973) combined a Q-sort approach with factor analysis in a lengthy scoring procedure that is of limited appeal. Mueller (1974) used a multidimensional scaling approach with some interesting results.

Perhaps the most commonly used variation of the Rep Test is the version developed by Bieri (1955) and later modified by Bieri et al. (1966) to measure cognitive complexity. In this version, 10 role types are identified. In contrast to Kelly's original procedure, the experimenter provides constructs for the subjects to use in rating each role type. As discussed later, a number of studies have demonstrated that analyses based on constructs provided by the experimenter yield data comparable to those based on constructs elicited from the subject.

The grid format used in the Bieri modification is illustrated in Figure 4.1. The 10 role types are designated along the top of the grid. Ten experimenter-provided bipolar constructs are also listed. Bieri reported that these constructs were selected because they were representative of constructs elicited from people with college educations. Each role type is rated on each construct on a six-point scale ranging from +3 to −3. This too is a departure from the original method, which utilized a two-point rating scale.

A score for cognitive complexity is derived by comparing the rating given one individual on a particular construct to ratings given that individual on the other constructs. That is, if "yourself" is rated as +3 on "outgoing" and +3 on "adjusted," a score of 1 would be obtained for that comparison. Anything other than a perfect match yields a score of zero for that comparison. For each role there are 45 comparisons ((10 × 9)/2). The higher the score (450 is the maximum possible for the entire grid), the lower the cognitive complexity. A subject who does not differentiate among constructs, as they are applied to an individual, views the world in a simple way. Gibson (1975) pointed out that reversing the pole position of provided constructs (e.g., shy–outgoing to outgoing–shy) affects the cognitive complexity score. This is important in comparing cognitive complexity scores in repeated administrations or across studies. Epting (1975) offered some suggestions for dealing with this problem.

PROVIDED VERSUS ELICITED CONSTRUCTS

In the original presentation of the Rep Test, Kelly utilized a technique that required subjects to generate their own constructs. This procedure was important for Kelly because it provided clinically useful information about each individual's construct system. In the modifica-

+3   +2   +1   -1   -2   -3

+3	+2	+1	-1	-2	-3
	Outgoing			Shy	
	Adjusted			Maladjusted	
	Decisive			Indecisive	
	Calm			Excitable	
	Interested in others			Self—absorbed	
	Cheerful			Ill humored	
	Responsible			Irresponsible	
	Considerate			Inconsiderate	
	Independent			Dependent	
	Interesting			Dull	
+3	+2	+1	-1	-2	-3

Elements:

1. Yourself
2. Person you dislike
3. Mother
4. Person you'd like to help
5. Father
6. Friend of same sex
7. Friend of opposite sex (or spouse)
8. Person with whom you feel most uncomfortable
9. Boss
10. Person difficult to understand

Figure 4.1. A modified Rep Test (Bieri et al., 1966, p. 191). Used by permission of John Wiley & Sons, Inc.

tion developed by Bieri and his associates (Bieri et al., 1966) the constructs were provided by the investigator. Because of the widespread adoption of this modification, it is important to compare this technique to the original. Although Bender (1974) and others have shown that elicited constructs yield more extreme ratings than provided constructs, we wish to determine whether the cognitive complexity (i.e., structural) scores of a subject would be similar across the two techniques.

Bieri et al. (1966) cited three studies with normal subjects that indicated similarity of cognitive complexity scores based on elicited and provided constructs. Adams-Webber (1970c), in a review of the relevant literature, concluded that for normal subjects the two techniques provide equivalent measures of cognitive complexity. He noted that subjects prefer to generate their own constructs (a conclusion made earlier by Bonarius, 1965) and that the modified version requires less time for administration. We would venture to guess that a larger proportion of subjects complete the protocol.

More recently, Stringer (1972) showed that although both elicited and provided constructs could be used to predict sorting behavior, more of the task variance was accounted for by using elicited constructs. In other research, Kuusinen and Nystedt (1975a, b) and Metcalfe (1974) found only partial support for the similarity of cognitive complexity scores derived from elicited and provided constructs. Wilkins, Epting, and Van De Riet (1972) found that elicited constructs produced a restricted range of cognitive complexity scores, as compared to provided constructs.

Little (1969) found no significant relationship between the Bieri procedure and a procedure developed by Crockett (1965) that derives a measure of cognitive complexity from elicited constructs. As part of an impression formation study, Miller (1969) administered Crockett's (1965) Role Category Questionnaire and Bieri's modified Rep Test to 240 male and female undergraduates. The correlations between the Bieri and Crockett measures were not statistically significant for males or females.

Leitner, Landfield, and Barr (1974) reviewed a variety of measures of cognitive complexity and concluded that measures using provided constructs do not correlate highly with measures using elicited constructs. The investigators questioned the validity of measures based on provided constructs. It should be noted that Leitner and his colleagues did not focus on the Kelly and Bieri approaches and thus may not negate the conclusion reached by Adams-Webber (1970c).

Considered as a whole, then, the evidence indicates that the Bieri technique, utilizing experimenter-provided constructs, is a useful alternative to the original technique.

RELIABILITY

In the earliest reported reliability study of the Rep Test, Hunt (1951) administered the instrument to nine psychiatric patients and 30 college students. He readministered the test one week later, using different role titles. The mean percent agreement between the constructs used on the two administrations was about 70%. Bonarius (1965), citing this study and studies by Pedersen (1958) and Fjeld and Landfield (1961), concluded that subjects use similar role figures and produce similar constructs when a second administration of the Rep Test is compared to a first.

Tripodi and Bieri (1963) reported a test-retest reliability coefficient of .86 for cognitive complexity scores based on administrations of their modified Rep Test one week apart. When subjects generated their own constructs, the reliability coefficient was .76. These data were obtained in a study of only 16 subjects. In another study, Tripodi and Bieri (1964) reported a test-retest reliability coefficient for cognitive complexity of .71 for Bieri's modification of the Rep Test (10 roles and 10 provided constructs). The subjects were 64 graduate students, and the judgments were spaced one week apart.

In a study by Meyers (1964) cited by Bieri (1965), three classes of high school students, varying widely in level of intelligence, were administered a modified Rep Test. The test was readministered about a month later. For cognitive complexity, the group of intermediate intelligence ($N = 23$) showed the highest test-retest reliability ($r = .80$); the low IQ group ($N = 21$) and the high IQ group ($N = 23$) were similar in reliability ($r = .58$ and $r = .46$, respectively). In addition, the retest scores for the low intelligence group were significantly higher than the original scores.

Epting (1972) developed three alternate forms of the Rep Test using social issues as the stimuli and provided the constructs to be applied to the stimuli. Ten-by-ten grids were generated by 99 college students for each of the three forms on each of two occasions. Following Bieri, a cognitive complexity measure was derived by requiring each subject to rate each social stimulus on the provided constructs, using a six-point rating scale. A new construct was counted when it did not match any of the others exactly. The grids were administered twice, at a one-week interval. The test-retest correlations for each of the three forms were .65, .62, and .64. Mueller (1974) administered the Bieri modification and an alternate form to 40 Australian undergraduates and obtained a correlation of .82 between cognitive complexity scores on the two instruments.

Although the test-retest reliabilities reported in these studies are statistically significant, they are somewhat below the level that is generally acceptable (cf. Bavelas, Chan, & Guthrie, 1976; Curry & Menasco, 1977). It appears to us that the Bieri test should be lengthened to improve its reliability.

RESPONSE SETS

Bieri (1965) provided some data indicating that cognitive complexity is related to social desirability. For a sample of high school students, he reported a significant correlation of .35 between cognitive complexity and scores on the Marlowe-Crowne Social Desirability Scale. Using the same instruments he reported a significant correlation of .29 for a sample of undergraduates. In the high school study a subsample of subjects with intermediate levels of intelligence accounted for the significant finding. In the college study, the relationship held for females but not males.

Goldstein and Blackman (1976) found a significant correlation of .46 between scores on Bieri's modification of the Rep Test and scores on Couch and Keniston's (1960) 15-item acquiescence scale for a sample of 48 undergraduates.

VARIATIONS

A variety of stimuli have been used in grid format to generate constructs. Bannister and Mair (1968) cited studies that employed films, paintings, inanimate objects, emotions, problem situations in a person's life, and types of bread as stimuli. Mazis (1973) used automobiles as stimuli, and Slater (1969), in his review of the Bannister and Mair book, cited additional applications of grid techniques. More recently, Slater (1976) reported on attempts to develop a generalized grid technique. Watson (1970) reported on the usefulness of the Rep Test as a method of studying outpatient psychotherapy groups using the patients as stimuli. Similarly, Fransella and Joyston-Bechal (1971) used this variation of the Rep Test to study changes in a psychotherapy group over time. Reid and Holley (1972) found the Rep Test useful in an investigation of British students' choice of university, by using the universities as stimuli. Duck (1972) and Duck and Spencer (1972) used the Rep Test in studies of friendship groups.

Vacc and Vacc (1973) modified Bieri's Rep Test so that it could be administered to children. They reworded the role titles and constructs so that the language was appropriate to a third-grade reading level and made the role titles more relevant for children (e.g., "boss" became "teacher"). Their Adapted Modified Role Repertory Test evidenced satisfactory test-retest reliability for a sample of 25 third graders over a four-week interval. They administered their modification and the Bieri modification to 83 undergraduates and obtained correlations between the two tests of about .53. Although the correlations were statistically significant, a higher relationship would be desirable. Reker (1974) was able to test 10-year-olds individually using an apparatus that he designed. However, the validity of this procedure is unknown.

DEMOGRAPHIC STUDIES

Deaux and Farris (1975), in a study of interpersonal judgment, found no differences in the cognitive complexity scores of their male and female undergraduate subjects, a finding they report to be consistent with those of other studies.

DEVELOPMENT

There is a paucity of developmental research on cognitive complexity. Bieri (1966) pointed out two major reasons for this. The first is that

Kelly was concerned with adult behavior, and the second is that the Rep Test and its variants are not suitable for administration to children. More recently, as already noted, Vacc and Vacc (1973) developed the Adapted Modified Role Repertory Test for use with children.

Bannister and Mair (1968) hypothesized that, with development, the construct system of the child tends toward greater integration. We have found virtually no data on such developmental issues. Bannister and Mair, however, cited two unpublished studies involving children by Ravenette (1964) and Salmon (1967). Adams-Webber (1970a) also argued that in the process of development constructs become increasingly more differentiated and the construct system becomes more integrated. This point is similar to that of a number of investigators, including Harvey, Hunt, and Schroder (1961). As we see in the next chapter, an increase in differentiation and integration with an increase in maturity is a central tenet of the theory of Harvey, Hunt, and Schroder.

Using the Adapted Modified Role Repertory Test, Vacc and Greenleaf (1975) studied the cognitive complexity of 368 children in the third, fifth, seventh, and ninth grades and found evidence for increased cognitive complexity with age. There were no statistically significant differences in cognitive complexity between the ninth graders and a sample of 83 adults who had been administered Bieri's (1955) modification of the Rep Test. Using a grid-type instrument of their own devising, Rushton and Wiener (1975) reported that 11-year-olds attained higher cognitive complexity scores than 7-year-olds, a difference that we found to be statistically significant.

Salmon (1970) speculated on how construct systems develop, noting the significance of the mother in providing the initial constructs for the child. Salmon stressed that the mother's construing of differences and similarities between herself and the child is crucial. Particularly harmful to development is the lack of any overlap between the mother's concepts of herself and her children, as well as a total sharing of constructs. As the child develops, he must go beyond the constructs he developed in his interaction with his mother to be able to interact with peers and other adults.

Bannister and Fransella (1971) cited an unpublished dissertation by Brierley (1967) in which changes in the constructs used by 90 children at ages 7, 10, and 13 years were studied. Brierley showed that, with increasing age, the content of the constructs was more likely to be categorized in terms of behavior (e.g., play instruments) and personality (e.g., are nosey) and less likely to be categorized in terms of social role (e.g., children) or appearance (e.g., skinny).

Some data on the relationship between cognitive complexity and maternal child-rearing practices was provided by Goldstein and Blackman (1976). Forty-eight undergraduates completed the Bieri modification of the Rep Test and the Children's Report of Parent Behavior Inventory (Droppleman & Schaefer, 1963; Schaefer, 1965). The Parent Attitude Research Instrument (Schaefer & Bell, 1958) was completed by the mothers of 37 of the students. The data indicated that students low in cognitive complexity had mothers whose attitudes reflected a rejection of the mothering role. The measures of the students' perceptions of their mothers' child-rearing practices did not increase the variance accounted for in cognitive complexity. It was also found that cognitive complexity was not related to sex. For a subsample of 20 students for whom the data were available, there was a statistically significant correlation of .44 between cognitive complexity and age.

RESEARCH

COGNITIVE COMPLEXITY AND OTHER MEASURES OF COGNITIVE STYLE

Bieri (1965) reported statistically significant correlations between cognitive complexity and scores on the F Scale for female ($r = .45$) but not male undergraduates. He also found a significant correlation between cognitive complexity and the Dogmatism Scale for female undergraduates ($r = .27$). Vannoy (1965) found a significant correlation of .20 between a Bieri-type modification of the Rep Test and a modified F Scale for 113 male undergraduates; the correlation of the Rep Test with Budner's (1962) Intolerance of Ambiguity measure was not statistically significant.

In the course of his study on the factorial structure of simplicity–complexity, Pyron (1966) administered a modified version of the Rep Test, a 28-item version of the F Scale, and the Dogmatism Scale to a sample of 80 college students. The number of constructs derived from the modified Rep Test was not significantly correlated with F-Scale or

Dogmatism-Scale scores (the latter scales correlated significantly at .53). When scores from these three instruments were combined in a factor analytic study with 10 other measures of cognitive style and attitudes, a three-factor solution was extracted. The Rep Test loaded on a factor of simplicity–complexity; the F Scale and Dogmatism Scale had their primary loadings on another factor. Starbird and Biller (1976) failed to find differences in cognitive complexity among 180 undergraduates varying in level of dogmatism.

In the course of a detailed study on differentiation and abstraction, Gardner and Schoen (1962) compared the performance of 70 women on a number of tasks reflecting cognitive style. Of particular interest here are the correlations between cognitive complexity as measured by two versions of the Rep Test, Rokeach's (1951a, b) Narrow-Mindedness Test, and two indices from Pettigrew's (1958) Category-Width Scale. One of the Rep-Test measures was significantly correlated with the Rokeach measure ($r = .45$, $N = 28$), but the Rep-Test measures did not correlate significantly with the Pettigrew measures. Thus the data indicated that high cognitive integration, as measured by the Rokeach test, was associated with lower levels of cognitive complexity, as measured by one of the Rep tests.

Rigney, Bieri, and Tripodi (1964) were interested in whether cognitively complex subjects could attain concepts more accurately. They were careful to point out that such a relationship would only be expected to obtain when the task required differentiation and articulation. The cognitively complex individual is one who differentiates among concepts and is able to make discriminations on each of these conceptual dimensions. The authors labeled the first capacity as differentiation, the second as articulation. When the complexity of the task (the number of dimensions and the articulations along dimensions) is great, one would expect better performance from cognitively complex subjects. In this study, the matching of stimulus complexity with the individual's cognitive complexity is an excellent paradigm of how research in cognitive complexity should be carried out (cf. Bieri, 1971).

The authors used two concept attainment tasks, one in the social domain, the other involving physical abstractions. The subjects were presented with a standard stimulus and asked whether each of 12 comparison stimuli matched the standard. For the 60 graduate student subjects of this study, there were essentially no overall differences in the accuracy of performance of high- and low-complex subjects, with complexity measured by the Bieri modification of the Rep Test.

Hornsby (1964), in a study cited by Bieri et al. (1966), also failed to demonstrate differences in overall concept attainment accuracy between high- and low-complex judges. Hornsby studied the performance of 211 judges who were either undergraduate or graduate students. He did find, however, that cognitively complex subjects were more likely than the low-complex subjects to make errors in judging exemplars. Bieri accounts for this in terms of Leventhal's (1957) finding that low-complex judges benefit more than high-complex judges from the addition of new information. However, Leventhal's finding was significant only at the 10% level of significance, casting some doubt on this interpretation. Further, the direction of Leventhal's finding is at variance with the general finding that high-complex individuals are better able to utilize new information. Leventhal's hypothesis is supported by data from the Rigney, Bieri, and Tripodi (1964) study, in which the greater improvement of low-complex subjects on the latter half of the task resulted from their improvement in judging exemplars in contrast to the stability in this regard of the high-complex subjects.

Hess (1966) obtained data suggesting that cognitive complexity, as measured by the Rep Test, is related to the number of concepts used by a subject on the Alternative Conceptualizations Test, a task requiring the categorization of small household items in as many ways as possible. For his sample of 43 college students, $\tau = .18$ ($p < .05$, one-tailed).

Zimring (1971) measured the speed with which cognitively simple and complex subjects responded on a word-association task. He administered a modified Rep Test to 22 college graduates. A cognitively simple subject was defined as one whose constructs were similar to each other, the measure of similarity being derived from Kelly's (1955) original nonparametric factor analysis technique. There was a significant correlation ($\rho = .82$) between complexity and the time taken to give a word association to the constructs the subjects had provided. The more complex the subject, the longer the reaction time.

Bieri and Blacker (1956) compared a Rep-Test measure of cognitive complexity to cognitive style measures derived from a modified

Rorschach inkblot test. The latter included measures based on the content of the responses to standard Rorschach inkblots, as well as to the characteristics of the stimuli (e.g., form and color) that led to the subject's perceptions. The subjects were 40 male undergraduates. Cognitive complexity was measured by a count of the number of different responses made on the Rep Test and the Rorschach test. For the Rep Test, six roles were delineated: yourself, brother (or brother type) closest in age, closest girl friend, most successful person you know, person you know whom you admire, and person you know whom you would like to help or for whom you feel sorry. The six stimuli were compared in triads, as outlined by Kelly, in all possible combinations. Altogether, 20 sorts were made. The complexity measure for the Rep Test was the number of different constructs given on the 20 sorts; the greater the number of constructs, the greater the cognitive complexity. For a construct to be considered the same as one given previously, it was necessary that the same word or words be used in both instances. As the authors noted, this criterion was quite stringent. With a possible score of 1–20, the mean number of constructs was 15.5, the median was 16.6, and the range was 9–20.

The six measures of cognitive complexity derived from the Rorschach correlated significantly with the Rep-Test measure of cognitive complexity. The average intercorrelation was .40; this supported the Bieri and Blacker hypothesis of the generality of cognitive complexity across stimulus domains. However, Caracena and King (1962) failed to replicate this finding, and have no clear explanation for the discrepancy in results.

Epting, Wilkins, and Margulis (1972) hypothesized that cognitively complex subjects would use more abstract labels for their constructs than would cognitively simple subjects. Ninety-six subjects completed a 20 × 20 grid version of the Rep Test with social issues as the stimuli. The grids were factor-analyzed using J. V. Kelly's (1964) nonparametric program. The 20 most cognitively complex subjects were contrasted with the 20 least complex subjects regarding the concreteness–abstractness of the verbal labels they used for their constructs. Two judges rated the 20 labels produced by each of the subjects on a five-point concreteness–abstractness scale. As hypothesized, the verbal labels used by the cognitively complex subjects were significantly more abstract than the labels used by the cognitively simple subjects.

The studies reviewed in this section indicate that cognitive complexity is at best only poorly related to other measures of cognitive style.

ACCURACY IN PERCEIVING OTHERS

Bieri (1955) was the first to present data on the relationship between behavior and cognitive complexity. Bieri predicted that cognitively complex individuals would predict the behavior of others more accurately. He formulated this hypothesis as a direct test of Kelly's theory, which states that an individual with a more highly differentiated construct system is able to predict events more accurately. Bieri also hypothesized that the more cognitively simple an individual, the more likely he would be to predict that other people would behave as he would. Bieri argued that since the cognitively simple individual does not make fine discriminations about others, he is more likely to assume that their behavior would be similar to his.

Bieri's subjects were 34 undergraduates. A social situations test involving behavioral choices for 12 situations was administered, along with a modification of the Rep Test. Each subject was to select one of four alternatives for each situation on the social situations test. He was also to predict how two of his classmates would respond to each item.

Bieri obtained a correlation of .29 between the accuracy of prediction and cognitive complexity. However, this correlation is significant at the .05 level only when a one-tailed test of significance is used. Further analyses indicated that the relationship obtained was due to the ability of high-complexity judges to accurately predict *differences* between themselves and others; cognitive complexity was unrelated to the accuracy of prediction of *similarities* between self and others. As hypothesized, cognitively simple subjects were more likely ($r = .32$) to view others as similar to themselves. Again, this correlation coefficient is statistically significant only with a one-tailed test. This relationship was due to the tendency of low-complexity judges to inaccurately view themselves as similar to others.

As part of a later study, Sechrest and Jackson (1961) replicated Bieri's finding of a positive relationship between predictive accuracy and cognitive complexity at the same level of significance. Their subjects were 60 female nursing students, who were administered a modified Rep

Test and a 12-item situations test highly similar to Bieri's. The authors' measure of predictive accuracy was the total number of correct predictions the subject made regarding how six other people would fill out the form. The correlation between this measure and the number of constructs the subject generated on the Rep Test was .22, significant at the .05 level with a one-tailed test.

Leventhal (1957) compared the accuracy of interpersonal judgment of cognitively simple and cognitively complex subjects. He predicted that cognitively complex judges would be more accurate predictors of reported behavior and that their accuracy of judgment would increase more than the accuracy of cognitively simple judges as the amount of information on which they based their judgments increased. Leventhal obtained scorable data on a modified Rep Test from 253 male undergraduates. The 35 subjects scoring most cognitively simple and the 35 subjects scoring most cognitively complex were selected. From each group seven subjects were selected to be interviewed and the remaining 28 to be judges. The interviews were tape recorded and the judges filled out a questionnaire as they thought the interviewee would respond. Under one condition, the judges listened to a 15-minute segment dealing with family background and school and job experiences; under another, they listened to a 35-minute segment that contained additional material about values and self-description. Overall, there were no significant differences in the accuracy of judgments made by simple and complex judges.

Crockett (1965) reviewed these studies, along with a dissertation by Campbell (1960) and concluded that subjects high in cognitive complexity differentiate other individuals more sharply and assume that other people are less similar to themselves. This suggested to Crockett that cognitively complex individuals make more inferences from a set of information than do cognitively simple ones.

Adams-Webber (1969) hypothesized that cognitively complex subjects would be more accurate judges of other people's constructs than would cognitively simple subjects. Thirty university students were administered the Rep Test in a form that generated 22 constructs. Then they interacted for 20 minutes in dyads, discussing hypothetical vacation plans. At the conclusion of the discussion, each member of the dyad was given a list of 44 constructs, 22 of which were supplied by the experimenter and 22 that had been previously generated by his partner.

The subject's task was to select the 22 constructs that had been generated by his partner. As hypothesized, the cognitively complex subjects identified more accurately the constructs used by their dyad partners.

In work related to earlier efforts, Adams-Webber, Schwenker, and Barbeau (1972) hypothesized that individuals who produce relatively undifferentiated constructs would be less accurate judges of the constructs used by others. An undifferentiated construct was defined as one in which the pattern of judgments regarding the self was similar to that of the judgments of people close to the person. The subjects in the investigation were 24 Canadian undergraduates. Three weeks after completing the Rep Test, the subjects were assigned to eight separate triads and were instructed to participate in a 30-minute discussion. Following the discussion period, each subject was given a list of 30 constructs, half of which had been used by his partners in the triad. He was asked to match the constructs with the partner that had produced them. As hypothesized, subjects with undifferentiated construct systems made less accurate judgments than the more differentiated subjects.

Vacc (1974) studied the ability of undergraduates to accurately judge the academic achievement and cognitive complexity of other students. Neither the low- nor high-complex students could accurately judge cognitive complexity. Both groups were able to predict academic achievement equally well.

In another investigation, Macrae (1969) found that high- and low-complex sixth graders did not differ significantly in the accuracy of their judgments of how a selected classmate would fill out the extraversion scale of the Eysenck Personality Inventory.

Adams-Webber (1973) pointed out that, although there have been a number of studies on the accuracy of interpersonal judgment by subjects differing in cognitive complexity, the complexity of the individuals judged has received little attention. Adams-Webber studied the accuracy with which undergraduates predicted the others' constructs after they had interacted in groups of three for 30 minutes. He found that the constructs used by subjects highest in cognitive complexity were predicted less accurately than those of subjects low or moderate in complexity. Unfortunately, the interaction between the cognitive complexity of the judge and the complexity of the target was not studied.

Leitner, Landfield, and Barr (1974), based on their review of the literature, concluded that individuals who are more cognitively complex are more accurate in predicting differences, but not similarities, between themselves and others. Based on our review of studies in this area, we believe that studies on the relationship between cognitive complexity and the prediction of behavior have not demonstrated convincingly that cognitively complex subjects are more accurate judges of others than cognitively simple subjects. It seems to us that both the complexity of the judge and the complexity of the environment must be considered simultaneously.

INTEGRATING INCONSISTENT STIMULI

Crockett (1965) pointed out that cognitively complex subjects, when presented with two descriptions of an individual, the second differing in valence from the first, should produce a more mixed description than cognitively simple subjects. The latter would be expected to produce a more univalent description. After being presented with the contradictory information, cognitively complex individuals would be expected to change their impression less than cognitively simple subjects. As we have seen, these hypotheses were also made with regard to the functioning of the dogmatic individual.

Crockett cited an unpublished dissertation by Rosenkrantz (1961), an unpublished thesis by Supnick (1964), and studies by Leventhal and Singer (1964) and Mayo and Crockett (1964) as providing only partial support for these generalizations. For example, Mayo and Crockett (1964) showed that subjects differing in cognitive complexity differentially modified their judgments in response to new information. Thirty-six undergraduates, selected from a pool of 80 subjects because of their extreme cognitive complexity scores, listened to tape-recorded statements about a fictitious character. In the first session approximately half the subjects listened to positive trait descriptions; the remaining subjects listened to negative descriptions. In the second session the valence of the descriptions was reversed, thus presenting the subjects with inconsistent information. It was found that, initially, all subjects were accurate judges of the stimulus person. After the second presentation, the high- and low-complex subjects differed. The low-complex subjects were greatly influenced by the second presentation (recency effect), shifting their descriptions strongly in the direction of the second presentation. Although high-complex subjects also shifted in the direction of the second presentation, their shift was less marked. The high-complex subjects produced a more ambiguous description than the low-complex subjects.

Crockett (1965) also cited an unpublished dissertation by Nidorf (1961) as evidence that cognitively complex subjects are better able to reconcile contradictory trait information into a unified description than are cognitively simple subjects. The six traits that were to be used by subjects as the basis of their written impressions were pessimistic, intelligent, competitive, kind, sensitive, and self-centered. The written descriptions were coded as integrated or unintegrated. A statistically significant correlation of .36 was found between the measures of cognitive complexity and integration.

Fertig and Mayo (1970) also investigated the ability of subjects differing in cognitive complexity to integrate discrepant information. The authors used an impression formation task to vary levels of environmental complexity. In the least complex situation, subjects were presented with a list of eight positive traits and asked to write an integrated description of an individual. In the situation of moderate complexity, two of the eight traits were negative. In the most complex situation, four of the eight traits were negative. Fertig and Mayo hypothesized that both simple and complex subjects would write more integrated descriptions in the moderately complex situation. They further hypothesized that the more complex subjects would write more integrated descriptions across all three conditions, their performance being most superior to the simple subjects in the moderately complex situation.

The subjects of the study were 60 cognitively simple and 60 cognitively complex female undergraduates, chosen from a pool of 211 volunteers because of their extreme scores on a modified Rep Test. As hypothesized, the most integrated descriptions were written for the moderately complex situation. Despite an attempt to tease out data supporting their other hypotheses, the authors did not find the hypothesized interaction between cognitive and situational complexity.

We find a number of problems with this study, including the authors' use of the three impression formation situations as a dimension of environmental complexity. It may well be that, depending on the dimensionality of the traits, writing a consistent description based on eight positive traits may be at least as complex a task as writing a consistent description based on mixed positive and negative traits.

Tripodi and Bieri (1966) argued that cognitively complex individuals are more likely to react to stimuli in a complex way. In an ambiguous situation, cognitively complex subjects should impose greater complexity on the material. In this study, the authors hypothesized that cognitively complex subjects would produce stories containing greater conflict than stories produced by less complex subjects, conflictual responses presumably reflecting greater information and complexity. The subjects in the study were 64 graduate students, who were administered the Rep Test with provided constructs. Each subject was presented with three brief descriptions of social situations and asked to compose a story regarding the situation. The Rep Test was scored for cognitive complexity, and the stories were scored for conflict. As hypothesized, the most cognitively complex subjects produced stories with the greatest amount of conflict. The authors also found that cognitively complex subjects were more certain of their judgments when presented with inconsistent information.

Based on his summary of the literature, Bieri (1968) concluded that a more cognitively complex subject ". . . will discriminate better among inconsistent stimuli, will prefer and be more certain of his judgments based upon inconsistent information, and will inject greater conflict into his judgments." He pointed out, and we agree, that these conclusions are tentative and in need of additional research.

In a study relating to these issues, Menasco (1976) provided some evidence that, for undergraduates in a laboratory setting, high cognitive complexity was related to greater difficulty and discomfort in making difficult decisions. In a field study involving housewives, high cognitive complexity was related to greater difficulty in making decisions regarding the purchase of major appliances. However, the measure of decision-making difficulty was based on the number of alternatives considered by the housewives (e.g., number of brands considered), so that here cognitive complexity was shown to relate to the complexity, rather than the difficulty, of decision making. Similar results were reported in the area of dogmatism by Lambert and Durand (1977).

Petronko and Perin (1970) showed that cognitively simple subjects, selected on the basis of a modified Bieri modification of the Rep Test, had difficulty integrating inconsistent information during an impression formation task. Press, Crockett, and Delia (1975) used Crockett's (1965) Role Category Questionnaire as a measure of cognitive complexity and administered an impression formation task. They showed that cognitively complex subjects, when given a set to understand the person about whom they were forming an impression, produced more complex descriptions than did cognitively simple subjects. There was no difference in the complexity of the material produced by the two groups under a set to evaluate the person being judged. Thus, under an instructional set to use a single dimension (evaluation), the performance of the complex and simple subjects was similar. Under a set designed to require the use of many dimensions, the output of the complex subjects became more complex.

Crockett (1965) also reviewed studies that indicate that cognitively simple subjects are likely to use either positive or negative attributes in describing stimuli, whereas cognitively complex subjects are more likely to use both positive and negative attributes when describing a stimulus. In his doctoral dissertation, Campbell (1960) showed that subjects high in cognitive complexity were less likely to group others into a good-bad dichotomy. Supnick (1964) showed that cognitively complex subjects were more likely than less cognitively complex subjects to mix positive and negative constructs in describing individuals.

In the study by Larsen (1971) cited in the chapter on dogmatism, the investigator hypothesized that cognitively simple subjects would be more likely to displace attitudinal statements when sorting them to create a Thurstone scale. There were no significant differences in performance among subjects differing in levels of cognitive complexity as measured by Bieri's (1966) modification of the Rep Test.

The findings of the studies reviewed in this section provide some evidence that cognitively complex individuals are more likely than cognitively simple individuals to integrate discrepant information.

In a related area that was also the subject of research in the area of dogmatism, Lundy and Berkowitz (1957) showed that subjects low in cognitive complexity were less likely than subjects high in cognitive complexity to change their attitudes in response to a communication endorsed by either peers or generals. A group of 63 undergraduates was administered a Bieri modification of the Rep Test. The first 10 rows and columns were analyzed to obtain cognitive complexity scores. Attitudes toward movies, tariffs, and punishment of criminals were measured. One month later, the attitude scales were readministered with either favorable or unfavorable endorsement of the issues attributed to college students or Army generals.

Although Lundy and Berkowitz presented a rationale for their expected findings, the results of their study are inconsistent, in part, with those of other research. Investigators undertaking research in other areas of cognitive style have shown that subjects with simple cognitive styles tend to be more influenced by authority than subjects with complex cognitive styles.

DISTANCE OF THE ROLE STIMULI

Miller and Bieri (1965) studied the Rep Test responses of 126 graduate social work students and showed that socially close role stimuli evoked less cognitively complex judgments than socially distant role stimuli. They hypothesized that, when confronted with a distant person, subjects assume greater vigilance, leading to increased differentiation of perceptions. They argued that this behavior is adaptive in that it facilitates flexibility in the anticipation of the other's behavior. The positive findings of this study were replicated by Supnick (1964) and Baldwin (1972).

Miller (1968) obtained similar results but added the dimension of situational stress. His subjects were 312 undergraduates, half of whom completed the Rep Test under standard instructions (nonstress condition), and half of whom were administered the Rep Test under the guise of its being a formal examination of social intelligence (stress condition). Students taking the Rep Test under the stress condition evidenced significantly less cognitive complexity than students in the nonstress condition. Miller proposed that the vigilance hypothesis takes into account the stress of the judging situation as well as stress engendered by the people being rated.

Irwin, Tripodi, and Bieri (1967) thought that the Miller and Bieri (1965) finding might have been due to differences in affect toward distant, as compared to close, role stimuli. To test this hypothesis, they studied 115 undergraduate members of fraternities or sororities. Each subject selected four liked, four neutral, and four disliked housemates as role figures for the Rep Test. Following the Bieri procedure, 10 constructs were provided, against which each of the role figures was rated. It was shown that cognitive complexity was greatest for the negatively evaluated role stimuli, intermediate for the neutral figures, and least for the positively evaluated figures. A second study with 80 subjects, with a somewhat modified procedure, yielded similar results. Carr (1969) also found that undergraduates rated negatively evaluated persons more complexly than positively evaluated persons.

In a similar vein, Soucar and DuCette (1971), in a study of 165 undergraduates, found that judgments of disliked political figures were more complex than those of positively evaluated political figures. Following a similar rationale, Soucar (1971) found that teachers ($N = 70$) exhibited greater cognitive complexity in their ratings of disliked students; graduate students ($N = 66$) exhibited greater cognitive complexity in their ratings of disliked instructors. Wilkins, Epting, and Van De Riet (1972) also found greater cognitive complexity elicited from negative role stimuli in their study of 82 undergraduates; similar findings were reported by Kuna and Williams (1976).

Koenig and Seaman (1974) required 146 undergraduates to rate eight role figures, half of whom were of positive affect, half of negative affect. The subjects also indicated whether the figures were threatening or nonthreatening. The subjects' responses on the modified Rep Test indicated greater complexity in the judgments regarding negative figures. The negative figures were also perceived as more threatening than the positive figures, substantiating the vigilance hypothesis.

When four positively evaluated novels and four negatively evaluated novels were used as stimuli for a modified Rep Test, Koenig and Edmonds (1972) found that their 31 undergraduate subjects demonstrated greater cognitive complexity in rating the negative stimuli. The authors pointed out that since the negatively evaluated books could not be viewed as threatening, the vigilance hypothesis was not applicable. Other investigators (Koenig, 1971; Kuna & Williams, 1976) also questioned the usefulness of the vigilance hypothesis. In a later study, Koenig (1975) derived cognitive complexity scores from ratings of liked and disliked sororities. He reported higher cognitive complexity in the ratings of the least liked groups, but we find the reported difference not statistically significant.

Bodden and Klein (1973) compared the cognitive complexity associated with liked and disliked vocations. Sixty-seven male undergraduates completed a Rep Test in which six liked and six disliked vocations served as the stimuli. Following Bieri's procedure, these vocations were rated on 12 provided, vocationally relevant constructs. As in other research, the negatively evaluated stimuli were associated with greater cognitive complexity.

Turner and Tripodi (1968) studied the differences in the cognitive complexity of therapists' judgments about their clients and significant others. Their subjects were 36 graduate social work students. One administration of the Rep Test utilized clients as role stimuli; a second utilized five positive and five negative role types. In both administrations, 10 constructs were provided by the experimenters. The data indicated that greater cognitive complexity was obtained when the clients were rated. As in previous research, negative role types were judged as more complex than positive role types. An attempt at a similar differentiation for positive and negative clients revealed no significant differences. It should be noted, however, that clients were merely ranked from most to least liked; thus one cannot assume that the first five clients were positively evaluated and the last five negatively evaluated.

These studies generally demonstrate that higher cognitive complexity is associated with negatively evaluated stimuli. However, it is questionable that the viligance hypothesis is an adequate explanation of these results.

GENERALITY ACROSS STIMULUS DOMAINS

A reappearing theme in the literature concerns the generalizability of cognitive complexity across different stimulus domains and over time. This issue may be restated as a question about whether cognitive complexity is a *trait*. That is, is cognitive complexity a relatively enduring attribute of an individual, or is it a characteristic of an individual, at a particular point in time, that may vary from one situation to another? Bannister and Mair (1968) take the position that, according to personal construct theory, the individual is in a constant state of change.

Crockett (1965) concluded from his review that cognitive complexity is not a trait that is generalizable across a number of content areas. Rather, cognitive complexity is specific to particular domains. On the other hand, Crockett admitted that subjects who are highly complex when measured with regard to stimuli of one domain are likely to be highly complex in other domains.

Allard and Carlson (1963) administered three versions of the Rep Test to a total of 41 undergraduate students. Each version used seven stimuli and required subjects to make 26 triad comparisons. One version used standard role figures; a second used famous figures, such as military leaders; a third used geometric designs. The three versions were scored for cognitive complexity; patterns of responding across rows and variety in descriptive adjectives were considered. The intercorrelations among the three cognitive complexity scores ranged from .67 to .57, all significant beyond the .001 level.

In the study by Epting (1972) cited in the section on reliability, three alternative forms of the Rep Test, using social issues as stimuli, were administered to 88 undergraduates. The correlations for cognitive complexity scores among the three alternate forms on the first administration were .56, .59, and .60; on the second administration, one week later, the intercorrelations were .72, .74, and .75, all statistically significant beyond the .001 level.

Another study with data relevant to the question of the generalizability of cognitive complexity across stimulus domains was conducted by Bodden (1970). Cognitive complexity was measured with Bieri's modification of the Rep Test using roles in the interpersonal realm. A second measure of cognitive complexity was developed using 12 occupational titles as the stimuli. Data were gathered from a sample of 200 undergraduates. The correlation of .43 between the two measures was statistically significant.

Durand and Lambert (1976) administered three versions of the Bieri Rep Test to 102 male business-administration students. The three domains sampled were automobiles, toothpastes, and interpersonal relations. Although cognitive complexity scores derived from the different domains were significantly correlated in two of the three comparisons, the magnitudes of the correlation coefficients were low (.33, .22, .18), indicating little generalization of cognitive complexity across the studied areas.

Koenig and Seaman (1974) administered a Bieri modification of the

Rep Test to 172 undergraduates. They found that male stimuli elicited higher cognitive complexity scores than female stimuli. They also found male subjects to be more cognitively complex than females.

The modifiability of cognitive complexity with experience would argue against a trait point of view. Wicker (1969) tested the idea that cognitive complexity would be greater if the subject had greater experience with the domain of stimuli being rated. He reasoned that students from small high schools would have more experience with a greater variety of behavior settings than students attending a larger school. Therefore, if a Rep Test utilized behavior settings rather than role descriptions as stimuli, it would be expected that students from the smaller schools would obtain higher cognitive complexity scores. Wicker presented data showing that students at smaller schools did, in fact, have more experience and involvement in a variety of behavior settings. As hypothesized, the 40 high-school students from the smaller schools had higher cognitive complexity scores than the 40 matched students from the larger school. Wicker also found that females had higher cognitive complexity scores than males.

Baldwin (1972) presented data on the modifiability of cognitive complexity, albeit not in the expected direction. Twenty-five government employees participated in a five-day training program designed to increase self-awareness, sensitivity, understanding of others, and interviewing skills. At the beginning of the program and again at its conclusion, the subjects completed a version of Bieri's modification of the Rep Test. Unexpectedly, there was a significant decrease in cognitive complexity scores. In a similar vein, Bodden and James (1976) found that providing subjects with additional information about vocations reduced the complexity with which they viewed those occupations.

These studies indicate that cognitive complexity scores are similar when different stimuli are used. There is some evidence that environmental factors may modify complexity.

INTELLIGENCE

The data available from a number of studies indicate that cognitive complexity is independent of intelligence. In Bieri's (1955) original report of the performance of 28 subjects, the correlation between cognitive complexity and scores on the Ohio State Psychological Examination, purportedly measuring verbal intelligence, was not statistically significant.

In a study by Leventhal (1957) the correlation between intelligence, as measured by American Council Psychological Examination scores, and cognitive complexity, was not significant for a randomly selected subsample of 95 students.

In the course of their investigation of 60 female nursing students, Sechrest and Jackson (1961) obtained a nonsignificant correlation between cognitive complexity and peer-rated academic intelligence, and a nonsignificant correlation with peer-rated social intelligence. Vannoy (1965) obtained a significant correlation of .19 between scores on a modified Rep Test and the verbal score on the Cooperative School and College Ability Test for a sample of 113 male undergraduates.

A study by Meyers (1964), cited by Bieri (1965), related intellectual functioning to cognitive complexity. The two variables were not significantly correlated. However, in this study there was a significant relationship between complexity and intelligence ($r = .44$) for 21 low intelligence subjects.

Crockett (1965) cited four studies that showed no significant relationship between various indices of IQ and measures of cognitive complexity derived from interpersonal stimuli. Wicker (1969) found no significant correlation between a Rep-Test measure of cognitive complexity using behavior settings as stimuli and an unspecified measure of IQ.

In a study of 36 college students, Kuusinen and Nystedt (1972c) found no significant relationship between a Miller-type verbal analogies test used as a measure of general intelligence and four measures of cognitive complexity using elicited and provided constructs. Standing (1973), in a study of 40 steel mill inspectors, found a nonsignificant correlation between the Otis Test of Mental Ability and cognitive complexity scores.

An interesting finding of the Bieri and Blacker (1956) study was that vocabulary scores on the Wechsler-Bellevue (Form I), taken as a measure of intelligence, correlated significantly with four of six Rorschach-derived measures of cognitive complexity; the significant correlations ranged from .37 to .46. However, the correlation of intelligence with a Rep-Test measure of cognitive complexity was not statistically significant.

INTERACTION WITH ENVIRONMENTAL COMPLEXITY

Miller (1969) required cognitively complex and cognitively simple subjects to interact with a confederate. After the interaction, the cognitively complex subjects (as measured by Crockett's Role Category Questionnaire) viewed the confederate as more complex than did the cognitively simple subjects. In this study, judgments of the confederate's cognitive complexity were made under conditions of high or low information about the confederate. The data indicated that the amount of information about the confederate did not affect the subjects' judgments of the confederate's level of cognitive complexity. Similarly, Delia, Clark, and Switzer (1974) showed that subjects high in cognitive complexity, as measured by the Crockett instrument, produced impressions of individuals with whom they were interacting informally that were more differentiated, integrated, and abstract than did subjects low in cognitive complexity.

Standing (1973) was interested in the relationship between cognitive complexity and complexity in the work world. He hypothesized that an inverted U-shaped relationship exists between the two variables. Standing measured the cognitive complexity and job satisfaction of 40 steel mill inspectors and hypothesized that the inspectors who were high or low in cognitive complexity would have low job satisfaction relative to those who were intermediate in cognitive complexity. Complexity was measured by a modification of the Rep Test in which aspects of the job were the stimuli. Individual protocols were factor analyzed, with cognitive complexity defined by the number of factors extracted from each analysis. The data obtained supported the hypothesized relationship. Implicit in Standing's study was the notion that the job of a steel mill inspector is of intermediate environmental complexity.

Standing's research is directed toward the study of the fit between individual and environmental complexity; when this fit is optimal, one would expect a maximum of job satisfaction. This issue is more central to the formulations of Harvey, Hunt, and Schroder (1961), discussed in the next chapter.

CRITIQUE

Soon after the appearance of Kelly's *The Psychology of Personal Constructs,* Bruner (1956) characterized the work as developing a theory of personality from a theory of cognition. He felt that this was an innovative approach and possibly ". . . the single greatest contribution of the past decade to the theory of personality functioning." Rogers (1956), like Bruner, commented that the theory is carefully formulated. In evaluating the general theory, Bruner wrote that Kelly's emphasis on the possibility of making choices as the basis of how one thinks and behaves was an overreaction to the picture of man as an irrational being strongly influenced by unconscious forces, or as an automaton whose behavior was subject to its reinforcement history. Mischel (1964) also critically reviewed Kelly's theory, arguing that constructs should be considered rules to determine behavioral choices rather than hypotheses regarding the outcome of events.

Despite Professor Kelly's untimely death in 1967, a number of investigators have continued work in the area of cognitive complexity. A clearinghouse has been established for the exchange of information, and bibliographies related to personal construct theory are issued from time to time. Personal construct theory was the subject of the Nebraska Symposium on Motivation in 1976, and an international congress has been proposed on a regular basis. Over the years, there have been adherents to, and detractors from, the theory. Our concern in this chapter is not to survey the research in the field as it concerns Kelly's general theory or its clinical applications. Rather, we are interested in those aspects of Kelly's theory that relate to cognitive style and the research relevant to that issue. Principally, this reduces to research on cognitive complexity as measured by the Rep Test and its derivatives.

A major difficulty is that investigators in the field of cognitive complexity seem unaware of the related work of others, as manifested by the lack of cross-referencing and systematic attack on the research issues. Many of the issues raised regarding cognitive complexity were also of concern to researchers in authoritarianism and dogmatism. There are virtually no references relating the three areas to each other. Although several investigators have intensively pursued specific areas (e.g., Bieri, Adams-Webber, Bannister), there appears to be little connection among the major themes.

Our overall impression of the data relevant to the cognitive complexity aspect of Kelly's work is similar to that expressed earlier about Kelly's theory by Bannister and Mair (1968): ". . . the evidence available is scanty and disproportionately small in relation to the size of the theoretical structure which has been erected." For a theory that was published over 20 years ago, Kelly's work has not stimulated the extensive research that should accompany such an innovative point of view. Much of this is undoubtedly due to the complexities of administering and scoring the original versions of the Rep Test. Bieri's modification, however, is much simpler to administer and score and should generate research from a wider circle of investigators. Especially important is the demonstrated independence of Bieri's measure of cognitive complexity and IQ.

One issue has been the validity of the measurement of cognitive complexity when constructs are provided by the experimenter rather than elicited from the subject. In his review of Bannister and Fransella (1971), Pervin (1973) questioned the practice of providing constructs, since subjects may interpret verbal labels differently. However, the studies reviewed in this chapter provide data that demonstrate the comparability of the two techniques in the measurement of cognitive complexity. Based on their review of cognitive complexity, Leitner, Landfield, and Barr (1974) found that many measures have been used over the years and concluded that they were generally unrelated to each other. They suggested that additional theoretical and operational work be applied to cognitive complexity so that the dimensionality of the construct and its measurement can be clarified. Bavelas, Chan, and Guthrie (1976) questioned both the reliability and validity of measures of cognitive complexity.

Research on developmental aspects of cognitive complexity is also lacking. As noted earlier, this is due partly to Kelly's lack of attention to development aspects of his theory and partly to the complexity of the measuring instruments, which are difficult even for adults. Vacc and Vacc's (1973) downward extension of the Rep Test represents one attempt to deal with this problem. There are also developmental research strategies that were used in the study of authoritarianism and dogmatism that could be applied in an attempt to uncover some of the relationships between child-rearing patterns and cognitive complexity. For example, measurements could be obtained of parents' cognitive complexity and their child-rearing patterns. Another design would relate recalled child-rearing patterns to measures of cognitive complexity.

Cronbach (1956) noted that, although the Rep Test is flexible and indirect, the complexity of the instrument and theory has led to errors of analysis. There are several situations in which a high score on the Rep Test may not be a valid indication of high cognitive complexity. Although we omit research on clinical populations from this survey, there is evidence to indicate that disorganized personalities score high on cognitive complexity. If the Rep-Test protocol is filled out at random, a high cognitive complexity score will result, since there will be few matches in comparing each row with every other row. One approach to distinguishing complex from disorganized responses would be to readminister the instrument and compare the responses on a row-by-row basis. The complex individual should show greater stability than the disorganized individual. On the positive side, the Rep Test by its very nature should not be subject to social desirability or acquiescence response sets, although data on this issue are scanty.

As mentioned in preceding chapters, the failure to report the absolute level of cognitive complexity makes the comparison of results of different studies difficult. A score sufficient to categorize a subject as high in cognitive complexity in one study may not be sufficiently high to categorize him as high in cognitive complexity in another study. A second problem with the presentation of results is the frequent failure to report the proportion of the variance that is being accounted for in the statistical analyses. Usually it is only the level of the significance of a difference between means that is reported. Another difficulty with the reporting of results is the failure of investigators to indicate the number of subjects who do not complete the Rep-Test protocols. This criticism was also made earlier in connection with research on Einstellung in the area of authoritarianism. Missing data from subjects who fail to complete an instrument may lead to systematic bias in results.

Schroder, Driver, and Streufert (1967) argued that the number of constructs (dimensions) that a subject may generate is limited to the number of rows analyzed in the Rep Test. They pointed out that this may confound moderately and highly cognitively complex subjects. As Adams-Webber (1970b) noted, Hunt (1951) showed that 20–25 rows are generally sufficient for even the most complex subjects. However, much of the research summarized in this chapter is based on Rep tests of about 10 rows, lending strength to the criticism by Schroder, Driver, and Streufert.

Finally, it should be noted that measures of cognitive complexity derived from the Rep Test provide a measure of differentiation, the number of constructs used by the subject. The Rep Test does not provide a measure of integration, the ways the constructs interrelate. Landfield and Barr (1976) and Landfield (1977) recently reported an attempt to derive a measure of integration (which they term "ordination") using a Rep-Test approach. In the next chapter, differentiation and integration are considered in the measurement of cognitive style.

CHAPTER FIVE
Integrative Complexity

The view of people as information processors is central to the position originally presented in Harvey, Hunt, and Schroder's *Conceptual Systems and Personality Organization* (1961) and later expanded in Schroder, Driver, and Streufert's *Human Information Processing* (1967). Briefly, the view presented is that people engage in two activities in processing sensory input: differentiation and integration. Differentiation refers to the individual's ability to locate stimuli along dimensions. Integration refers to the individual's ability to utilize complex rules, or programs, to combine these dimensions.

The individual who is low in differentiating and integrating ability is said to be *concrete;* the individual who is high in differentiating and integrating ability is said to be *abstract.* All people may be ordered along a continuum from concrete to abstract, depending on their ability to differentiate and integrate information. This continuum was termed *integrative* or *conceptual complexity.*

Behavior is viewed, following Kurt Lewin (1935), as a function of the person and the environment. Just as individuals vary in levels of integrative complexity, so the environment varies in levels of informational complexity. According to the Harvey, Hunt, and Schroder approach, the individual's behavior is best understood as an interaction of his differentiating and integrating ability (integrative complexity) and the informational complexity of his environment.

The individual's ability to differentiate and integrate mediates between stimulus input and behavioral output. The input field consists of a range of stimuli that are filtered, or processed, by the mediating structure. This mediating structure allows the individual to differentiate environmental elements and integrate the elements to produce behavioral output.

DIFFERENTIATION

Aspects of the individual and the environment determine the dimensions along which the individual views his environment. For most individuals, color has three dimensions: hue, brightness, and saturation. When people are asked to judge the similarity of different color patches, they consider these three dimensions. For individuals who are totally color blind, the dimension of hue is nonexistent. Such individuals would make color judgments in terms of only two dimensions, brightness and saturation. As another illustration, pure sound has only two dimensions: pitch and loudness. The normal individual can differentiate these two, and only these two, dimensions of pure sound.

In everyday life individuals are called on to process information that is more complex than color patches or pure sound, and the differentiations that are made about more complex objects show greater interindividual variation. For example, what are the dimensions used when information about dogs is processed? For one person, dogs vary in size, coat, and color. For another, dogs vary in size, coat, color, strength, intelligence, longevity, resistance to disease, and country of origin.

There is another way in which individuals may vary in their differentiating ability. Assume that two individuals think of dogs only in terms of size, coat, and color. For one of these individuals, size may mean "large" or "small." For the other person, size may be much more differentiated. The French poodle, for example, exists in various sizes: pocket, toy, miniature, standard, royal, and imperial. The individual making these distinctions is making greater differentiations along the dimension of size than is the person who views dogs simply as large or small. Some evidence is presented in the section on development that the number of dimensions utilized by an individual is determined by his past training. The more familiar one is with objects, the more likely one is to differentiate more among the objects.

INTEGRATION

The second aspect of the mediating process is the individual's ability to integrate the dimensions that he has differentiated. The dimensions are integrated by the application of rules (programs, schemata). Integration is related to differentiation in that the greater the number of dimensions, the greater the potential for complex schemata. At any given level of differentiation, there are likely to be individual differences in integrating ability.

Individuals varying in their levels of integrative complexity will vary in the weightings they assign to the dimensions they differentiate and the ways they combine the information generated by differing dimensions. The rules or schemata that individuals use for integrating information may be simple or complex. These differences are best illustrated by the four nodal points along the concrete–abstract dimension posited by Harvey, Hunt, and Schroder (1961) in their earliest formulation.

System I: Dependence.   The most concrete type of functioning is found in the system I, or dependent, individual. This individual has poor differentiating and integrating abilities. That is, he views his world in terms of only a few dimensions, and his rules for combining these dimensions are simple. The dependent person tends to compartmentalize; he is capable of maintaining contradictory beliefs. There are also tendencies to bifurcate, to see things in terms of black–white distinctions, and to overgeneralize. The system I individual attempts to avoid ambiguity and, as a consequence, minimizes conflict.

System II: Negativism.   This stage is characterized by the emergence of alternate schemata for organizing dimensions. At this level of functioning the individual is capable of generating different perceptions of a situation. The system II individual is capable of a simple branching alternative: if *A*, then *X*; if *B*, then *Y*. The individual's level of integration is conditional; that is, what is interpreted as "good" may depend on the particular condition. However, given the particular condition, the individual's behavior is fixed. System II functioning is also associated with a break with absolutism, a pushing against rules or control; hence, *negativism.*

System III: Independence. At the system III level of functioning, differentiation and integration become more complex. Decisions become more difficult and are marked by weighting and compromise among the elements. The individual at this stage demonstrates an empirical orientation toward the environment, and many of his concepts develop from independent, exploratory behavior.

System IV: Interdependence. The most abstract level of functioning is found in the system IV, or interdependent, individual. Such a person has reached the point at which schemata are developed for putting together comparisons made between alternatives. It is this individual who can process a maximum amount and complexity of information and who shows the greatest tolerance of stress.

The differences between concrete and abstract individuals were summarized by Harvey and Schroder (1963). According to the authors, greater concreteness is characterized by the following:

1. Poor differentiation and incomplete integration
2. A bifurcated view of the environment
3. Reliance on authority
4. Intolerance of ambiguity
5. Rigidity under low levels of stress
6. Collapse under high stress
7. The inability to see alternative solutions to problems
8. A poorer ability to role play and to think in hypothetical terms
9. A poorly defined self-concept

On the basis of a review of research using the "This I Believe" Test as a measure of integrative complexity, Miller and Harvey (1973) arrived at a number of conclusions regarding ways in which highly concrete subjects function differently from highly abstract subjects. Miller and Harvey concluded that concrete subjects tend toward extreme and polarized judgments, are more reliant on status and power, are less tolerant of ambiguity and uncertainty, have a greater need for cognitive consistency, are more rigid, are less sensitive to subtle environmental cues, are less well able to role-play, and tend to generalize about others from incomplete information.

The early work on integrative complexity centered around identifying representatives of the four major conceptual systems and studying differences in behavior among them. Harvey's (1964) study of conformity is an example of this approach. Across a variety of conformity situations, Harvey showed system III subjects to be heavily dependent on external cures provided by either the physical or interpersonal environment. System I subjects were dependent on authority figures, whereas system II subjects rejected authority. System IV subjects were generally uninfluenced by external cues. In later research, this interest in the performance of system-specific subjects was replaced by an interest in the dimension of integrative complexity as it varies along a continuum.

ENVIRONMENTAL COMPLEXITY

Research in the area of intrinsic motivation, that is, motivation occurring in the absence of any known tissue deficit (need for exploration, manipulation, stimulation, etc.) has introduced the concept of the inverted U-shaped curve (Berlyne, 1960). As illustrated in Figure 5.1, this

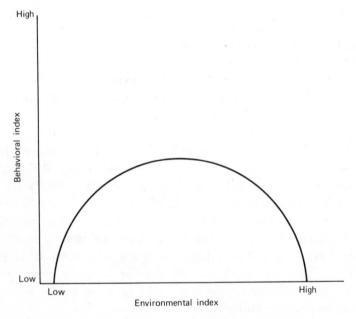

Figure 5.1. An illustration of an inverted U-shaped curve.

curve relates a behavioral variable to some aspect of the environment. It is often found that organisms function best at intermediate levels of arousal, stimulation, or complexity. For example, if environmental stimulation falls to too low a level (sensory deprivation) or rises to too high a level (sensory bombardment, or sensory overload), the organism does not function well.

In Schroder, Driver, and Streufert (1967), the concept of the inverted U-shaped curve is extended to the study of integrative complexity. The hypothesized difference in the functioning of concrete and abstract individuals is illustrated in Figure 5.2. The more abstract the individual, the higher the level of performance of which he should be capable. Abstract individuals are hypothesized to perform at least as well as concrete individuals in environments of low informational complexity, but they should perform better in environments of high informational complexity. The level of optimal performance attained by abstract individuals is hypothesized to occur at a higher level of informational complexity than the level of optimal performance for concrete individuals.

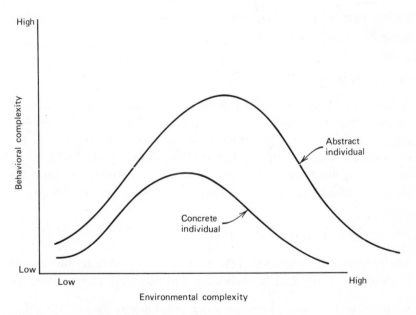

Figure 5.2. Functioning of concrete and abstract individuals in relation to environmental complexity (after Schroder, Driver, & Streufert, 1967).

Hunt and Sullivan (1974) applied the concept of matching the integrative complexity of the individual to the structure of the educational experience, an environmental variable. They provided evidence showing that children low in integrative complexity do better in a structured environment (e.g., lectures), whereas children high in integrative complexity do better in less structured environments (e.g., student-centered approaches).

GROUPS

Integrative complexity theory has also been applied to the study of the functioning of social systems (Schroder & Harvey, 1963). Groups may be viewed as similar to individuals in that the functioning of the group may be located along a continuum from concrete to abstract.[1] As individuals evolve concepts to define situations, groups evolve norms. Also similar is the developmental progression; all groups are hypothesized to function initially concretely, but, given the appropriate training conditions, they will progress to more abstract levels of functioning. Another interesting application is the Suedfeld and Rank (1976) finding that the success of revolutionary leaders can be understood in terms of integrative complexity theory.

MEASUREMENT

A number of procedures have been used to measure integrative complexity. One of the earliest measures was the Situational Interpretation Experiment (Hunt, 1962b). More common measures are the Sentence Completion Test and the Paragraph Completion Test, the "This I Believe" Test, the Impression Formation Test, the Interpersonal Topical Inventory of Integrative Complexity, and multidimensional scaling.

PARAGRAPH COMPLETION TEST

The Paragraph Completion Test (PCT), first reported as the Sentence Completion Test (SCT) by Schroder and Streufert (1962), is a major

---

[1] In this chapter we review studies involving groups only to the extent that data are analyzed and reported for individuals in the group. It is beyond the scope of our review to consider the functioning of groups per se (e.g., Tuckman, 1964).

method for assessing levels of integrative complexity. The SCT presents the subject with a number of sentence stems (e.g., "When I am in doubt . . . ," "Rules . . . ," "When I am criticized . . ."). For each stem, the subject is required to complete a sentence and write one or two additional sentences in the same vein. The response to each stem was usually scored on a five-point scale, from concrete to abstract, on the basis of the *structure* that underlied the response. The individual's total score was originally the sum of the scores of the single items. The items represent each of three major areas tapped by the SCT: stems that implied the presence of alternatives (e.g., "When I am in doubt . . ."), stems that implied the imposition of external standards (e.g., "Rules . . ."), and stems that implied interpersonal conflict (e.g., "When I am criticized . . .").

The SCT evolved into the Paragraph Completion Test (Schroder, Driver, & Streufert, 1967). In the PCT the subject is presented with five sentence stems and allowed 90 seconds to write three sentences for each stem. An example of a concrete response to the stem "Rules . . ." is "are made to be followed. They give direction to a project or life or anything. They should not be broken except in extreme circumstances" (Schroder, Driver, & Streufert, 1967). An example of an abstract response to the same stem is "Rules . . . are made for everyone but are interpreted in many ways. It depends on the point of view of the interpreter. It is in this very process of interpretation that a society stays dynamic and changes and grows" (Schroder, Driver, & Streufert, 1967). It may be noted that the more abstract of these responses evidences greater differentiation and a more complex system of integration.

In scoring the PCT, Schroder, Driver, and Streufert suggested using the mean of the two most abstract responses to provide the integrative complexity score. They argued that completing the PCT is a tedius task; thus the maximum cognitive integration produced is the best index of overall complexity.

Reliability estimates for the PCT are generally at a satisfactory level (cf. Gardiner & Schroder, 1972). Schroder, Driver, and Streufert (1967) reported that, after a four-day training period, interjudge reliability for the PCT ranged between .80 and .95.

Hunt (1962a) presented a manual for scoring responses to the SCT for 10- to 16-year-old children. Six of the sentence stems are scored for concreteness–abstraction and three for negativism. Hunt reported inter-rater reliabilities of .80 and .84 for the two scales, respectively. Scores on the scales are combined to yield a single measure of integrative complexity. In their study of 20 male and 20 female 12-, 14-, and 17-year-olds, Sullivan, McCullough, and Stager (1970) reported an inter-rater reliability of .76 for Hunt and Halverson's (1964) Conceptual Levels Questionnaire, an SCT-type instrument for children.

Bottenberg (1969) reported on a German adaptation of the PCT with an inter-rater reliability of .91 and a split-half reliability of .75, based on a sample of 100 university students.

"THIS I BELIEVE" TEST

A test that is similar to the PCT is the "This I Believe" or TIB Test, developed by O. J. Harvey (1963b, 1964). The TIB Test requires the subject to complete, in two or three sentences, the phrase "This I believe about ————." The dash is replaced by such referents as friendship, guilt, myself, majority opinion, people, and compromise. As with the PCT, scoring of the protocol requires intimate knowledge of integrative complexity theory:

> Some of the more important bases for classifying a subject include the relative degree of absolutism and evaluativeness of his expressed beliefs, positivity–negativity of statements about authority, triteness and normativeness of the statements, ethnocentrism, avidity of subscription to socially approved modes of behavior, concern with interpersonal relations, and the simplicity–complexity of expressed beliefs. (Harvey, 1964)

Unlike the PCT, for which the responses to each stem are scored, on the TIB Test a single global score is assigned after reading responses to all the stems. As Schroder (1971) pointed out, a major difference between the TIB Test and the PCT is that the former is scored partly on the basis of content (e.g., reliance on external authority), whereas the latter is scored solely on the basis of structure.

Like the PCT, the TIB Test was reported by Harvey (1964) to have high predictive and construct validity. Harvey (1963b) reported inter-judge reliabilities of .90 or more across seven different samples of subjects. Harvey and Felknor (1970) reported that interjudge reliabilities for the TIB Test generally range between .85 and .95. They also reported a one-week test-retest reliability of .90 and an eight-month test-retest reliability of .85. Greaves (1971) cited data from his dissertation and other research of his that indicated satisfactory interjudge and test-retest reliability for TIB-Test scores. Harvey (1966a) reported that of 1400 scored TIB tests, 30% were scored system I, 15% system II, 20% system III, and 7% system IV. The remainder were scored as some combination of the above.

Cox (1974) administered the PCT and TIB Test to a total of 349 undergraduates at three universities. The correlations between the two tests were studied separately for males and females at each university. None of the six correlation coefficients was statistically significant, nor was the correlation based on the total sample. Based on his data, Cox cautioned against using results obtained from the TIB Test interchangeably with those derived from the PCT to support integrative complexity theory. However, the range of the PCT scores obtained from Cox's sample was severely restricted, and the TIB Test was scored by untrained judges. Supporting Cox's findings, Epting and Wilkins (1974) obtained a nonsignificant correlation between the PCT and a modified version of the TIB test for a sample of 90 undergraduates.

An objective version of the TIB Test, the Conceptual Systems Test (CST), was reported by Harvey, Prather, White, and Hoffmeister (1968). The CST was developed from responses by subjects to the TIB Test. The CST consists of 49 statements with which the subject agrees or disagrees. A profile is derived on the basis of prior factor analyses, and a determination is made of appropriate system placement based on this profile.

IMPRESSION FORMATION TEST

The Impression Formation Test (IFT) was developed by Streufert and Schroder (1962) as a measure of integrating ability. It was theorized that two individuals with equally high levels of differentiating ability might differ in their uses of integrative schemata.

Asch (1946) found that subjects presented with a list of adjectives developed a "consistent view" when asked to form an impression of a person described by the adjectives. Later investigators (e.g., Gollin, 1954) found that individuals varied in the ways in which they integrated adjectives. In another study, Nidorf (1961) found that subjects whose solutions to the impression formation task involved integration were high in differentiating ability. Working specifically within the integrative complexity framework, Wolfe (1963) found his abstract subjects superior to concrete subjects on the impression formation task.

In the IFT the subject is presented with a set of three adjectives and is asked to write down impressions of a person described by the adjectives. He is then presented with another set of three adjectives, inconsistent with those used in the first set, and again asked to write his impressions of a person described by this set of adjectives. Finally, the subject is told that both sets of adjectives actually refer to the same person and that he is to write his impressions of this person. The descriptions are used as the basis for assessing the individual's level of integrative complexity. The subject who evidences more complex rules for integration and places greater importance on the cognitive processes of the person described is considered to be more abstract (Streufert & Schroder, 1962).

Streufert and Driver (1967) reported on a revision of the IFT and presented a manual for scoring IFT responses for integrative complexity and differentiation complexity. They presented test-retest reliabilities for the five adjective sets that ranged from .72 to .92. When scored for integrative complexity, the five sets correlated from .41 to .60 with the SCT; when scored for differentiation, the five sets correlated from .09 to .21 with the SCT. The data were obtained from an unspecified sample.

Streufert and Driver (1967) reported correlations between the earlier version of the IFT and the SCT as ranging between .26 and .88, with a median correlation of .52. Schroder, Driver, and Streufert (1967) reported correlations from .40 to .80 between the PCT and IFT. Schroder, Driver, and Streufert (1967) reported that interjudge reliability for the IFT can reach .85 after one day's training when IFT training follows PCT training.

Suedfeld (1968) showed that verbal instructions could be used to modify responses on the IFT and PCT. Twenty-two integratively simple and 22 integratively complex undergraduates were each assigned to one of three experimental conditions. One condition was designed to increase complexity, one to decrease complexity, and one was neutral. The data showed that the experimental manipulation resulted in a number of complicated changes in integrative complexity scores, indicating the importance of standardized instruction.

INTERPERSONAL TOPICAL INVENTORY

The Interpersonal Topical Inventory (ITI) is a forced-choice instrument developed by Tuckman (1966) as a measure of integrative complexity. It is a modification of an instrument developed in 1959 by Schroder and Hunt (cf. Schroder, 1971). On the ITI the subject is presented with six stems: "When I am criticized . . . ," "When I am in doubt . . . ," "When a friend acts differently toward me . . . ," "This I believe about people . . . ," "Leaders . . . ," and "When other people find fault with me. . . ." For each stem, the subject is presented with six pairs of responses. His task is to complete the sentence by indicating his choice of one of the statements from every pair of statements. Each of the 12 statements for each stem (six pairs of statements) represents a system I-, II-, III-, or IV-level response. The six pairs of statements make possible all paired combinations of the four systems: I versus II, I versus III, I versus IV, II versus III, II versus IV, and III versus IV. The subject is given four scores; each score represents the total number of times he has chosen one system's response over the others. A subject is considered to be functioning at a specific system level if he scores high on that level and low on the other three.

Tuckman (1966) presented data from over 100 Naval recruits indicating significant differences in the SCT-measured level of abstractness for subjects that were classified on the basis of the ITI. He also presented data indicating a significant relationship ($C = .54$) between the SCT and ITI. Suedfeld, Tomkins, and Tucker (1969) reported a significant correlation of .19 between the SCT and the ITI for a sample of 178 undergraduates. Russell and Sandilands (1973) cited an unpublished study by Jacobson (1973) in which a significant correlation of .18 was obtained between the PCT and ITI for a sample of 120 subjects. In their own study of about 160 undergraduates, Russell and Sandilands also obtained a significant correlation of .18 between the two measures. Schroder (1971) reported unpublished studies by himself and Hunt indicating that the correlation between the ITI and SCT decreases as level of education increases. Stewin and Anderson (1974) found no relationship between the ITI and the SCT. Stewin (1976) failed to find significant relationships between the ITI and either the PCT or the TIB Test for a sample of 100 eleventh graders. The correlation between the PCT and the TIB Test was a significant .41.

MULTIDIMENSIONAL SCALING

The most mathematically sophisticated of all attempts to measure integrative complexity is the application of multidimensional scaling (MDS). In the most common MDS format, the subject is required to make judgments of similarity between pairs of complex objects. The resulting matrix of similarity judgments is analyzed to determine the minimum number of dimensions the subject might have used to generate the pattern of similarity ratings. MDS also yields weightings to indicate the importance of each dimension.

It has been hypothesized that the number of dimensions yielded in an MDS analysis relates to the individuals differentiating ability and that the weightings of the dimensions yielded in the MDS analysis, or their obliqueness, relate to the individual's integrating ability. Although MDS studies have yielded some interesting results (e.g., Cohen & Feldman, 1975; Warr, Schroder & Blackman, 1969a, b), it is unclear whether MDS will solve the measurement problem for integrative complexity theory. The parallel between dimensionality and differentiation is promising, but the relationship between the weightings of the dimensions and integration is unclear (Blackman, 1966; Fraser, 1976). Another realistic difficulty is the expense involved in the computer processing of each subject's similarity ratings.

SOCIAL DESIRABILITY AND ACQUIESCENCE

Schroder and Streufert (1962) failed to find a significant correlation between the concrete–abstract scale of the SCT and a measure of social desirability for a sample of 40 male high school students. Scores on Bottenberg's (1969) German language adaptation of the PCT were not significantly correlated with a German adaptation of Bass' Social Acquiescence Scale. In their study of 107 eleventh graders, Stewin and

Anderson (1974) failed to obtain significant correlations between either the ITI or the CST and the Couch and Keniston (1960) measure of agreement response tendency.

DEVELOPMENT

A basic concept of the integrative complexity approach is that the individual's information-processing abilities develop as he progresses through a number of stages. It is hypothesized that, early in life, all children function at a concrete level. If environmental conditions are appropriate, the child progresses to more abstract stages. Because of environmental or training conditions, the child's development may be arrested at any point; thus in adults the entire continuum of integrative complexity is represented. The progression from concrete functioning to abstract functioning is a developmental one. In the process of developing to levels of more abstract functioning, the individual must generate new differentiations (i.e., new interpretations of events) and must evolve new and more complex rules for integration.

In integrative complexity theory, the most important aspect of the environment is the style of training to which the child is exposed. The theory proposes two major styles of training. The first is termed *unilateral,* under which rules for behavior are generated externally; the second is termed *interdependent,* under which rules are generated internally. Schroder, Driver, and Streufert (1967) also refer to these training approaches as *deductive* and *inductive,* respectively.

UNILATERAL TRAINING

In unilateral training, the parent (or teacher or other trainer) provides the child with a ready-made schema. A schema is a rule describing a relationship between stimuli (input) and the responses (output) the individual is to make to the stimuli. The paradigm for this type of training is illustrated in Figure 5.3. In this diagram, the rule or behavior to be learned is represented by the curve labeled *schema.* The schema describes the relationship between stimulus and response. Given stimulus S_1, the appropriate response is R_1. In unilateral training, the schema

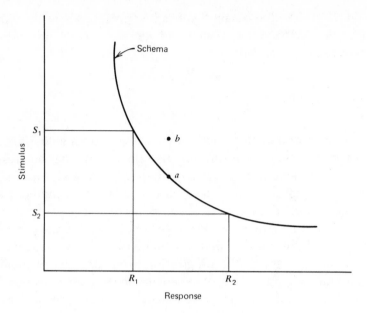

Figure 5.3. Paradigm for unilateral training.

to be learned is provided for the child. If the child makes the appropriate response to a given stimulus, he is likely to be rewarded. This situation is illustrated by point *a*, where the child's response to a stimulus falls on the curve. If the child makes an inappropriate response to a stimulus, he is likely to be punished. This situation is illustrated by point *b*, where the child's response to a stimulus does not follow the schema. Conceptualized in this way, the child is rewarded and punished until he learns the given schema for relating his responses to environmental stimuli.

Under unilateral training, the child learns to adapt to his environment by seeking externally provided schemata to govern his behavior. These schemata provide him with information about how to behave. Such an oversimplification of the environment leads to a restriction of perceptions and responses. Ambiguous situations in which, by definition, the schemata are not clear are threatening and are warded off. The individual also develops a tendency to distort the world to fit his available schemata, because he is unable to generate new ones.

Schemata can be conveyed to the individual directly or indirectly.

When schemata are expressed directly, they take the form of orders, directions, or explicit statements. Schemata expressed indirectly involve an implicit use of a predetermined criterion—the trainer rewards and punishes without an explicit statement of the schema.

Unilateral training leads to concrete functioning, but whether it leads to system I or system II functioning depends on whether the training has been applied reliably or unreliably. In reliable unilateral training the schemata are furnished reliably and consistently, and alternative interpretations or behaviors are generally ignored or punished. This type of training is similar to dominant, autocratic training and leads to system I functioning. In unreliable unilateral training there is an inconsistency of control, and the trainer may hold expectations for behaviors that are beyond the limits of the subject. The training lacks affectionate, benevolent, or rewarding components. This type of training is employed by the driving parent who obtains the child's dependence by arbitrary and irregular control, resulting in a distrustful relationship and system II functioning.

INTERDEPENDENT TRAINING

In unilateral training the concepts, or schemata, that the child is to learn are provided by the trainer. In interdependent training, the trainer allows the subject to generate his own rules and schemata for behavior. The basic task of the trainer is to provide a suitable learning environment for the child. If the environment provided by the parent is overly simple, the child will be understimulated and will not progress to abstraction; if the environment is overly complex, the child will be overwhelmed and will not progress to abstraction.

In unilateral training the child receives feedback on the appropriateness of his behavior through the rewards and punishments administered by his parent. In interdependent training feedback reaches the child as a consequence of his own behavior. The parent does not provide ready-made schemata or feedback. The child develops his own schemata by interacting with the environment and experiencing the consequences of this interaction.

The paradigm for interdependent training is illustrated in Figure 5.4. Note that there is no externally provided schema. Instead, the individ-

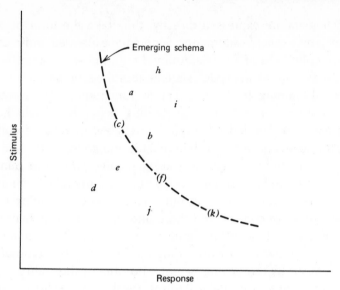

Figure 5.4. Paradigm for interdependent training.

ual emits a series of behaviors, a, b, c, d, ... As a consequence of
the behaviors several of the stimulus–response associations—(c), (f), (k)
—are preserved and contribute to the development of the schema. The
emergent schema is represented by the dotted curve. The difficulty
with interdependent training is the provision of an environment appropriate to the emergence of schemata. It is through the exploration of
his environment that the child learns to generate alternatives and to
integrate the dimensions of his experiences. The parent may reward
exploratory behavior, but he does not teach the schema.

Whether interdependent training leads to system III or IV functioning depends on whether the training has been protective or informational; protective interdependent training leads to system III functioning, whereas informational interdependent training leads to system IV
functioning. In protective interdependent training the parent helps the
child and provides an example, or model, of the behavior to be
learned. The trainer anticipates the child's failures and enters into his
exploratory behaviors as a helpful, supportive figure before the failure
occurs. In informational interdependent training the parent is more in
the background, providing environments for learning that are appropriate to the child's level of development. Basically, learning occurs

through the child's independent exploration of progressive barriers. The parent may participate by clarifying the feedback the child is experiencing, but he does not help or model. An example of such training is found in the autotelic environment developed by Anderson and Moore (1960), in which very young children are taught to read and write by progressing through an intrinsically rewarding environment.

The four major types of training proposed by Harvey, Hunt, and Schroder (1961) were equated by the authors to the four major types of attitudes generally found in studies of parental child rearing. These latter studies have, rather consistently, yielded two major dimensions of child rearing: autonomy–control, and cold–warm (or hostility–love). The two dimensions are independent of each other, and the relationship between them is illustrated in Figure 5.5 (cf. Schaefer, 1959). As shown, each of the four major types of training proposed in integrative complexity theory may be associated with one of the quadrants of the figure.

Cross (1966) performed the first study designed to provide direct evidence on the relationship between integrative complexity and parental child-rearing patterns. The subjects were 377 boys in the eighth grade of one school. Integrative complexity was measured by Hunt and Halverson's (1964) Conceptual Level Questionnaire (CLQ), an SCT-type

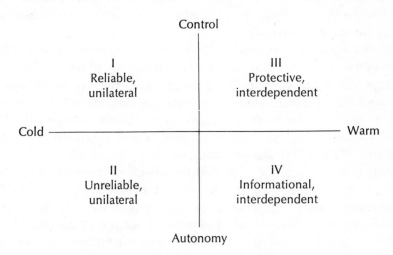

Figure 5.5. Relationship of unilateral and interdependent training to the two major dimensions of child rearing.

instrument for children. The 33 boys with the highest complexity scores were matched on the basis of IQ and grade level with 33 concrete subjects. The parents of these 66 children were administered a seven-item interview developed by Cross (1964) to measure unilaterality–interdependence of child rearing. The parents of all the eighth grade boys were requested to complete the Parent Attitude Research Instrument (PARI) developed by Schaefer and Bell (1958). PARI data were available from 182 of the families.

Cross' data indicated that families whose sons were extremely concrete were more unilateral in their approach to child rearing than families whose sons were extremely abstract. Across the larger sample, the PARI data indicated that parents of concrete boys tended to be authoritarian ($r = .23$); the relationship between integrative complexity and parental warmth was not statistically significant.

In a study of parent–child relationship antecedents of level of integrative complexity, Harvey and Felknor (1970) selected 106 undergraduates from a larger pool on the basis of their TIB-Test scores. In addition to the TIB Test, the subjects also completed a 70-item questionnaire on parent–child relations. Cluster analyses were performed to reduce the number of parent–child relations variables. For both mothers and fathers, 11 clusters were found. A large number of t tests were calculated to compare differences between representatives of each of the four levels of integrative complexity; analyses were also done separately for males and females.

By our count, Harvey and Felknor (1970) performed almost 400 t tests in the analysis of their data. Given the number of tests performed, a large number of statistically significant differences could be found on the basis of chance alone. It is therefore difficult to interpret the results of the study. However, Harvey and Felknor interpreted their data as supporting the theoretical expectations regarding the antecedents of level of integrative complexity.

Bishop and Chace (1971) studied the effects of parental integrative complexity on the home-play environment and on the novelty of children's responses in a play situation. The subjects were 72 three- and four-year-old children attending nursery school and 79 parents whose TIB tests could be scored reliably. The data for fathers indicated no relationship between the father's level of integrative complexity and either the play environment or the novelty of the children's responses.

The authors presented data that suggested that abstract mothers are supportive of a nonrestrictive, flexible play environment and their children tend to make more novel responses—responses the investigators interpreted as indicative of complexity.

The scant data available on the relationship between child rearing and integrative complexity thus provide some support for the developmental aspects of the theory.

AGE

Harvey, Hunt, and Schroder (1961) hypothesized that integrative complexity increases with age. Several studies provide data on this point. Hunt (1962b) studied the relationship between integrative complexity and age in a sample of 136 boys in the sixth through twelfth grades. The subjects were selected from a pool of 910 boys to provide an even distribution across the four stages of integrative complexity as measured by the Situational Interpretation Experiment. The correlations between age and integrative complexity was not statistically significant. In a second aspect of the study, 484 boys from the fifth through tenth grades were administered a sentence completion test to measure integrative complexity. There was little variation in the integrative complexity scores; thus there could not be a significant correlation between complexity and age or any other variable.

Cross (1966) failed to find a significant correlation between age and integrative complexity, as measured by an SCT, across a sample of approximately 175 eighth to twelfth grade boys. Sullivan, McCullough, and Stager (1970) administered Hunt and Halverson's (1964) CLQ to 20 male and 20 female 12-, 14-, and 17-year olds. CLQ scores were significantly related to age for the two sexes combined ($r = .65$).

Thus the available evidence on the relationship between age and integrative complexity is insufficient to support the hypothesized relationship.

OTHER DEMOGRAPHIC VARIABLES

In their study of 20 male and 20 female 12-, 14-, and 17-year-olds, Sullivan, McCullough, and Stager (1970) failed to find sex differences on

Hunt and Halverson's CLQ. Hunt and Dopyera (1966), in a study of 969 lower- and middle-class junior high-school aged children, found significantly higher integrative complexity scores, as measured by a six-item SCT, for females in both SES groups. Hunt and Dopyera also found lower levels of integrative complexity among 277 lower-class junior high-school students when compared to 692 middle-class students, despite the relatively concrete performance of both groups. There was significantly greater variability in the integrative complexity of the lower-class subjects.

Bishop and Chace (1971) presented data on the relationship between TIB-measured integrative complexity and demographic variables for a sample of 45 mothers of nursery school children. Mothers who differed in integrative complexity did not differ in age or education; there were no differences in their husbands' incomes, occupational levels, ages, or levels of education.

Russell and Sandilands (1973) reported data from their own study of about 160 undergraduates, as well as data from unpublished studies by Corfield (1971) and Jacobson (1973), as indicating no differences in the levels of integrative complexity for males and females. Russell and Sandilands also found no statistically significant relationships between either ITI or PCT measures of integrative complexity and age or birth order.

There are insufficient data to reach a clear conclusion on the relationship of integrative complexity to such demographic variables as sex and socioeconomic status.

RESEARCH

INTEGRATIVE COMPLEXITY AND OTHER MEASURES OF COGNITIVE STYLE

Streufert and Driver (1967) reported a significant correlation between the IFT and the F Scale ($r = .18$) for a sample of 124 male undergraduates. IFT scores were not significantly correlated with scores on the Dogmatism Scale. Schroder, Driver, and Streufert (1967) reported correlations from .25 to .55 between scores on the F Scale and either the SCT or IFT in a variety of studies; most correlations reportedly did not exceed the .40 level. The investigators stated that the relationships between measures of integrative complexity and the Dogmatism Scale were lower.

Schroder and Streufert (1962) obtained a correlation between scores on the SCT and the F Scale of .34 for a sample of 147 male high school students. Correlations of the SCT and both the Dogmatism Scale and the Gough and Sanford (1952) Rigidity Scale were not statistically significant. Streufert and Driver (1967) reported a significant correlation of .23 between the IFT and an unspecified measure of rigidity for a sample of 124 male undergraduates. Scores on Bottenberg's (1969) German adaptation of the PCT were significantly correlated ($r = .28$) with a German adaptation of Budner's (1962) Intolerance of Ambiguity Scale.

In the course of a factor analytic study of cognitive structure, Rule and Hewitt (1970) administered the ITI, a 28-item F Scale, and the Dogmatism Scale to a sample of 91 male and 113 female undergraduates. The correlations between the ITI and the F Scale was statistically significant for both sexes ($r = .39$ for males, $r = .29$ for females). The ITI was significantly correlated with the Dogmatism Scale for males ($r = .23$), but not for females.

In his study of 136 sixth through twelfth grade boys varying in integrative complexity, Hunt (1962b) found a significant correlation of .37 between integrative complexity and a measure of cognitive complexity derived from the work of Bieri, Bradburn, and Galinsky (1958). Streufert (1970) reported that, on the basis of his own research, correlations between the SCT and Rep Test are consistently low and sometimes negative. Epting and Wilkins (1974) correlated scores on Bieri's modification of the Rep Test with scores on the PCT and a modification of the TIB Test for a sample of 90 undergraduates. The correlations in both cases were a statistically significant .31. However, whereas the correlation with the TIB Test was positive and in the expected direction, the correlation with the PCT was unexpectedly negative. We reported earlier that, in this sample, the correlation between the modified TIB Test and the PCT was not statistically significant.

Carr (1965a, b) developed the Interpersonal Discrimination Test, an instrument similar to Kelly's Rep Test, to distinguish between differentiation and discrimination. Differentiation was interpreted as the number of dimensions an individual uses to describe the characteristics of several people. Discrimination was interpreted as the number of categories that are used within dimensions to group the people that served as stimuli. The subjects in Carr's study were 63 undergraduates selected from a larger group of undergraduate males on the basis of their SCT scores. Subjects were classified as system I, II, or III, with no differences in intelligence among the subjects in the three groups. Carr found no significant differences in differentiation among the three groups. When discrimination along the three most commonly used dimensions was studied, Carr found that system III subjects used more categories (i.e., were more discriminating among the stimuli) than system I subjects. Although it is not reported, we assume that system II subjects did not differ significantly on discrimination from the other two groups.

In another study, Carr (1969) presented data that are relevant to the vigilance hypothesis encountered in Chapter 4. Twenty-seven male medical students were divided into concrete and abstract groups on the basis of their SCT scores. A modification of the Rep Test was used to provide a measure of differentiation. The data indicated that abstract subjects made greater differentiations among the stimuli, that negatively evaluated stimuli were differentiated to a greater degree than positively evaluated stimuli, and that concrete subjects demonstrated greater differentiation when rating negatively evaluated people than when rating positively evaluated people.

Smith and Leach (1972) developed what they called a "hierarchical measure of cognitive complexity" from Rep-Test data. They studied a sample of 13 subjects classified as system I and 14 subjects classified as system IV on the basis of TIB-Test scores. Concreteness on the measure of cognitive complexity was associated with concreteness on the TIB Test. Scores on Bieri's measure of cognitive complexity were not related to TIB-Test scores.

Harvey, Reich, and Wyer (1968) found that concrete subjects were more likely than abstract subjects to differentiate among both the stimuli and the attributes used to rate stimuli when members of both groups were not intensely involved with the stimuli. However, abstract subjects demonstrated greater differentiation when they were highly involved with the stimulus material. The subjects were 40 undergraduates selected on the basis of their TIB-Test scores. As the authors pointed out, these results demonstrating that differentiation is related to intensity (and not to direction) contradict the vigilance hypothesis that states that greater differentiation is related to negaive evaluation of the stimulus object (Irwin, Tripodi, & Bieri, 1967).

Vannoy (1965), in a study of the similarity of cognitive style measures, administered the SCT along with a variety of other measures to a group of 113 male undergraduates. A factor analysis of a 20-variable intercorrelation matrix with an eight-factor solution indicated the SCT to be independent of the other measures. Specifically, the SCT did not correlate significantly with a modified Rep Test or a modified F Scale. Vannoy concluded that there is no general dimension of cognitive style.

Harvey (1966b) summarized construct validity data relating the TIB Test to a number of measures of cognitive style, including a modified Rep Test, the F Scale, the Dogmatism Scale, the Gough and Sanford Rigidity Scale, the Gottschaldt Embedded Figures Test, and the Denny Doodlebug Problem. Harvey reported that, in general, the "expected" relationships between integrative complexity and the other measures of cognitive style were obtained. However, the data were not available in the report for our review.

On the basis of the results of the studies summarized in this section we note some relationships between integrative complexity and other measures of cognitive style. However, the data are contradictory, and when significant relationships between measures are obtained, the correlations never exceed moderate levels.

INTELLIGENCE

In his study of the generality of cognitive complexity, Vannoy (1965) reported a statistically significant correlation of .23 between the SCT and verbal scores on the SCAT for a sample of 113 male undergraduates. In a study of Naval recruits with IQs in excess of 105, as measured by the GCT, Tuckman (1966) found no significant differences in intelligence among groups varying in levels of integrative complexity as measured by either the ITI or SCT. Streufert and Driver (1967) reported a significant correlation of .22 between the IFT and the verbal score on the College Entrance Examination for a sample of 124 male undergraduates. Schroder, Driver, and Streufert (1967) reported previous studies to yield correlations between integrative complexity and IQ ranging from .12 to .50.

Pohl and Pervin (1968) studied 150 male undergraduates and showed that abstract subjects received better grades in social sciences and humanities, and concrete subjects received better grades in engineering. They reported a nonsignificant correlation between PCT scores and verbal scores on the SAT and a significant correlation of —.20 between PCT scores and math aptitude scores on the SAT. In a study of 84 undergraduates, Miller and Harvey (1973) failed to find statistically significant differences between concrete and abstract subjects as measured by the TIB Test on two measures of intelligence (WAIS digit symbol and a vocabulary measure derived from the WAIS and Otis). However, abstract subjects performed better on an arithmetic measure derived from the WAIS and Otis. Bottenberg (1969) failed to find a significant correlation between scores on his German language PCT and a measure of intelligence.

Cox (1974) correlated performance on the PCT and TIB Test with SAT verbal and quantitative scores. Data relating the PCT to SAT scores were available for 328 undergraduates. PCT scores were significantly related to SAT verbal ($r = .18$) and quantitative ($r = .23$) scores. Data relating the TIB Test to SAT scores were available for 295 undergraduates. TIB-Test scores were significantly related to SAT verbal ($r = .27$) and quantitative ($r = .23$) scores.

Several investigators reported on the relationship between integrative complexity and intelligence in children. In his study of 136 boys in the sixth through twelfth grades, Hunt (1962b) also obtained IQ scores from the California Test of Mental Maturity. The obtained correlation of .26 between integrative complexity and IQ was statistically significant. Cross (1966) reported a significant correlation of .24 between SCT-measured integrative complexity and IQ (primarily Thorndike-Lorge) for a sample of approximately 175 eighth- to twelfth-grade boys. In their manual on the SCT, Schroder and Streufert (1962) reported a correlation of .57 between a group-administered OTIS IQ test and the SCT for a sample of 40 male high school students.

Thus, although only some studies with adults report statistically significant relationships between integrative complexity and intelligence, the studies with children consistently yield significant correlations between the two variables.

CONSISTENCY

Harvey (1965) hypothesized that when people are required to argue against their own beliefs, concrete subjects would, after making the argument, modify their beliefs in the direction of the argument they had made more than would abstract subjects. Harvey's 80 subjects were selected from a pool of 220 male undergraduates on the basis of their TIB-Test scores. Subjects assessed as system I or II were categorized as concrete; those assessed as system III or IV were categorized as abstract. The data indicated that the concrete subjects did in fact change their attitudes more than the abstract subjects when retested immediately after role playing. The concrete subjects also maintained this change more than abstract subjects when attitudes were measured one week later.

Crano and Schroder (1967) showed that when subjects low in integrative complexity are presented with attitude-discrepant information, they tend to be consistent in their reactions to the information when the reactions are measured along several dimensions (e.g., acceptance of the message and evaluation of the source). Subjects high in integrative complexity are more likely to react to the material in a less internally consistent way.

In a study of role-playing ability, Harvey (1963b) required 10 subjects from each of the four levels of integrative complexity to argue in opposition to their own beliefs. He hypothesized better performance by abstract subjects because of their ability to tolerate conflicting ideas without the need to resolve the inconsistency. Harvey presented data indicating that system IV subjects performed better than system I, II, and III subjects on virtually all measures of role playing. In a later study of 84 undergraduates, Miller and Harvey (1973) also noted the predicted superiority in role playing by abstract subjects.

Harvey and Ware (1967) selected 17 concrete and 17 abstract undergraduates on the basis of their TIB-Test scores. The subjects were presented with two descriptions of an individual. One of the descriptions contained six statements describing a person in a highly favorable way and three statements describing him in a highly unfavorable way. The other description of the person consisted of six unfavorable and three favorable statements. The subjects were required to rate the relative consistency of the statements in the descriptions and to write at least two paragraphs accounting for the perceived consistency or inconsistency.

The theoretically derived hypotheses of the study were generally confirmed. Harvey and Ware found that concrete subjects experienced greater discomfort from the inconsistency, did not give many explanations of the inconsistencies, and used stereotyped labels to describe the inconsistent behaviors.

Ware and Harvey (1967) studied the degree to which concrete and abstract subjects differed in their tendencies to accept as plausible the presence of consistent and inconsistent traits in an individual. The TIB Test was used to assess integrative complexity; 36 undergraduates, 18 concrete and 18 abstract, were studied. Each subject was presented with items of information about a person. After being presented with these items, the subjects were asked to rate the plausibility that additional items of information were also characteristic of the person. When the initial information and the additional information were consistent (i.e., all negative or all positive), concrete subjects accepted the additional information as plausible more than the abstract subjects. However, when the additional information was inconsistent with the initial information, abstract subjects were more accepting of the additional information. The data also indicated that, regardless of the consistency of the information, concrete subjects were more certain of their judgments than the abstract subjects.

Halverson (1970) argued that individuals low in integrative complexity would rely heavily on the evaluative dimension in forming impressions of others. He predicted that subjects low in integrative complexity would tend to integrate descriptions of personality well when the descriptors were similar on an evaluative dimension; when the descriptors were dissimilar, the subjects would have difficulty integrating them. Halverson's hypothesis was confirmed in his study of 96 male undergraduates selected on the basis of extreme scores from a pool of 180 subjects.

The data of these studies show that concrete subjects are less tolerant of inconsistency than abstract subjects.

TASK AND ENVIRONMENTAL COMPLEXITY

In his doctoral dissertation, Claunch (1964) hypothesized that abstract subjects would perform better than concrete subjects on essay examinations, but that the two groups would perform similarly on objective tests. He reasoned that achieving a good grade on an essay examination requires the integration of learned material, whereas achieving a high grade on an objective test requires the recall of isolated concepts. Using the SCT, Claunch selected 40 concrete and 40 abstract subjects from a pool of 180 male undergraduates. Matching the two groups on IQ required the elimination of a few subjects. The concrete and abstract subjects performed similarly on objective tests administered during a semester's course in personality theory. The abstract subjects performed better than the concrete subjects on the final examination for the course, an essay test requiring the student to make contrasts and comparisons among the theories and theorists studied in the course.

Suedfeld and Hagen (1966) used a word association task to compare the information-processing ability of concrete and abstract subjects. The subjects were required to guess a stimulus word when presented with a sequence of five responses associated with that stimulus. The response lists were of two types. One type contained five words that previous research had shown to have equal probabilities of use as response words to the stimulus words. The other type of list contained one word with a very high probability of being used as a response to a particular stimulus word, along with four others of lesser probabilities.

The abstract subjects did not differ as much as the concrete subjects in their ability to guess the stimulus words when presented with the two types of response list. For the concrete subjects, the list containing the high probability response word led to a greater number of correct solutions than the list containing words of equal probabilities of use. The data suggest that concrete subjects perform worse than abstract subjects in a complex situation. Suedfeld and Hagen also reported some data suggesting that the abstract subjects integrated more clues by utilizing more response words in arriving at their decision.

Hill and Kuiken (1975) hypothesized that integratively complex subjects would perform worse than concrete subjects when presented with a task in which irrelevant cues were provided. The subjects of the study were 32 integratively complex and 32 integratively simple subjects chosen on the basis of extreme scores on the ITI from a pool of 300 undergraduates. One of the two tasks was to identify the artists who produced a set of representational paintings; the other was to identify the artists who produced a set of abstract paintings. The subjects viewed each work of art for either 2.5 or 12.5 seconds. The authors hypothesized that there would be no differences between the groups with the short exposure time; they hypothesized that for the longer exposure, abstract subjects would perform better in identifying the artists of the abstract art, but worse in identifying the artists of the representational art. The significant three-way interaction effect that is required to support the hypothesis was not obtained. The hypothesis was reportedly validated, in part, by simpler analyses. The results of this study provide merely suggestive support for the hypothesis that irrelevant cues are detrimental to the performance of more integratively complex subjects.

A number of studies were conducted exploring decision-making processes under conditions of varying environmental complexity (cf. Streufert, 1973). We limit our review to a sampling of the studies in which the integrative complexity of the individual was one of the variables under investigation; we omit those studies in which environmental complexity was related to decision making when no individual measures of integrative complexity were taken.

One procedure for studying the relationship between environmental complexity and the performance of subjects differing in integrative complexity is the use of simulations that allow the control of the amount of information flow. In one such study, Streufert and Driver (1965) used the SCT and IFT to select 40 highly concrete and 40 highly abstract subjects from a pool of 236 undergraduate males. The concrete subjects were divided into 10 four-man teams, as were the abstract subjects.

The similation used in the study was described by Streufert, Clardy, Driver, Karlins, Schroder, and Suedfeld (1965). The simulation involved the teams' making decisions about the invasion of an island. The complexity of the situation was varied by manipulating the amount of information presented to the team during each of the seven half-hour game periods. After each period, each subject responded to a series of questions about his and the "enemy's" tactics. These protocols were scored for differentiation and integration.

As hypothesized, the relationship between the level of complexity of the environment and the complexity of the subjects' perceptions of the environment was in the shape of an inverted U-curve; that is, the complexity of the subjects' perceptions of the environment was great-

est when the information load in the environment was at an intermediate level. The data also indicated that concrete subjects perceived
the environment in a more concrete way than abstract subjects.

In another report analyzing how the subjects performed in this situation, Streufert and Schroder (1965) used different indices of performance and obtained similar results. For example, they derived a measure
of the integration of one decision with another and showed that integration was highest at intermediate levels of information load. Consistent with the results of the first report, the performance of the
concrete subjects evidenced less integration than the performance of
the abstract subjects.

In still another paper analyzing the performance of the same subjects, Streufert, Suedfeld, and Driver (1965) found differences between
concrete and abstract subjects in information search as a function of
information load. The two measures of information search, however,
yielded somewhat different results. When requests for information to
an outsider were considered, the abstract subjects tended to reduce
information search in environments with higher information load.
When the measure was the efforts made by the group to gain more information, it was the concrete subjects whose requests for information
decreased more sharply as information load in the environment increased. A measure of the integration of the information obtained
yielded data suggestive of the inverted U-shaped curve found in other
studies.

Suedfeld and Streufert (1966) reported a partial replication of the
study by Streufert, Suedfeld, and Driver (1965). In this replication, individuals rather than groups were run. Eighteen concrete and 18 abstract
subjects were selected on the basis of their SCT scores. It was shown
that information search decreased as information load increased and
that concrete subjects requested more information than the abstract
subjects in the low and moderate information-load conditions. The
authors interpreted this finding as consistent with the theory, which
predicts that concrete subjects need more information because they
cannot use items of information in combination with others. Later in
this section, investigators using sensory deprivation as a low information-load condition predict *greater* information search by abstract subjects on the basis of this theory.

Stager (1967) used the same island invasion task and showed that four-man groups that had a high percentage of abstract subjects engaged in more information search than groups with a lower percentage of abstract subjects.

Susan Streufert (1973) raised the question of whether the results of earlier studies on the relationship between information load and decision making were due to information load or to the relevance of the information presented. In previous research, all information presented to subjects was relevant; thus the two variables were confounded. In a study of 12 dyads formed with male undergraduates who participated in a simulation game, Streufert found that simple decision making was unaffected by relevance, but integrated decisions increased under conditions of increased relevance.

Karlins (1967) also used a complex problem-solving situation to study the information utilization characteristics of subjects of varying levels of integrative complexity. The simulation task required the subjects to obtain the cooperation of natives on a South Sea Island in the construction of a hospital (cf. Karlins & Schroder, 1967). The subjects were 60 male undergraduates selected on the basis of extreme scores on the PCT and Mednick's (1962) Remote Associates Test, a measure of creativity. The groups were matched on intelligence. As hypothesized, the abstract subjects asked a broader range of questions when working on the task, and the categories in which the questions were asked were more evenly weighted. The former was said to indicate the superior differentiating ability of abstract subjects, the latter to reflect, in part, their superior integrating ability. Since the subjects were formed into groups on the basis of two measures, however, the concrete and abstract subjects may not be completely representative of concrete and abstract subjects in general.

In a study utilizing the same task, Karlins and Lamm (1967) showed that 30 abstract Peace Corps volunteers asked more questions than 30 concrete volunteers who were matched on intelligence. In a war game simulation, the same findings were obtained for a sample of 12 concrete and 12 abstract subjects matched for intelligence (Karlins, Coffman, Lamm, & Schroder, 1967).

In these studies the attempts to relate integrative complexity to environmental conditions are noteworthy. Although the results are not always consistent with theoretical expectations, there is clearly sufficient indication of the value of this type of research to stimulate continued work in this area. Streufert in particular has pursued this line of research (e.g., Streufert, 1969, 1970, 1972; Streufert & Castore, 1971; Streufert & Streufert, 1969).

As already shown, the simulation tasks provided opportunities to study performance in highly complex environments. Sensory deprivation (SD) has been used to study performance in an environment of low complexity. Subjects varying in level of integrative complexity are hypothesized to be affected differently by extremely high or low levels of environmental complexity. The theory states that structural regression, that is, a reduction in differentiating and integrating abilities, should occur in environments of low complexity.

Suedfeld (1963, 1964a) used SD to study the effects of low environmental complexity on attitude change. He argued that structural regression should be especially marked for concrete subjects because of their dependence on external referents for their behavior. Abstract subjects should show less structural regression in an environment of low complexity because of their utilization of internally generated schemata. In an environment of low complexity, in which externally provided schemata are virtually nonexistent, concrete subjects should readily accept a schema provided for them; abstract subjects should be less likely to accept such a schema.

Suedfeld located a large pool of potential subjects whose attitudes toward the Turks were neutral. From this pool he selected 20 system I subjects, 20 system II subjects, and 20 system III subjects. There was an insufficient number of system IV subjects to create a group of this type. One-half the subjects in each group were subjected to SD; the other half were assigned to an untreated control group. Suedfeld's SD subjects were placed in a dark, sound-proofed chamber and were required to lie quietly in bed. About 24 hours after the beginning of the experiment, a recorded pro-Turk message was played for all the subjects. The experimental subjects were still in SD; the control subjects had been allowed to follow a "normal" routine. When both groups of subjects were retested regarding their attitudes toward the Turks, it was found that the concrete subjects had shifted from their original neutral position. When system I, II, and III subjects who had undergone SD were compared, the system I subjects evidenced the greatest change; the system II subjects also evidenced a significant change in the pro-Turk direction, but the system III subjects' attitudes did not change.

Hewitt (1972) studied attitude change as a function of integrative complexity, salience of the communication, and environmental complexity. Integrative complexity was measured with the ITI, and there were three levels of environmental complexity: sensory deprivation, overstimulation, and normal stimulation. The subjects were 97 female undergraduates, 48 system I and 49 system IV, selected from a pool of 534 female students. Although abstract subjects recalled more of the communication than the concrete subjects, there were no differences in attitude change associated with integrative complexity, either alone or in interaction with the other two variables.

Suedfeld and Vernon (1966) studied the effects of sensory deprivation on the differences between concrete and abstract subjects in information seeking. The subjects were 14 concrete and 14 abstract males chosen from a pool of 248 male undergraduates on the basis of their SCT scores and the neutrality of their attitudes about Turkey and the Turks. The subjects were presented with more information if they made pro-Turk responses to a series of test questions based on statements about Turkey. It was hypothesized that, because of their higher need for information, abstract subjects would exhibit greater compliance than concrete subjects in order to receive additional information. The data supported this hypothesis. However, when attitude change was studied by comparing initial to postexperimental attitudes toward Turkey, it was found that concrete subjects who underwent deprivation became more favorable toward Turkey than abstract subjects. This supported the investigators' hypothesis that abstract subjects would not change their attitudes; it is consistent with Suedfeld's (1963, 1964a) earlier findings.

MacNeil and Rule (1970) studied whether concrete and abstract subjects differ in their preferences for structurally simple or complex messages. Using the ITI, 20 system I and 20 system IV male subjects were chosen from a pool of 900 undergraduates. One-half of each group were subjected to sensory deprivation, and one-half of each group were controls. The sensory deprivation condition consisted of a four-hour confinement in an 8 × 10 foot illuminated room; an audio tape provided masking noise, translucent goggles reduced form perception, and arm bands reduced tactile stimulation.

The investigators rewrote a selection from a novel in structurally simple and complex forms. The simple message used simple, declarative sentences to present information in an isolated, independent manner. The complex message used complex sentences with many clauses to present information in an interrelated, dependent manner. The messages lasted approximately 2½ minutes. At any time during the four-hour test period, the subject could press a switch to listen to either the simple or complex message.

The data indicated that there were more than twice as many requests to listen to either of the messages during sensory deprivation as there were in the control condition. During sensory deprivation, concrete subjects preferred the simple message to the complex message; abstract subjects preferred the complex message to the simple message. There was no difference in requests for simple or concrete messages under the control condition. The study thus showed that concrete and abstract subjects differed in the *type* of information they preferred under conditions of low environmental complexity.

The studies employing sensory deprivation generally support the theoretically derived hypotheses concerning differences in performance between concrete and abstract subjects. For example, it was found that abstract subjects tend to seek information more than concrete subjects in the sensory deprivation situation, but concrete subjects evidence greater attitude change.

STRESS

As noted in Schroder, Driver, and Streufert (1967), stress (e.g., war during the internation simulation task) lowers the level of integrative complexity. Suedfeld (1964b) hypothesized that abstract subjects would be more stressed after an experience of 24 hours of deprivation than would more concrete subjects. He argued that abstract people are more strongly motivated to seek information and hence would be more stressed in a situation of reduced information flow. Ten concrete and 10 abstract subjects were chosen from a pool of 100 undergraduates on the basis of their responses to the SCT. The subjects were placed in a condition of "darkness, silence, and restricted motility" for 24 hours, at the end of which time a 15-item scale to assess subjective stress was administered. The hypothesis was supported.

In the chapter on authoritarianism we saw that stress was often induced by informing the subjects that their performance reflected intelligence. Sieber and Lanzetta (1964) used the same technique in a study relating information search to level of integrative complexity. The subjects were 15 concrete and 15 abstract undergraduate women, chosen from a pool of over 300 on the basis of extreme scores on the SCT. Stress had no effect on the performance of abstract subjects compared to that of concrete subjects. It was found, however, that abstract subjects sought more information before making decisions; under conditions of increased uncertainty, the information search by abstract subjects increased, whereas that of concrete subjects remained unchanged. In a subsequent study of 30 concrete and 30 abstract subjects, Sieber and Lanzetta (1966) found that abstract subjects engage in more predecision information search and are more uncertain about their decisions than are concrete subjects. The authors also provided evidence that subjects could increase the complexity of their decision making with training.

CREATIVITY

In a study of over 100 Naval recruits, Tuckman (1966) used the SCT and ITI as measures of integrative complexity and found that 70 system I subjects performed worse on measures of creativity and creativity motivation than the more abstract subjects. In the course of a study of information utilization, Karlins (1967) obtained a nonsignificant correlation between PCT scores and scores on a measure of creativity, Mednick's (1962) Remote Associates Test, for a sample of 300 male undergraduates.

OTHER CORRELATES OF INTEGRATIVE COMPLEXITY

Marx (1970) attempted to study the relationship between integrative complexity and concept formation. His subjects were 144 female high school students whose integrative complexity was assessed with the PCT. The subjects were presented with a concept formation task that confounded intentional–incidental learning with the level of task complexity. Marx interpreted his data as indicating that concrete subjects do significantly worse on an incidental learning task compared to subjects with both medium and higher levels of integrative complexity. This difference disappeared in a covariance design with intelligence covaried out, suggesting that differences in intelligence may have accounted for the performance differences. There were no significant differences among the three groups differing in integrative complexity in performance on an intentional concept formation task.

Greaves (1972) selected groups of subjects varying in integrative complexity as measured by the TIB Test. The subjects were shown slides containing descriptive material about the United States and Sweden. Some subjects received a verbal presentation that was biased toward the United States along with the slides. Other subjects received a verbal presentation that was biased toward Sweden. Concrete subjects recalled the information in the direction of the biased presentation better than information that was contradictory. Abstract subjects were less influenced by the verbal presentations, tending to recall pro-United States information better under both conditions of bias.

In a study of 115 undergraduates, Frauenfelder (1974b) showed that subjects scoring low on the PCT were more likely than high PCT scorers to make extreme judgments on the basis of a vignette describing a person. In another report regarding the performance of these subjects, Frauenfelder (1974a) found that females low in PCT-measured integrative complexity were more influenced than females high in integrative complexity in forming impressions by a positive or negative set created by the experimenter. This finding did not hold for males.

CRITIQUE

The two most important features of integrative complexity theory concern the articulation of personality and environmental variables and the strong emphasis on developmental considerations. Although social scientists generally agree on the importance of considering both personality and environmental variables in the understanding of human behavior (e.g., Ekehammer, 1974), the concept is rarely used in research. What is especially valuable about the integrative complexity viewpoint is that the personality variable is related to the environmental variable in an articulated manner. Individuals vary in the complexity of their abilities to process information; the environment varies in the complexity of the information it contains. The dimensions are related to each other, and the result has been productive and important research.

One of the most interesting aspects of integrative complexity theory, the concern with environmental training conditions that lead to greater complexity, has not received sufficient attention. Given the plethora of research on child-rearing attitudes and behaviors and their relationship to child development, the lack of research here is especially evident. As is true of research on integrative complexity in general, part of the difficulty is related to instrumentation. In this case the lack of an instrument designed to assess training conditions along the unilateral–interdependent dimension has limited research relating integrative complexity to child rearing.

Another related problem is that, although developmental considerations are important to the theory, much of the research on development must be retrospective or longitudinal in nature, because the child progresses through stages, and all young children are concrete. It is difficult to determine whether a child functioning at a concrete level is in a transitional stage or his progression to higher levels of integrative complexity has been arrested. Such a distinction has important implications for functioning.

The major stumbling block to widespread research on integrative complexity theory is the problem of measurement. The PCT and the TIB Test require scoring by trained individuals; the IFT is also projective, and multidimensional scaling is time consuming, costly, and has unclear relationships to differentiation and integration. Tuckman's objective ITI is an instrument that can be used readily by others and should receive additional attention and validation. The same is true of the Conceptual Systems Test.

Although it is a major measure of integrative complexity, the PCT is not without its critics. Specifically, Streufert and Driver (1967) outlined a number of problems with the instrument: lengthy training supervised by one of the few qualified investigators is necessary for scoring; test-retest reliability has been unstable, and an alternate form does not exist. Similar criticisms are applicable to the TIB Test.

Schroder, Driver, and Streufert (1967) reported that objective measures of integrative complexity (e.g., the ITI) are unsatisfactory for research. The correlation between objective measures and the PCT or

IFT, although statistically significant, are low, and predictions from the two types of measure are said to demonstrate the superiority of the PCT and IFT. Schroder, Driver, and Streufert believe that objective measures are unlikely to be suitable for the measurement of integrative complexity, because concrete subjects can respond abstractly when an abstract response is presented to them.

An unfortunate situation occurs when investigators administer a number of tests of cognitive style and neglect to report the intercorrelations among them. For example, Harvey (1963b) administered his TIB, the Dogmatism Scale, the Doodlebug problem, the F Scale, the Gough Rigidity Scale, and the WAIS, among other tests, to a sample of 80 subjects in a study of role playing. He did not report the intercorrelations among these measures.

There are also problems in the measurement of environmental complexity. Differences in environmental complexity are generally established by making distinctions among low, moderate, and high levels of complexity. Greater precision in the differentiation of levels of environmental complexity would undoubtedly yield more precise relationships between integrative complexity and environmental conditions.

Also in need of investigation is the possibility that the level of integrative complexity may vary from one domain to another. For example, an individual who is complex in the interpersonal domain may be simple in the mathematical domain. Virtually all work in integrative complexity has been concerned with complexity in the interpersonal area because of the centrality of such functioning for the individual. Research on the consistency of complexity across various domains may prove useful in further improving the accuracy of prediction.

CHAPTER SIX
Field Dependence

In this chapter we consider the work of Witkin and his associates, an approach to the measurement of cognitive style based on the study of perception. Witkin, Oltman, Raskin, and Karp (1971) defined cognitive styles as ". . . the characteristic, self-consistent modes of functioning which individuals show in their perceptual and intellectual activities. These cognitive styles are manifestations in the cognitive sphere of still broader dimensions of personal functioning which cut across diverse psychological areas."

Witkin's interest in cognitive style dates back to 1942, when he studied factors that related to perception of the upright (Witkin et al., 1954). Many subjects were used in the early studies, and Witkin was intrigued by the large individual differences in perception that were noted. He felt that to understand the perceptual phenomena, it was necessary to study the characteristics of the individual as well as aspects of the situation. Witkin noted that an individual's characteristic way of perceiving was consistent from one situation to another, that it was not easily altered, and that it was stable over periods of years.

Witkin's next step was to study the relationship between performance on his perceptual measures and on other measures. In the major portion of his first book, *Personality through Perception* (Witkin, Lewis, Hertzman, Machover, Meissner, & Wapner, 1954), investigations of the relationship of personality to perception were summarized. On the basis of these studies, individuals designated "field dependent" were found to be passive and to have poor impulse control, low self-esteem, and an undifferentiated and primitive body image. The results of these early studies supported the hypothesis that ". . . the individual differences we have been observing are definable in terms of degree of dependence on the structure of the prevailing visual field, ranging from great dependence, at one extreme, to great ability to deal with the presented field analytically, or to separate an item from the configuration in which it occurs, at the other" (Witkin et al., 1954).

The Rod-and-Frame Test (RFT) was the major instrument used in this early research. The subject taking the RFT is seated in complete darkness and views a luminous rod suspended within a luminous frame. Both the rod and frame can be tilted independently. Initially, the rod and frame are both tilted, and the subject is told to direct the experimenter to adjust the rod to a position that the subject believes is vertical. Some subjects are successful at this task and are termed *field independent*. Others orient the rod in relation to the tilted frame and are termed *field dependent;* that is, their perceptions are dependent on the surrounding environment.

Another instrument used in these early studies was the Embedded Figures Test, or EFT (Witkin, 1950). On the EFT the subject is required to recognize a geometric figure within a complex background. At first, performance on the EFT was narrowly construed as reflecting a perceptual dimension of field dependence–independence (Witkin et al., 1971). When performance on this task was found to be related to performance on nonperceptual intellectual tasks, the underlying construct was broadened to a "global-articulated" dimension, a dimension on which individuals differ in their tendency to structure their perceptual field. The relationships between performance on the EFT and measures of personality led Witkin to postulate an underlying dimension of differentiation. The more differentiated the individual, the more field independent he is. Differentiation may be understood as the capacity to distinguish gradations of a stimulus dimension. Witkin showed that individuals whose judgments about the rod are not independent of the frame have more limited articulation across a variety of experiences.

Witkin et al. (1971) pointed out that this broadened concept includes differences in body concept, the nature of the self, and defenses. The more differentiated person perceives the field as more discrete and structured, has a more definite sense of body boundary, a sense of individuality, internalized standards, and is less likely to use primitive, indiscriminate defenses, such as massive repression and primitive denial.

Witkin, Dyk, Faterson, Goodenough, and Karp (1962) distinguished between formal and content aspects of personality systems, a distinction similar to that between style and content. Witkin's interest is with the formal, or stylistic, aspect, which he conceives as divided into components of differentiation and integration. In writing of differentiation, Witkin refers to the complexity of a system's structure. The less differentiated the system, the more homogeneous the structural state. The highly differentiated system is specialized and divided into subsystems, each of which mediates specific functions. In such a system, thinking would be differentiated from acting, feeling from perceiving. In an undifferentiated system, specific functions are either not possible or are mediated by the system as a whole. Witkin distinguished between the complexity and effectiveness of integration. Complexity refers to the elaborateness of the subsystem relationships; effectiveness refers to how smoothly the subsystem components function together. Differentiation must precede integration, but its presence does not necessarily imply that integration will follow. Witkin noted that the highly differentiated individual is capable of functioning in a differentiated or undifferentiated manner. There is also a tendency for the person who is differentiated in one area to be differentiated in other areas.

Witkin was concerned with the relationship between field independence and the individual's performance in a wide variety of areas. He suggested that the dimension of differentiation ". . . pervades the individual's perceptual, intellectual, emotional, motivational, defensive, and social operations" (Witkin et al., 1962). Recently, Witkin and Goodenough (1976) reviewed the development of the field-dependence construct and noted that adaptive qualities are associated with each pole of functioning. For example, field-dependent individuals are more socially sensitive, whereas field-independent individuals are superior in some cognitive areas.

As in previous chapters, our concern here is limited to a consideration of the research on field dependence that relates to cognitive style.

MEASUREMENT

Over the years, Witkin used a variety of instruments to measure field dependence.

TILTING-ROOM–TILTING-CHAIR TESTS (TRTC)

For these tests, a chair is suspended in a room that measures 70 × 71 × 69 inches. Both room and chair may be tilted left or right. In the Room-Adjustment Test (RAT), the room is tilted 56 degrees and the chair 22 degrees. With the chair remaining in its tilted position, the subject's task is to instruct the examiner to reorient the room to an upright position. The RAT is comprised of eight trials; in four trials the room and chair are tilted in the same direction, and in four trials the room and chair are tilted in opposite directions. The Body-Adjustment Test (BAT) consists of six trials. In half the trials the room and chair are tilted in the same direction, and in the other half they are tilted in opposite directions. While the room remains tilted, the subject is required to direct the experimenter to bring him to the upright. These tests are scored similarly to the RFT, as discussed below.

ROD-AND-FRAME TEST (RFT)

The RFT was described briefly earlier in this chapter. The standard administration of the RFT consists of three series of eight trials each. In the first series, the frame and the subject's body are both tilted 28 degrees in the same direction; the rod is tilted 28 degrees in the same or opposite direction. The subject is required to bring the rod to a vertical position. In the second series, the body of the subject and the frame are both tilted 28 degrees to opposite sides. In the third series, the subject remains erect while the frame is tilted 28 degrees to the left or right. The total score is calculated by first converting the subject's score on each series (the mean absolute error for the eight trials) into a standard score on the basis of the age and sex group to which the subject belongs. The three standard scores are averaged to produce an overall score. Witkin et al. (1962) suggested using only the third series of the RFT instead of the complete test.

OTHER VERSIONS OF THE RFT

Handel (1972) cited a number of studies using variations of the original RFT that do not require a light-proof room or a tilting chair and that are portable. He also cited procedures in which the subject himself adjusts the apparatus, rather than having the experimenter carry out the manipulations. Performance with these modified instruments generally correlates well with performance on the original instrument. It should also be noted that there have been a number of studies of testing variations that affect performance on the RFT (e.g., Long, 1973).

One of the more widely used modifications is Oltman's (1968) portable RFT. In a standardization study with 163 college students, Oltman reported a correlation of .89 between performance on his portable measure and performance on the standard RFT. Stuart and Murgatroyd (1971) reported on an especially light-weight portable RFT. For a sample of 148 college students, a correlation of .86 was obtained between scores derived from their instrument and scores from Oltman's (1968) apparatus.

Busch and Simon (1972) reported on a method for instructing 5- to 7-year-olds in the use of a portable RFT. Fiebert (1967) developed a system for administering the RFT to deaf children. Keogh and Tardo (1975) compared the performance of 63 third graders on two versions of the RFT. They found that Nickel's (1971) version, although significantly related to Gerard's (1969) version, was more reliable and yielded scores with greater variability. It also related better to the CEFT (see below).

Hurley (1972) reported an unsuccessful attempt to develop a group-administered RFT.

EMBEDDED FIGURES TEST (EFT)

The EFT requires the subject to locate a simple figure within a complex context. Witkin selected 24 figures from a set originally developed by Gottschaldt (1926) and superimposed colored patterns to make the task more difficult. The subject was originally given a maximum of five minutes for each figure. The score was the mean amount of time taken to find all 24 figures. The raw score was converted into a standard score. As with the RFT and TRTC, a positive standard score is indicative of field dependence. Witkin et al. (1971) prepared a manual giving detailed instructions on the administration and scoring of the EFT.

Witkin, on the basis of his own work (Witkin et al., 1962) and that of Jackson (1956), recommended the use of the first 12 items of the EFT, with a three-minute limit for each item, for research purposes.

OTHER VERSIONS OF THE EFT

Jackson, Messick, and Myers (1962, 1964) compared performance on five group-administered versions of the EFT with performance on an individually administered short form of the EFT derived from Jackson (1956). Their subjects were 112 undergraduates. They found all five group-administered forms to correlate significantly with the individually administered form, the correlation coefficients ranging from .62 to .84. For economy of administration, they recommended that their Form V be used. This form requires only ten minutes for administration and can be printed at a lower cost than the chromatic versions of the test.

Spotts and Mackler (1967) also presented data on the relationship between individual- and group-administered versions of the EFT. Their subjects were 40 male undergraduates. They administered the Jackson (1956) short form of the EFT individually and a Jackson, Messick, and Myers (1964) group-administered Hidden Figures Test. Spotts and Mackler obtained a statistically significant correlation of .55 between the two measures. This correlation is lower than the .84 reported by Jackson and his colleagues.

A Group Embedded Figures Test (GEFT) is also available for group administration (Witkin et al., 1972). Although the GEFT was shown by Witkin et al. (1971) to relate to other measures of field dependence, the authors pointed out the need for additional validity studies for this instrument. This suggestion is consistent with the findings of a study by Renna and Zenhausern (1976). A sample of 337 undergraduates was found to be more field dependent than expected on the basis of Witkin et al.'s (1971) norms. Evans (1969) showed that correlations between the EFT and an early version of the GEFT were higher when subjects had prior opportunity to practice the group task. For 62 inexperienced college student subjects, the correlation was .41; for 43 experienced subjects, the correlation increased to .73.

The EFT is suitable for subjects 10 years of age and older. Goodenough and Eagle (1963) developed a children's version of the EFT, the CHEF. They administered the CHEF along with the RFT, BAT, and EFT to 30 ten-year-old boys. The correlations between CHEF scores and the other three tests were all statistically significant (.70, .46, and .63, respectively). (The intercorrelations among the other three tests were also significant and ranged from .59 to .68.) The CHEF was modified for easier administration by Karp and Konstadt (1963) and became known as the Children's Embedded Figures Test (CEFT). Witkin et al. (1971) recommended using the CEFT for children five to nine years old. Their manual presents some reliability and validity data. A preschool EFT (Coates, 1972) was developed for children three to five years of age.

Banta (1970) also developed a version of the EFT for use with very young children, the Early Childhood EFT. The task requires the identification of cut-out figures from a context. Herkowitz (1972) developed the Moving Embedded Figures Test (MEFT) for use with elementary school children. The subject views a 20-minute film and is required to discriminate figures moving against stationary backgrounds. Unfortunately, the author presented no data relating performance on the MEFT to performance on the CEFT. The data relating to several of these preschool instruments were reviewed by Kogan (1976). Various published versions of the EFT (the EFT, Group EFT, Children's EFT, and Preschool EFT) are available from the publisher, Consulting Psychologists Press, Palo Alto, California. Bowd (1976) presented evidence that item difficulty on the CEFT is not monotonic, and suggested reversing items T4 and T5.

A number of foreign language forms of the Witkin tests have been used, including a translation of the instructions of the CEFT into Ibo (Okonji, 1969). To administers CEFT to a group of Mexican children, Mebane and Johnson (1970) translated the directions into Spanish. Vojtisek and Magaro (1974) developed a short form of the EFT suitable for use with hospitalized psychiatric patients. Pizzamiglio and Pizzamiglio (1974) presented norms for an Italian version of the CEFT. Axelrod and Cohen (1961) employed a tactile version of the EFT in their research on the elderly.

Comrey, Backer, and Glaser (1973) cited a convention presentation by Evans (1969) reporting the development of a questionnaire measure of field dependence. Evans' 50-item Psychological Differentiation Inventory was designed for use with undergraduates and was developed to correlate with the EFT. Evans reported significant correlations between his measure and the EFT of .76, .64, and .46 for samples of 73, 60, and 154 undergraduates, respectively.

Finally, Rosenblum, Witkin, Kaufman, and Brosgole (1965) reported on a version of the EFT designed for administration to monkeys. Their initial data indicated that monkeys, like humans, differ from one another in "perceptual disembedding."

RELIABILITY

Witkin et al. (1962) reported the results of their own research and that of others on the reliability of the RFT, BAT, and EFT. In all the studies reported, the reliabilities were satisfactorily high, clustering in the high .80s to low .90s when tests were readministered at one-week intervals. Test-retest reliabilities over a three-year period are somewhat lower for the RFT and BAT, but remain satisfactory.

Adevai and McGough (1968) compared RFT scores for a sample of 36 undergraduate males tested as freshmen and again four years later. There were no statistically significant differences between the mean error scores between the two testings; the correlation between the two sets of scores was .86. Adevai and McGough reported that Bauman (1951) found a similar correlation of .84 for a sample of 32 males tested three years apart.

Dreyer, Nebelkopf, and Dreyer (1969) administered the CEFT to a sample of 46 kindergarten and first-grade children. The test-retest correlation was a significant .87. They also noted a one-month test-retest reliability of .96 for portable RFT scores for a sample of 90 kindergarten children. Bowd (1974) administered the CEFT to 53 kindergarten children and readministered the test to 47 of the children 10 months later. He obtained a significant correlation of .80.

Busch and Simon (1972) reported very high split-half reliability coefficients for five- to seven-year-old children on their RFT (cf. Rusch & Lis, 1977). The test-retest reliability over periods ranging from about one month to more than two months was .57 for their 70 subjects. Using a portable RFT, Rusch and Lis (1977) found test-retest correlations ranging between .26 and .90 for a sample of 113 children retested after a three-year interval.

The results of these and other studies indicate that the major measures of field dependence have satisfactory reliability.

PARAMETRIC FACTORS

A number of investigators have made parametric studies of the RFT measure. For example, Corah (1965b) demonstrated that the starting position of the rod was of great importance, and Cegalis and Young (1974) found that a 180 degree rotation of the rod and frame significantly increased scores of field dependence. Reinking, Goldstein, and Houston (1974) showed that factors in the RFT testing situation combine with cognitive style to influence performance. Lester (1968) summarized a number of studies showing that a variety of factors in the testing situation (e.g., the instructions that the subject is given) influence RFT scores. As Lester implied, work on standardization of the administration of the RFT is likely to result in improved reliability and validity (cf. Lasry & Dyne, 1974, who obtained different correlations between the EFT and RFT when the latter was administered under differing conditions).

Small (1973) provided an excellent brief summary of studies reporting attempts to modify RFT performance. Generally, RFT performance is not modifiable by drugs or alcohol, but it can be improved by psychotherapy, supplying feedback, and practice. Goodenough and Witkin (1977) also noted that EFT and RFT performance shows greater field independence with practice or training. In his own study, Small showed that the RFT performance of normal college students could be improved through the administration of verbal reinforcement; it is unclear from Small's data whether verbal reinforcement can worsen RFT performance. Pelletier (1974) showed that training in Transcendental Meditation increases EFT- and RFT-measured field independence. Taken together, the results of these studies suggest that the experimenter should use naive subjects to avoid any bias in his subjects' scores.

INTERCORRELATIONS AMONG MEASURES
OF FIELD DEPENDENCE

There are two considerations with regard to intercorrelations among measures of field dependence. The first involves the degree of the relationship between different versions of the same measure (e.g., RFT and Portable RFT, EFT, and Group EFT). It has generally been found that scores derived from various versions of the RFT are highly related (cf. Handel, 1972). The same is true for correlations between versions of the EFT (cf. Witkin et al., 1971).

The second issue involves the degree of the relationship between different measures of field dependence (e.g., RFT and EFT). Witkin et al. (1962) proposed that a perceptual index be derived by taking the mean score on the RFT, BAT, and EFT. They excluded the RAT from this index because it proved to be a poor measure of field dependence. Intercorrelations among the three tests indicated that significant relationships existed among them. The correlations were generally in the range of .30–.60. The authors cited this finding as an indication that individuals are consistent in their perceptual functioning. The correlations between the RAT and other tests, however, were lower; this was especially true for younger subjects (8–12 years).

As part of a study attempting to determine whether the ability to overcome embeddedness is a specific aspect of a more general ability to overcome distraction, Karp (1963) administered the RFT, EFT, and BAT, along with a variety of other measures, to 150 male undergraduates. A factor analysis of the intercorrelations among the 18 measures showed the three measures of field dependence to load on a common factor and, in fact, to have the highest loadings of any of the items, on both four- and eight-factor rotations. On the basis of this data, Karp concluded that the ability to overcome embeddedness is distinct from distractibility.

In their study of developmental differences in field dependence, Witkin, Goodenough, and Karp (1967) generally found statistically significant correlations between the EFT and both the RFT and BAT at various ages from eight years to college level; there were also some significant correlations between the BAT and RFT. Arbuthnot (1972) reviewed 40 studies in which more than one measure of field dependence was used. He concluded that the Kohs Block Design and Draw-A-Person Test should not be used as substitutes for the RFT and EFT in the measurement of field dependence; he recommended using the latter two together. Weissenberg (1973), in a review of 12 studies, found a median correlation of .51 between the HFT and the EFT, RFT, or figure-drawing scale.

We reviewed 16 reports representative of the research on the relationship between versions of the RFT and versions of the EFT (Adevai,

Silverman, & McGough, 1968; Barrett, Cabe, & Thornton, 1968; Denmark, Havlena, & Murgatroyd, 1971; Dreyer, Dreyer, & Nebelkopf, 1971; Dubois & Cohen, 1970; Dumsha, Minard, & McWilliams, 1973; Elliott, 1961; Fiebert, 1967; Goldberger & Bendich, 1972; Gough & Olton, 1972; Gruenfeld & Arbuthnot, 1969; Keogh & Ryan, 1971; Keogh, Welles, & Weiss, 1972; Nevill, 1974; Wolitzky, 1973; Young, 1959). Almost all the correlations were statistically significant and were generally in the .30–.65 range.

SOCIAL DESIRABILITY

Pearson (1972) used the lie scale of the Eysenck Personality Inventory as a measure of social desirability. For a sample of 30 neurotic young adults, he obtained a statistically significant correlation of .48 between this measure and the Jackson (1956) short form of the EFT, indicating that greater need for social approval is related to field dependence, at least among young, neurotic subjects.

In a later study, Farley (1974) administered the HFT and the lie scale of the EPI to a sample of 61 undergraduates. The two measures were not significantly correlated. Farley also administered the Marlowe–Crowne Social Desirability Scale and again failed to find a statistically significant relationship with HFT performance. Similarly, Evans (1969) failed to find a significant relationship between the Marlowe–Crowne measure and his questionnaire measure of differentiation.

SEX DIFFERENCES

In their early work, Witkin et al. (1954) found females to be more field dependent than males, the differences being largest among adults. Since this early report, it has often been maintained that females are more field dependent than males. However, a close examination of the literature brings this finding into question. We have located a number of studies in which there were no statistically significant differences in field dependence between males and females for both children (Bigelow, 1971; Bowd, 1974b, 1976a; Busch & Simon, 1972; Coates, Lord, & Jakabovics, 1975; Crandall & Sinkeldam, 1964; Domash

& Balter, 1976; Dreyer, Nebelkopf, & Dreyer, 1969; Erginel, 1972; Keogh & Tardo, 1975; Massari, 1975) and undergraduates (Bieri, 1960; Eisner & Williams, 1973; Jackson, Messick, & Myers, 1964; Willoughby, 1967). Indeed, in one study with children (Coates, 1974) and one with undergraduates (Constantinople, 1974), females were found to be significantly more field independent than males.

Naditch (1976) concluded that evidence regarding sex differences in field dependence is inconclusive. Bowd (1976a) concluded that research on the CEFT failed to reveal sex differences. Recently, Goodenough and Witkin (1977) concluded that consistent sex differences have not been found in studies using EFT-type instruments. On RFT measures, however, they reported that males were generally more field independent.

There are some data that indicate that sex differences can also be related to factors in the test situation. Goldstein and Chance (1965) presented data indicating that initial sex differences in EFT performance disappear with practice. They found the performance of all subjects to improve with practice. Naditch (1976) compared performance on a portable RFT under two conditions. In one condition the RFT was described as a test to perceptual abilities. In the other condition the rod was replaced with a female figure and the subject told that the RFT was a test of empathy. In the standard condition, males were more field independent than females; there were apparently no sex differences under the female figure/empathy condition.

INTELLIGENCE

A number of studies have shown a positive relationship between field independence and intelligence. In a factor analytic study involving a relatively small number of children, Goodenough and Karp (1961) found some indication that performance on measures of field dependence is related to performance on the WISC subtests of block design, picture completion, and object assembly. They interpreted this finding as providing evidence that these intellectual tests share with the measures of field dependence the requirement of overcoming an embedding context. In a later study of 150 male undergraduates, Karp (1963) obtained similar results. In their test manual, Witkin et al. (1971) summarized the results of several studies on the relationship of EFT performance and intelligence. They presented evidence that the moderate correlations between the EFT and the Wechsler IQ scales were due to the relation between EFT performance and a Wechsler "analytical factor" (i.e., block design, object assembly, and picture completion). Similarly, Coates (1975) found that performance on the Preschool EFT was related to performance on the block design and geometric design scales of the WPPSI.

From our own review of 20 studies, we find generally consistent indications that various measures of field dependence are related to various measures of both verbal and performance intelligence. These studies involve both children (Bigelow, 1971; Busch & Simon, 1972; Canavan, 1969; Crandall & Lacey, 1972; Crandall & Sinkeldam, 1964; Dreyer, Hulac, & Rigler, 1971; Erginel, 1972; Massari & Massari, 1973; Pedersen & Wender, 1968; Riley & Denmark, 1974; Satterly, 1976; Stuart, 1967; Weisz, O'Neill, & O'Neill, 1975) and undergraduates (Bieri, Bradburn, & Galinsky, 1958; Dubois & Cohen, 1970; Elliott, 1961; Gough & Olton, 1972; Houston, 1969; Spotts & Mackler, 1967; Wachtel, 1971). The correlations between field dependence and intelligence are mostly in the .40–.60 range; correlations between field independence and academic achievement and aptitude tests are somewhat lower.

DEVELOPMENT

AGE

In the first major report of field-dependence research, Witkin et al. (1954) presented data on the relationship between age and field dependence. Of special interest is their finding that field independence increased sharply between the ages of 10 and 13 years. Between the ages of 13 and 17 years, slight increases in field independence continued. There was no significant difference in field independence between the 17-year-olds and a group of adults with a mean age of about 20 years.

An important study of developmental differences in field dependence was reported by Witkin, Goodenough, and Karp (1967). Both cross-sectional and longitudinal studies were undertaken, with subjects varying in age from eight to 24 years. In the longitudinal study of RFT performance, one group of subjects ($N = 60$) was tested at 10, 14, and 17 years; the 30 boys in this group were also tested at 24 years of age. A second group of subjects ($N = 53$) was tested at eight years and again at 13 years. The RFT, BAT, and EFT were administered cross sectionally to approximately 25 boys and 25 girls at the following ages: 8, 10, 11, 12, 13, 15, 17, and about 20 years. The data indicated an increase in field independence with increasing age, until the age of about 17 years, at which time there was a leveling off. In addition, there was evidence that individuals maintained their relative positions along the field-dependence–field-independence dimension with increasing age. That is, a subject high in field independence relative to his peers at one age level was likely to remain high relative to his peers at later age levels.

In their study of correlates of field independence, Crandall and Sinkeldam (1964) obtained a significant correlation of .74 between performance on a modified EFT and age for a sample of 50 grade school children ranging in age from 6 years, 10 months to 12 years, 5 months. The correlations for both males and females ranged from .50 to .83 when three measures of EFT performance were correlated with age (Crandall & Lacey, 1972). Canavan (1969) reported on a developmental study of field dependence involving 1510 children in kindergarten through the sixth grade. Field dependence was measured with a modification of the RFT in which the silhouette of a man replaced the illuminated rod. An analysis of variance indicated grade, sex, and ethnic group differences. The older children and boys were more field independent. White subjects were more field independent than Mexican-American children, who in turn were more field independent than Black children. These results obtained even when the effect of IQ, measured by a full-scale WISC, was eliminated by covariance analyses.

Handel (1972) used a portable RFT device to study changes in field dependence as a function of age among 563 Israeli boys in grades seven through 11. He found a statistically significant correlation between age and total error scores ($r = .27$), indicating that older boys were more field independent than either the six- or seven-year-olds. Saarni (1973) found a significant correlation of .55 between RFT performance and age for a group of 32 boys in the sixth through ninth

grades; it is unclear whether data for girls were analyzed. Vaught, Pittman, and Roodin (1975) studied the RFT performance of 10 groups of
20 children each, ranging in age from four to 13 years. They found
that both boys and girls increased in field independence with increasing age.

GERIATRIC SAMPLES

There has been considerable interest in the level of field dependence
of older people. Axelrod and Cohen (1961) found that 30 older men
(63–78 years) performed worse than 30 younger men (20–36 years)
on Gottschaldt EFT tasks and a tactile EFT. Comalli (1965) studied the
RFT performance of twenty 80–90-year-old Spanish American War
veterans and fifteen 65–80-year-old volunteers, all of whom were
healthy and ambulatory. The data on their performances were presented in a graph, as were data on the performances of younger subjects. Comalli concluded that the performance of the elderly subjects
was field dependent and similar to that of children. There were no
statistical tests of this contention.

Another study of field dependence in older people was conducted
by Schwartz and Karp (1967). Their subjects were 17 male and 17 female subjects, ranging in age from 58 to 82 years, who were attending
a day center. The BAT, RFT, and an abridged version of the EFT were
administered. The performances of these subjects were compared to
those of two younger groups (17-year-olds and 30–39-year-olds). The
data indicated that, for both sexes, the older subjects were significantly
more field dependent. The frequently reported finding that women are
more field dependent than men did not hold for the geriatric subjects
of the study. In evaluating the results of this study, it is important to
note that the older subjects were predominantly foreign born and had
markedly less formal education than the younger groups. Tramer and
Schludermann (1974) administered the CEFT to 94 males, aged 52–88
years, who were in a veterans hospital for treatment of acute illnesses.
The majority of subjects had not completed elementary school. The
investigators found that field dependence increased with increasing
age.

In other research, Karp (1967) studied a group of 20 elderly men
who were gainfully employed. He compared the performance of this

group with that of a group of unemployed elderly males, some of whom had been previously studied. The EFT performances of the employed elderly were significantly more field independent than those of the unemployed elderly.

These studies, along with that of Markus (1971), provide some evidence that the elderly and the infirm elderly are more field dependent than younger subjects. However, infirmity and advanced age have been confounded in these studies; thus a definitive statement on the relationship between these variables and field dependence must await further research. Markus and Nielsen (1973) provided data on this issue by administering an abridged CEFT to five samples of geriatric subjects, ranging from healthy residents of a senior citizens' center to infirm institutionalized patients. The data were obtained from a total of 604 subjects. Based on their tabular and graphic presentations, Markus and Nielsen concluded that older subjects (over 75 years of age) were more field dependent than younger subjects, the institutionalized more field dependent than the noninstitutionalized subjects, and the female subjects no less field dependent than the male subjects.

Eisner (1972) presented data suggesting that the poor EFT performance of the elderly is related to inaccuracies in perception. For a sample of 20 males with an average age of 69 years, Eisner showed that the ability to reproduce accurately simple geometric figures was related to EFT performance.

These data indicate that both advanced age and infirmity are associated with field dependence.

PARENT-CHILD SIMILARITY

Corah (1965a) studied the relationship between the field dependence of parents and their children. The subjects were 30 boys and 30 girls between the ages of eight and 11 years and predominantly Jewish. The children were administered the CEFT, the parents a modified EFT. There were no significant correlations between the children's scores and their parents' scores. However, this study is often cited as indicating that there is a relationship between the field dependence of children and parents. This conclusion is based on an index of field dependence derived from EFT and Draw-a-Person (DAP) scores. When these scores were combined, a significant relationship was found between this measure of field dependence in boys and their mothers ($r = .39$) and girls and their fathers ($r = .41$). However, since the DAP was not central to the measurement of field dependence in the work of Witkin and his associates, this frequently cited conclusion must be questioned.

In an investigation by Dyk and Witkin (1965), mothers' performance on the EFT was studied in relation to their 10-year-old sons' perceptual index (BAT, RFT, EFT). For 26 mother–son pairs, a nonsignificant correlation coefficient was obtained. Goldstein and Peck (1973) studied the RFT performance of 181 eight- to 15-year-old children and their mothers on their initial visits to a child psychiatric outpatient clinic. A statistically significant correlation of .27 was obtained after the variance attributable to the child's age had been partialled out.

These studies, then, do not clearly demonstrate that the level of field dependence of children is related to that of their parents (cf. Goodeneough & Witkin, 1977).

MOTHER-CHILD RELATIONS

A study of greater value for its approach than for its results was reported by Dyk (1969). Detailed data on 72 infants had been gathered in an earlier study by Escalona and Leitch (1953). When these children were between the ages of six and nine years, a comprehensive battery designed to assess field dependence was administered. The aim of this research was to study the infant variables that may have been precursors of later levels of field dependence. Dyk proceeded by selecting the 12 children highest in field independence and comparing their experiences in infancy to those of the 12 children highest in field dependence. The author studied three types of variables: mother–child interaction, maternal characteristics, and characteristics of the infant. The detailed results are presented on an individual basis, without extensive statistical analyses. The study provides fertile material for the generation of hypotheses. For example, in nine of the 12 infants of the field-dependent group, maternal handling in infancy had been judged as lacking in sensitivity; this was true for only two of the 12 infants in the field-independent group.

As part of a previously cited report, Dyk and Witkin (1965) studied two groups, one consisting of 21 mother–son pairs. All the boys in the study were 10 years old and were volunteers from a New York City public school. Based on responses to an extensive, open-ended interview about family activities, mothers were categorized as either interfering with or fostering the development of field independence. A mother's self-realization and self-assurance in child rearing, encouragement of separation, and encouragement of the child to achieve mature goals were hypothesized as leading to field independence in the child. There were significant correlations between maternal characteristics and an index of field dependence based on the child's performance on the RFT, BAT, and EFT. For the first group, the point-biserial correlation was a significant .85; for the cross-validation group, the correlation was a significant .65.

In another investigation reported by Dyk and Witkin (1965), children's perceptions of parents were measured from stories they produced in response to TAT pictures. The subjects were 38 ten-year-old boys. When parents were mentioned in the TAT protocol, the story was scored for parental support or nonsupport. Parental nonsupport was characterized by coerciveness, anger, and physical punishment. The data indicated that field-independent boys were more likely to attribute supportive characteristics to parent figures than field-dependent boys. The field-dependent boys tended to view their parents as arbitrary, rigid, and tyrannical. In addition to these data, the results of two validation studies were reported. The relationships between the perceptual index and the ratings for mothers, father, and both parents combined were calculated for each of the samples. The results of the three studies were somewhat discrepant but, overall, five of the nine correlations were statistically significant and corroborated the original finding that field independence is associated with parental support.

In briefly summarizing the literature on the origins of field independence, Witkin et al. (1971) noted the general finding that interactions between parents and child that encourage separation and autonomous functioning lead to field independence. However, Domash and Balter (1976) recently failed to find a significant relationship between authoritarian control in mothers, as measured by the PARI (Schaefer & Bell, 1958), and CEFT performance for a sample of ninety-two 5½-year olds.

Crandall and Sinkeldam (1964) studied the relationship between field independence and the ratings of achievement behavior for a sample of 50 grade school children who were attending day camp. The authors hypothesized that such a relationship would exist because they viewed the EFT as a testing situation in which an achievement orientation would be likely to lead to success. Achievement behavior was reflected in such variables as independent achievement efforts and task persistence. The correlations between these ratings of achievement and EFT scores were generally significant.

Pedersen and Wender (1968) failed to find significant relationships between field dependence and attention-seeking behavior (comprised of two scales: seeking help without need and seeking attention or recognition) for a sample of 30 boys. The social behavior was rated at age 2½ years; field dependence was measured four years later. Coates, Lord, and Jakabovics (1975), in their study of preschoolers, found that children who tended to play in isolation were more field independent than those who were socially oriented in their play. In the research cited above, Crandall and Sinkeldam (1964) also studied the relationship between field dependence and dependent social behavior. Variables such as help and affection seeking from adults were rated by observers. Generally, the children's dependency behavior was unrelated to their EFT performances. Elliott (1961) too failed to establish any significant relationships between field dependence and dependency. The subjects in his study were male undergraduates, and dependency was assessed by statements made by the subjects while attempting to solve a very difficult puzzle.

In a paper reviewing cross-cultural studies of field dependence, Witkin (1967) concluded that the parent-child interactions associated with field dependence in the United States are also found in other cultures. The finding of greater field independence among males was also reported. In general, we include in our review studies using western subjects. In the area of field dependence in particular, there have been a number of investigations of members of other cultures (e.g., MacKinnon, 1972; Mebane & Johnson, 1970; Smith, 1971; Templer, 1972). Although these studies have developmental implications, we decided not to review them because of the difficulties involved in generalizing the results of these studies to Western society.

The results of the studies summarized in this section indicate that parental encouragement of autonomy leads to greater field independence in the child, a conclusion also reached by Goodenough and Witkin (1977). However, autonomous functioning in the child is not always related to the child's level of field independence.

OTHER FACTORS

Bieri (1960) studied the relationship between EFT performance and parental identification for a sample of 30 male and 30 female undergraduates. Using a two-tailed significance criterion, we find that there were no significant differences in EFT scores for subjects who identified with their mothers versus their fathers (analyzed separately for males, females, and the combined sample). Using several measures to assess identification with parents, Constantinople (1974) found only slight evidence indicating that field-independent male and female undergraduates were more closely identified with their fathers than were field-dependent subjects. Barclay and Cusumano (1967) argued that the development of field independence is an aspect of masculine identity and hypothesized that adolescent boys whose fathers were absent from the home would evidence greater field dependence than boys from intact homes. Their analysis of the RFT data from a study of 40 male adolescents supported the hypothesis.

Dershowitz (1971) compared the field dependence of 50 Orthodox Jewish boys, 56 nonobservant Jewish boys from the original sample of 10-year-old boys studied by Witkin et al. (1962), and 30 white, Anglo-Saxon Protestant boys. From the data presented by the author, it is unclear whether the groups differed in SES; IQ scores, however, were similar. Dershowitz administered two BAT series and the first 12 designs of the EFT, along with various other measures. The differences in field dependence among the three groups were significant for one of the BAT series, but not for the EFT. When a field-dependence index was developed by combining all three measures, the Orthodox Jewish boys were most field dependent, the Protestant subjects least field dependent, and the nonobservant Jewish subjects were in the middle.

Ramirez and Price-Williams (1974) administered the portable RFT to 180 fourth-grade Catholic parochial school children. Sixty of the children were Mexican-American, 60 were Black, and 60 were Anglo-American. One-half of each ethnic group was male, the other half female. The data indicated that the Anglo children were more field independent than the children of the other two groups. Females were found to be more field dependent than males. Ramirez and Price-Williams interpreted their findings, along with those of Dershowitz and others, as indicating that children from families emphasizing respect for family and authority tend to be field dependent. Children from families emphasizing individuality and the questioning of authority tend to be field independent. In a study comparing the performance of 20 Black and 20 White sixth-grade children, half boys and half girls, with IQs between 110 and 120, Perney (1976) found the Black girls to be more field dependent than the other three groups. All children were tested by a White female.

In the course of a study of over 3000 adult, employed males, Schooler (1972) found low but statistically significant relationships between EFT-measured field independence and such variables as younger age, father's education, and urban (vs. rural) upbringing. These findings support the author's hypothesis that the more complex the child's environment, the more likely he is to be field independent. Roodin, Broughton, and Vaught (1974) failed to find differences in RFT-measured field dependence on the basis of birth order or family size for a sample 186 undergraduates.

Gruenfeld, Weissenberg, and Loh (1973) reported data relating group-administered EFT scores to background material for a sample of 186 male high-school seniors. They obtained significant differences in EFT performance among six categories of social class; however, there is no report of statistical testing to determine which groups differ significantly from each other, and the relationship is not monotonic. In the course of a study of moral maturity, Schleifer and Douglas (1973) observed no differences on Banta's (1970) Early Childhood EFT between 35 middle-class and 37 lower-class preschool children. Bowd (1974) failed to find a significant relationship between CEFT scores and scores on a measure of socioeconomic status for a sample of 47 first-grade children.

RESEARCH

FIELD DEPENDENCE AND OTHER MEASURES OF COGNITIVE STYLE

In the course of their study of social perception, Rudin and Stagner (1958) administered a 30-item F Scale, the RFT, and a version of Gottschaldt's embedded figures to 34 male college undergraduates. The RFT and embedded figures were significantly correlated ($r = .55$). Scores on the F Scale were significantly related to RFT performance ($r = .45$), but not to the embedded figures measure. The data indicated that high-authoritarian subjects were more field dependent than low-authoritarian subjects. Stuart (1965) reported nonsignificant correlations between the F Scale and a short form of the EFT for two groups of undergraduates.

Bieri (1960) used a 20-item Acceptance of Authority Scale (Bales & Couch, 1956) as a measure of authoritarian submission. This scale had previously been shown to correlate highly with the F Scale (Bieri & Lobeck, 1959). The Acceptance of Authority Scale was administered, along with an eight-item EFT, to 30 male and 30 female undergraduates. The two tests were significantly correlated for the males ($r = .38$) and for both sexes combined ($r = .28$). Witkin et al. (1962) cited a personal communication from Mednick as evidence that, although field-dependent individuals are higher on authoritarianism than field-independent subjects, both groups may be more authoritarian than subjects who are intermediate in field independence.

Clark (1968) studied the relationship between field dependence and authoritarianism/dogmatism. Authoritarianism was measured by the administration of a scale of 38 items chosen from both the F and Dogmatism scales on the basis of the earlier factor analysis by Kerlinger and Rokeach (1966). Clark selected the 40 highest and lowest scorers from among 264 male undergraduates, and administered Jackson's short form of the EFT to these subjects. The low-authoritarian subjects were significantly more field independent than the high-authoritarian subjects.

Levy and Rokeach (1969) administered the Dogmatism Scale to 400 undergraduates and selected the 17 highest and the 17 lowest scorers matched for intelligence. These subjects were administered the Jackson short form of the EFT. There were no significant differences between the two groups in time of solution for any of the 12 EFT items. Hellkamp and Marr (1965) studied the relationship between field dependence and dogmatism among 38 undergraduate Catholic males. The Dogmatism Scale and RFT were administered. The relationship between the two measures was not statistically significant. Victor (1976) failed to find a statistically significant relationship between scores on the Dogmatism Scale and the HFT for a sample of 50 graduate students.

Elliott (1961) related scores derived from Bieri's modification of the Rep Test with EFT and RFT scores for a sample of 128 male undergraduates. The derived Rep-Test score was the number of psychological constructs used by the subjects. There were no significant correlations between this derived score and either of the measures of field dependence. It should be noted that the number of psychological constructs may not be related to the total number of constructs and thus may not be a measure of cognitive style.

Wolfe, Egelston, and Powers (1972) showed that 16 abstract college students failed to perform differently from 16 concrete students on the EFT. Integrative complexity was measured by a six-item PCT. Stewin (1976) failed to find significant correlations between the Group EFT and measures of integrative complexity (ITI, PCT, TIB Test) for a sample of 100 eleventh-grade students.

As part of a study on the relationship between field dependence and incidental recall of photographed faces, Messick and Damarin (1964) administered a group EFT and Pettigrew's (1958) Category-Width Scale to 50 undergraduates. The scores on the two measures were not significantly correlated. Hochman (1971) administered the Stroop Color-Word Interference Test (Messick, 1964) and the HFT to 48 female undergraduates. The data indicated that the more field-independent subjects performed better on the Stroop test, a finding interpreted by Hochman as indicating that field-dependent subjects are more susceptible to stimulus competition. Similar results were reported by Smith and Klein (1953) and Eisner (1972).

In their study of preschoolers, Keogh, Welles, and Weiss (1972) failed to find significant relationships between performance on Banta's (Banta et al., 1969) modification of the MFF and various indices of field dependence. More recently, however, Massari (1975) found that children considered to be reflective on the basis of their MFF scores were more field independent, as measured by the CEFT, than children considered to be impulsive. The subjects were 60 Black first-grade boys and girls and 54 Black third-grade boys and girls; the third graders evidenced more field independence than the first graders.

Thus there appears to be a significant relationship between field dependence and authoritarianism, but not between field dependence and dogmatism, cognitive complexity, or integrative complexity. Field-independent subjects are also less susceptible to stimulus competition than field-dependent subjects.

RIGIDITY AND INTOLERANCE OF AMBIGUITY

In a review of some of his work, Witkin (1964) noted a relationship between field dependence and performance on the Einstellung water jar task. In Chapter 2 a number of studies were discussed showing that individuals high on authoritarianism tended to be more rigid in their Einstellung performance. Witkin hypothesized that field-dependent subjects, because of their inability to overcome embeddedness, would have difficulty breaking the set induced by the initial problems. He cited a study by Guetzkow (1951), a doctoral dissertation by Fenchel (1958), and an unpublished study by Goodman (1960) as supporting his hypothesis. In addition to citing the Fenchel and Goodman studies, Breskin and Gorman (1969) also cited a master's thesis by Zaks (1954) and concluded that field-independent subjects manifest less rigidity on the Einstellung task than field-dependent subjects. Busse (1968), for his sample of 62 fifth-grade boys, reported a significant correlation of .33 between performance on the Einstellung water jar task and a version of the EFT (Crandall & Sinkeldam, 1964) utilizing the 10 easiest figures.

Hritzuk and Taylor (1973) compared subjects differing in field dependence on a task developed by Uznadze (1961) that is claimed to be similar to the Einstellung problem. The subjects were eighth-grade students who were classified as either field dependent or field independent on the basis of their RFT and EFT performances. There were statistically significant differences in the set-breaking ability of subjects in the two groups. However, the data indicated that in two of the cases field-independent subjects broke the set more easily, whereas in one case field-dependent subjects broke the set more easily.

Breskin and Gorman (1969) studied the performance of subjects varying in level of field dependence on a nonverbal test of rigidity developed by Breskin (1968). Their subjects were 47 undergraduates who were administered the Jackson (1956) group form of the EFT. Groups of males and females were each divided at the median on field dependence. There was no statistically significant difference in rigidity for males; for females, field-dependent subjects were more rigid than field-independent subjects.

Witkin et al. (1962) cited a dissertation by Gump (1955) in which adults differing in field dependence (on the Thurstone-Gottschaldt embedded figures) were tested on a picture recognition task. The pictures were projected at varying levels of blurriness. Each picture was presented initially in a very blurry form and then was made clearer on succeeding presentations. Gump was reported to have found that field-independent subjects were more accurate in their recognition of the blurry pictures. Witkin et al., on the other hand, presented a similar task to 29 ten-year-old boys and found no relationship between field dependence and picture recognition.

In an attempt to reconcile these differences, which might have been due to differences in the ages of the subjects, the operational definition of field dependence, or the different formats of the picture recognition tests that were used, Campbell, Dyer, and Boersma (1967) studied the performance of 30 ten-year-old boys and 30 adults males. Their task required the recognition of 36 familiar objects, each presented in fragmented form. For the adults, field dependence was measured by the Jackson short-form EFT; the CEFT was used for the children. The data indicated no significant relationships between field dependence and picture recognition ability.

Nebelkopf and Dreyer (1970) also studied the relationship between field dependence and the perception of ambiguous stimuli. Their subjects were 37 kindergarten and first-grade boys of average intelligence. The children were administered the Tent Series of the CEFT and Elkind's (1964) standardized version of the Ambiguous Pictures Test (APT). The APT consists of seven pictures, each of which contains an ambiguous figure capable of being interpreted in at least two ways. Nebelkopf and Dreyer found a statistically significant correlation of .83 between CEFT scores and the number of figures perceived on the APT. Performance on the APT appeared to be a function of both the ability to perceive a figure as distinct from its context (a task similar to the EFT) and to overcome the initial perception and shift to another (a task somewhat similar to the Einstellung task). The number of ambiguous figures perceived by the children suggests to us that it is this similarity to the EFT that accounts for the high correlation.

Lefever and Ehri (1976) studied the ability of subjects varying in levels of field dependence to correctly identify the two meanings of ambiguous sentences. The subjects were 69 undergraduates whose field dependence was assessed with an EFT-type measure. As hypothesized, field-independent subjects performed significantly better on the task.

Thus, although early studies provided evidence of a relationship between field dependence and rigidity, later work did not support this finding. The data on the relationship of field dependence and intolerance of ambiguity also present an inconsistent picture.

CONCEPT FORMATION

Ohnmacht (1966) studied the relationships among field independence, dogmatism, and concept formation. Forty subjects were split at the median on dogmatism and on the basis of EFT performance; they were required to master a concept-formation task. The data indicated a statistically significant difference in performance between the high- and low-dogmatic subjects, but no significant difference in performance between high- and low-field-dependent subjects; the interaction between field dependence and dogmatism was also not significant.

In a later study, Grippin and Ohnmacht (1972) again studied the relationship of field dependence and dogmatism to performance on concept attainment tasks. The subjects were 23 undergraduates who were administered the HFT, the Dogmatism Scale, and concept attainment tasks. Multiple regression analyses were performed, using HFT, dogmatism, and HFT-by-dogmatism interaction scores to predict performance on each of three concept attainment tasks. None of the three multiple correlations attained statistical significance.

Dickstein (1968) compared the performance of high- and low-field-dependent subjects on a concept attainment task. The subjects were selected from a pool of 96 female undergraduates and nursing students on the basis of extreme scores on the Thurstone CFT. A short-form EFT was also administered, and 20 subjects with high CFTs and EFTs were compared to 20 subjects with low CFTs and EFTs. There was some evidence that the field-independent subjects performed better on several of the indices of concept attainment.

DISCRIMINATION AND SYNTHESIS

Messick and Damarin (1964), on the basis of an earlier observation by Witkin et al. (1962), hypothesized that field-dependent subjects, having a greater need for the support of other people, would be more attentive to the physical appearance of other people. A group-administered EFT provided a measure of field dependence for their sample of 50 undergraduates. The subjects were shown photographs of the faces of 79 people and asked to estimate their ages and note whether the people resembled individuals known to the subjects. At the end of the testing session the subjects were shown 40 pictures, 20 of which had been among the first group of photographs. The subjects were asked to estimate the ages of the people pictured and to judge whether each of the photographs had been in the first group. A significant correlation of .29 was found between field dependence and correct recall; the field-dependent subjects were more likely to identify the photographs correctly. The authors cited similar results from a study by Crutchfield, Woodworth, and Albrecht (1958). On the other hand, Westbrook (1974) showed that field independence is also significantly related to accuracy in judging emotions from recorded conversations. In this direction too was the finding by Lavrakis, Buri, and Mayzner (1976) that Caucasian field-independent undergraduates were better able to recognize photos of Black individuals whom they had previously viewed. Similarly, Hoffman and Kagan (1977) found that field-independent male undergraduates were more accurate than field-dependent males in the recognition of photographed human faces, a finding for which they cite the support of other studies. Differences in the picture recognition performances of females differing in field dependence were not statistically significant.

A series of reports provides data on the relationship between RFT-measured field dependence and performance on tactile form-discrimination tasks. Vaught and Ellinger (1966) found significant correlations between field dependence and form discrimination for groups of 20 male and 20 female undergraduates. Vaught and Augustson (1967a) divided 42 female undergraduates into three groups differing in level of field dependence; they found no significant differences among the groups on form-discrimination tasks. Vaught and Augustson (1967b), in a study of 42 male undergraduates, reported that the more field-independent groups performed the form-discrimination tasks with fewer errors. Vaught and Roodin (1973) concluded that for females, the more field-dependent subjects tended to make fewer errors in form discrimination; for males the more field-dependent subjects tended to make more errors in form discrimination. The partitioning of the study into the three reports noted above seems unwarranted.

In a weight-discrimination task, Blasi, Cross, and Hebert (1972) found that 20 field-dependent undergraduates were more influenced by a comparison weight than were 20 field-independent undergraduates, a finding interpreted as illustrating that field-dependent subjects are more influenced by context than are field-independent subjects.

Fine (1973) studied the relationship between field dependence and the ability to discriminate colors and weights. His subjects were 56 soldiers who were extreme scorers on both the Gottschaldt Hidden Figures Test and the extraversion–introversion scale of the MMPI. The data indicated superior discriminating ability with regard to colors for field-independent subjects; there was little evidence of similar superiority with respect to weight discrimination.

A study that compared the synthesizing ability of subjects differing in field dependence was conducted by Kessler and Kronenberger (1967). The investigators selected the 30 highest and 30 lowest scorers on the Dogmatism Scale from among a sample of 110 undergraduates. These 60 subjects were administered the Jackson (1956) short form of the EFT, and, on the basis of the test results, four groups of eight subjects each were created. Following Levy and Rokeach (1960), the subjects were administered the Kohs block design test as a measure of synthesizing ability. The field-independent subjects evidenced significantly greater synthesizing ability than the field-dependent subjects; however, contrary to the Levy and Rokeach findings, there was no significant difference in the synthesizing ability of high- versus low-dogmatic subjects. This finding of superior performance on the Kohs test is consistent with Witkin's personal communication to Dawson (1967) stating that the Kohs test may be used as a measure of field dependence.

Wachtel (1971) administered the RFT to 46 male undergraduates who had been selected on the basis of extreme EFT and DAP scores. The subjects were required to learn to associate a nonsense syllable with a complex design. Field dependence was unrelated to performance on this task. However, Wachtel reported that field-independent subjects had better recall of the identifying label when presented with fragments of the complex design. This finding was based on a correlation that is just statistically significant at the .05 level using a one-tailed test.

In a task similar in some respects to the Doodlebug problem used in the study of dogmatism, Ehri and Muzio (1974) asked a sample of 61 college students whether horses on the outside of a merry-go-round moved faster than horses on the inside. On the basis of an EFT-type test, subjects were classified as field dependent, middle range, or field independent. Field independence was significantly related to the ability to solve the problem correctly. As in the Doodlebug problem, additional hints were given to subjects who could not solve the problem immediately. These hints were of little help to the field-dependent subjects. The investigators interpreted the results of the study as indicating the superior analyzing and synthesizing ability of field-independent subjects.

The results of these studies provide some evidence that field-independent subjects are superior to field-dependent subjects in discriminating and synthesizing abilities.

STRESS

We examined the relationship between stress and cognitive style in preceding chapters. Hill and Feigenbaum (1966) provided some data on this relationship with regard to field dependence. They administered the RFT to 17 female undergraduates. One week after the initial testing, stress was induced in 13 of the subjects by critical remarks threatening their self-esteem. The subjects who experienced this stress became more field dependent. However, Loo and Cauthen (1976) failed to find differences in EFT performance under ego-involving (stress) conditions versus non-ego-involving (nonstress) conditions for their sample of 60 female undergraduates.

Reinking, Goldstein, and Houston (1974) classified 181 female undergraduates as high analytic (field independent) or low analytic (field dependent) on the basis of their scores on the Jackson EFT. The subjects' RFT performances were then studied under various conditions. In one condition, the subjects' RFT performances under stress were evaluated. Stress was induced in half the subjects by instructing them that electric shocks would be administered to their wrists at random times during their RFT testing. The stressed high-analytic subjects evidenced more field independence than the nonstressed high-analytic subjects. The stressed low-analytic subjects evidence more field dependence than the nonstressed low-analytic subjects. Thus stress increased the field independence of field-independent subjects and the field dependence of field-dependent subjects. In a more recent study, Sarris, Heineken, and Peters (1976) used a flickering light to generate stress. Using the RFT, they found increased field dependence under the stress condition for a sample of 60 German university students.

Minard and Mooney (1969) offered evidence that subjects varying in level of field dependence perform differently on a task in which emotional content is a factor. Thirty male undergraduates were administered the BAT, EFT, and the DAP Test. The subjects were ranked according to their scores on each of the three tests, and the rankings were averaged across the three tests for each subject. The task required the recognition of tachistoscopically presented neutral and emotionally laden words. The data indicated that field-dependent subjects identified fewer emotionally laden words than neutral words; there was no difference in this regard for field-independent subjects. Subjects in the middle range of field dependence recognized more emotionally laden than neutral words.

Schimek and Wachtel (1966) studied the relationship between field dependence and the capacity to perform a task under different conditions of distraction. The subjects were 42 male undergraduates, 20 of whom had been administered both the RFT and an EFT, and 22 of whom were administered a group EFT. The task required the subjects to emit letters of the alphabet in a random order, one every two seconds for 3½ minutes. Various types of tape-recorded material were presented to the subjects during this period. The data indicated that field dependence was unrelated to distractibility. However, there was some evidence that field-independent subjects were better able to recall the prose passage played to them while they were engaged in the other task. From the results of these last two studies and other research, Goodenough (1976) concluded that the memories of field-dependent subjects are more adversely affected by stress than those of field-independent subjects. This conclusion is contained in Goodenough's comprehensive review of the relationship of field dependence to learning and memory.

Houston (1969) studied the performances of field-dependent and field-independent subjects under normal and distracting conditions.

He hypothesized that field-independent subjects would be less distracted by extraneous environmental conditions. Two groups of 20 female undergraduates were differentiated on the basis of the EFT scores and matched on anxiety level, need achievement, and intelligence scores. Each subject performed three tasks, digit span, anagrams, and the Stroop Color-Word Interference Test, first under normal conditions and again three weeks later while listening to high-intensity, tape-recorded noises. There were no significant differences between the two groups in performance on any of the tasks. In a pair of studies, Blowers (1974, 1976) failed to find differences in the susceptibility to distraction of field-dependent and field-independent subjects. The auditory distractors used in the studies had no differential effect on the subjects' reaction times.

Markus, Blenkner, Bloom, and Downs (1970) hypothesized that elderly people who are relocated would be more stressed if they were field dependent than if they were field independent. They administered a modified CEFT to 176 residents of a home for the elderly prior to a move to a new facility. Six months after the move, it was noted that none of the 34 field-independent but 20 of the 142 field-dependent subjects had died ($\chi^2 = 5.40$, $p < .025$).

These studies provide only partial support for the hypothesis that the performance of field-dependent subjects is more affected by stress than that of field-independent subjects.

CONFORMITY

Linton (1955) studied the conformity behavior of subjects varying in levels of field dependence. Data from about 50 male undergraduates were analyzed. Four measures from the TRTC and another from the EFT were used as measures of field dependence. The subjects' performances were studied in three conformity situations: the autokinetic situation, a syllogisms test that provided an index of the tendency of the subject's logic to be biased by his attitudes, and an attitude change test designed to measure the extent to which written material from authoritative sources is likely to result in the subject's changing his attitudes. When five measures of field dependence were used in multiple regressions to predict conformity, statistically significant relationships were found. The field-dependent subjects were more conforming.

Rosner (1957) studied the conforming behavior of 88 student nurses. In each of three conformity situations, the subjects were scored on whether they made independent judgments or conformed to the erroneous judgments of three confederates of the experimenter. From the total group, Rosner selected 20 high- and 20 low-conformers and administered the EFT. There were no significant differences in EFT performance between these two groups.

In a study in which field-dependent subjects were paired with field-independent subjects, Solar, Davenport, and Bruehl (1969) showed that field-dependent subjects tended to be influenced by the field-independent subjects. The investigators used the Thurstone EFT to select 10 extremely field-dependent and 10 extremely field-independent subjects from a pool of 203 female undergraduates. The RFT was first administered to each subject individually, then to the subjects in pairs. The RFT performances of the mixed pairs indicated greater field independence than was expected on the basis of the individual performances. On subsequent individual administrations of the RFT, the field-dependent subjects reverted to their earlier levels of field dependence. The researchers concluded that field-dependent subjects are socially dependent and conforming. In a related study, Oltman, Goodenough, Witkin, Freedman, and Friedman (1975) found that in dyads in which one or both of the members were field dependent, there was easier resolution of conflict than when both members were field independent. Wolitzky (1973), based on his study of 36 undergraduates, made the point that, although field-dependent subjects may be more responsive to social stimuli, field-independent subjects are more accurate in their social perceptions.

Simon, Langmeyer, and Boyer (1974) studied the performance of groups comprised of field-independent, field-dependent, and both field-dependent and field-independent subjects on a task involving the assemblying of squares from component parts. They showed that the groups composed of field-independent subjects performed the task more quickly. They pointed out that this finding might have arisen because of the more efficient sharing behavior in the field-independent groups or because of the superior perceptual functioning of the members of these groups.

Mausner and Graham (1970) also studied the conforming behavior of subjects varying in levels of field dependence. Field dependence was measured by the HFT. The conformity task involved making judgments of the speed at which a light flickered. The subjects were 36 male 10th-grade students, selected on the basis of extreme HFT scores from a pool of 132 subjects, tested in pairs. In the first stage of the experiment, one member of each pair was positively reinforced on four of six trials, whereas the other member was positively reinforced on two of six trials. In the second stage of the experiment, an attempt was made to influence the judgment of each subject by providing him with falsified data, supposedly from his partner. Overall, there was no difference in conforming behavior between the high- and low-field-dependent subjects. However, field-dependent subjects who, in the initial stage of the experiment had been positively reinforced on only two trials ("wrong" subjects), converged toward their partners' judgments. Field-dependent subjects who, in the initial stage of the experiment had been positively reinforced on four of the trials ("right" subjects), did not converge toward their partners' judgments. It should be noted that in this conformity state, a "right" subject was always paired with a "wrong" subject. Thus this finding may be the result of the interaction between field dependence and prior reinforcement, or field dependence and the responses of a partner who is seen as right or wrong.

Busch and DeRidder (1973) studied the effects of field dependence on the conformity behavior of disadvantaged children. Their subjects were 24 field-dependent and 24 field-independent Head Start children chosen from a pool of 96 children on the basis of extreme scores on a modified RFT. The children were asked to choose the larger of a pair of stimuli, some being presented with bogus information to induce conformity. There were no differences in conformity behavior between the field-dependent and field-independent children.

The conforming behavior of individuals varying in level of field dependence was studied by Greene (1976) in a natural setting. The subjects were 40 field-dependent and 40 field-independent female clients of a weight-reduction clinic, with field dependence assessed by the EFT. While the field-dependent women expressed greater willingness to adhere to the dieting program recommended to them by an interviewer, it was the field-independent women who were more likely to lose weight.

Thus there is some evidence that field dependence is related to conformity. In this connection, Laird and Berglas (1975) stated that when subjects are required to argue against their own beliefs, field-independent subjects would be more likely than field-dependent subjects to change their attitudes. They stated that in a conformity situation pressure for change comes from the external environment; in their counterargument situation, the pressure for change comes from the subject himself. Laird and Berglas correlated scores on the HFT with an attitude-change score for 25 undergraduates and obtained a statistically significant correlation of .43, indicating greater attitude change on the part of field-independent subjects.

CREATIVITY

Bieri, Bradburn, and Galinsky (1958) related performance on an eight-item EFT to scores on Guilford's (1956) Bricks Test, a test that has often been used as a measure of creativity. The Bricks Test requires the subject to list as many uses as he can for a brick. The correlations between field dependence and scores on the Bricks Test for both male and female ($N = 110$) undergraduates were not statistically significant. Similarly, Busse (1968), in his study of fifth-grade boys, failed to find a significant correlation between field dependence and performance on an "unusual uses" test.

Spotts and Mackler (1967), in their previously cited study, found no significant differences on 14 measures of creativity, derived from four separate tests, among groups of undergraduates categorized as field dependent, field central, and field independent. The analyses were performed once for a group of 45 subjects matched for intelligence and again for the larger sample of 114 unmatched subjects.

Moore, Gleser, and Warm (1970) studied the ability of subjects differing in field dependence to provide creative organization to ambiguous stimuli. Their subjects were 35 male undergraduates who were administered the RFT as a measure of field dependence. The subjects were shown 30 ambiguous line drawings from the Obscure Figure Test (Acker & McReynolds, 1965) and were required to describe what each figure represented. The responses were scored on a five-point scale from no response to highly creative response. There was a significant correlation of .44 between field independence and this creativity score.

Ohnmacht and McMorris (1971) administered the Dogmatism Scale, the HFT, and a measure of creativity, the Remote Associates Test (Mednick & Mednick, 1967), to an unspecified sample of 74 subjects. The data were analyzed separately for males and females. Two-by-two analyses of variance were performed, with subjects divided at the median on field dependence and dogmatism. There were no significant main effects or interactions for either males or females.

The results of these studies provide little support for a relationship between field dependence and creativity.

SENSATION SEEKING

The findings with regard to the relationship between field dependence and sensation seeking are mixed. Zuckerman, Kolin, Price, and Zoob (1964) reported a significant correlation of .49 between scores on the Thurstone EFT and their sensation-seeking scale for a sample of 32 males and a nonsignificant correlation for 30 females. Zuckerman and Link (1968) reported a significant correlation of .33 between scores on the EFT and the sensation-seeking scale for a sample of 40 males and a significant correlation of .42 between scores on the RFT and sensation-seeking scale for the same subjects. Bone and Choban (1972) failed to find a significant relationship between scores on the RFT and the sensation-seeking scale for either males or females. Farley (1974) failed to find significant correlations between scores on the HFT and the sensation-seeking scale for either a group of 30 female undergraduates or a group of 30 male undergraduates.

CRITIQUE

There have been many studies concerned with field dependence. In a review of field dependence through 1972, Long (1974) cited over 350 papers. These investigations are themselves only a sampling of the many studies in this area. In a bibliography covering the period 1954–1972, Witkin, Oltman, Cox, Ehrlichman, Hamm, and Ringler (1973) list and categorize some 1500 papers in the public domain. Witkin, Cox, Friedman, Hrishikesan, and Siegel (1974) added about 400 reports for the period ending mid-1974. Witkin, Cox, and Friedman (1976), for a two-year period ending September 1976, added over 600 new papers.

As in preceding chapters, we review research in this section that is relevant to the study of cognitive style. A number of studies are excluded that, although interesting, deflect us from our central concern with cognitive style. For example, Bard (1972) presented data suggesting that field-dependent subjects do better at team sports (e.g., volleyball), whereas field-independent subjects do better at individual activities (e.g., dancing).

In the course of his work, Witkin's view of the construct under study underwent change. At first there was a narrow view of performance on the experimental tasks having to do with the perception of the upright. With the introduction of the EFT and the interest in locating an object within an embedding context, the construct was broadened to field dependence/field independence. When EFT performance was related to performance on intellectual tasks, the construct was broadened further to a dimension that distinguished between the global and the articulated. Finally, with the demonstration that performance was also related to personality measures, the construct of differentiation was introduced. Most of the literature concerns field dependence and the dimension of differentiation. However, the distinction between field dependence and differentiation is not a central point in research; the dimension of global articulation seems to have had a relatively short life. Further, we have not found it useful to distinguish between field dependence and differentiation, a practice that is shared by most researchers.

For some reason, investigators seem to be impelled to modify the basic measures of field dependence. Although it is clear that a short form, a group form, and a children's form serve useful functions, it is not as clear that the many variations of each of these serve a useful purpose. The relationships among these many variations and the standard measures are often unclear. This makes difficult the task of comparing the results of studies with contrasting results and different instruments.

Another difficulty in comparing the results obtained in different studies is the way in which field-dependent and field-independent subjects are delineated. Vaught (1968), commenting on an exchange between Immergluck (1968) and Pressey (1968), showed that when an average deviation on the RFT of 10 degrees or more is used as the criterion for defining field dependence, only about 17% of the undergraduate population is defined as field dependent. Many investigators, who do not have access to large pools from which to draw samples, simply divide their subjects on the basis of median or quartile scores and therefore are likely to fail to include in the field-dependent group subjects who are clearly field dependent.

In this chapter we saw that the various versions of the RFT and EFT correlate about .30–.60. The magnitude of these correlations has been taken as an indication that a single dimension underlies performance on both tests. We also reported that the correlations between field independence and measures of intelligence are in the .40–.60 range. However, the magnitude of these correlations is not taken by Witkin to be evidence for a single dimension underlying both field dependence and intelligence.

The relationship between field dependence and intelligence has been an issue of considerable concern to researchers in this area (cf. Zigler, 1963a, b; Brody, 1972). Witkin has acknowledged the existence of a high relationship between some subtests of IQ measures (principally block design, picture completion, and object assembly from the Wechsler tests) and field dependence; he argued that these subtests involve the same perceptual skills as the measures of field dependence. However, we also noted substantial correlations between field dependence and verbal measures of intelligence, for which there is no common perceptual basis. Wachtel (1972) criticized research in the area for not controlling for intelligence and thus confounding the effects of field dependence and intelligence.

As Wachtel (1972) and Kogan (1973, 1976) have pointed out, Witkin's measurement techniques are more closely akin to techniques used to measure ability than to techniques used to measure alternative approaches to problem solving. That is, good performance on the RFT and EFT is measured in terms of correctness. Performance on the Paragraph Completion Test, on the other hand, is assessed on the basis of the strategy employed rather than on the correctness of the response.

We have been especially interested in locating studies relating the various indices of cognitive style to one another. In this chapter we reported studies in which both field dependence and dogmatism were assessed in the course of investigating other variables. Unfortunately, the authors usually neglected to report the relationship between the two measures.

Another troublesome factor, also encountered in other areas we have reviewed, is the relative lack of a direct, systematic attack on specific issues. Although Witkin and his colleagues should be commended for their continuing, detailed studies, such coherence is lacking in the work of other investigators. We have the impression that field dependence is not the central concern in many of the studies in which it is employed as a variable. Rather, the researchers are interested in some dependent measure and, for ease of administration, or fashion, find it convenient to administer the RFT or EFT. This impression is bolstered by our experience in surveying the literature. When we contacted authors for reprints of particular studies employing measures of field dependence and asked for reprints of related studies, more often than not the reprints of related studies that were sent to us were concerned with the dependent variable investigated in the original study, rather than field dependence.

CHAPTER SEVEN
Conclusion

The five preceding chapters were presented in a sequence that reflects decreasing emphasis on content and increasing emphasis on structure. The initial interest in research on authoritarianism was the personality dynamics of the anti-Semitic individual. Later, this research interest was broadened to a study of authoritarianism of the right. In this content-laden research, work on cognitive style, as reflected in the study of rigidity and intolerance of ambiguity, was not of central concern.

In the next chapter we saw that Rokeach attempted to deemphasize content by developing a measure of authoritarianism designed to be independent of political orientation of the right or the left. His approach to the measurement of content-free dogmatism incorporated into his measuring instrument items designed to measure cognitive style rather than the content of thought.

The work of Kelly and Bieri on cognitive complexity went still further toward the development of a content-free measure of cognitive style. In its original presentation, the formulation was a theory of personality that was to have clinical applications. That is, the content of the subject's responses would be of interest to a therapist. However, as we have seen, cognitive complexity developed as a measure of cognitive style in its own right.

Harvey, Hunt, and Schroder designed measuring instruments to assess the dimensionality underlying subjects' responses, as well as the hierarchical organization of these dimensions. The content of the subject's responses was entirely irrelevant, since it was posited that the subject brings a particular structure of thinking to a wide variety of content areas.

212

Similarly, Witkin and his associates began their research with no ties to content. Their approach to the measurement of cognitive style originated with the study of the perception of the upright and evolved to an interest in the individual's style of thinking.

Of overriding concern is whether cognitive style can be construed in a manner similar to a personality variable, that is, as a trait that is enduring over time and across situations (cf. Mischel, 1973). Regarding the question of stability over time, the measures of cognitive style are satisfactorily reliable over short intervals. There is some evidence of developmental changes, with a decrease in field dependence until the age of 17 years and a decrease in dogmatism at least through the college years; there is some evidence that with old age and infirmity there is a decrease in field independence.

Regarding the consistency of cognitive style across situations, the picture is less clear. It is questionable whether an individual's cognitive style would vary across different situations. We have seen that, although there are a number of general trends that emerged in the literature, even within a single approach to the measurement of cognitive style, the relationship of style to situation often yields mixed results. For example, the results of studies relating authoritarianism to Einstellung rigidity did not yield consistent findings.

On the basis of the results of his factor analytic study, Vannoy (1965) concluded that no unitary dimension was being measured by the various indices of cognitive style included in his investigation. Based on our own review of the literature, the same conclusion is warranted. However, it must be kept in mind that the five measures considered here are a sample of various approaches to the study of cognitive style. As noted, there has been a development in the approach to the measurement of cognitive style, beginning with content-laden instruments and culminating in projective and perceptual measures. From this historical vantage point, one would not necessarily expect significant relationships among the content-laden and content-free measures.

Cognitive style is best construed as a generic construct, much like personality. There are various approaches to the measurement of personality, and investigators differ in the number of aspects, or dimensions, they use in the study of personality. Eysenck (Eysenck & Eysenck, 1973), for example, has gone from a two-factor to a three-factor instrument, whereas Cattell (Cattell, Eber, & Tatsouka, 1970) has developed a 16-factor approach.

In reviewing the literature on cognitive style we have presented five approaches to the study of the construct. Clearly, to best predict information-processing behavior, studies using a number of the instruments should be conducted. It would be expected that increased variance in behavior could be accounted for by the unique contributions made by the different instruments.

RELATIONSHIPS AMONG THE FIVE INDICES OF COGNITIVE STYLE

A major concern is the extent to which the approaches to cognitive style outlined in the preceding chapters have a common basis. Because the tests were developed from different theoretical perspectives and for different purposes, there is reason to believe that the correlations would be less than perfect. Further, the methods of measurement differ widely, again mitigating against perfect correspondence among them. For example, the F Scale was designed as a measure of beliefs maintained by a certain type of person, whereas Witkin's work stems from an interest in perceptual style. The attitudinal format of the Dogmatism Scale shares little method variance with Kelly's Rep Test or the variety of techniques used to measure integrative complexity.

In spite of these difficulties, a number of investigators have shown moderate overlap between performance on these various tests. In addition to intercorrelating scores on the measures, some investigators have utilized two or more of the tests in factor analytic studies. The correlational studies are summarized in Table 7.1.

The data that have been reviewed indicate substantial correlations between scores derived from the F Scale and the Dogmatism Scale, possibly because these scales share method variance. However, we have seen that the two scales are factorially discriminable (Kerlinger & Rokeach, 1966; Warr, Lee, & Jöreskog, 1969). Most studies in the area have indicated moderate correlations between scores on the F Scale and scores on the other three measures of cognitive style: cognitive complexity, integrative complexity, and field dependence. However, the relationships between scores on the Dogmatism Scale and these three measures are generally not significant. The data indicate a lack of consistent relationships among measures of cognitive complexity, integrative complexity and field dependence.

Table 7.1 Summary of Studies Relating Two or More Tests of Cognitive Style

Study	Instruments	Correlation	Sample
1. Authoritarianism × Dogmatism			
Hession & McCarthy (1975)	29-item F Scale	.54	28 Irish graduate students
	Dogmatism Scale (Form D)		
Kahoe (1974)	30-item F Scale	.66	188 undergraduates
	Dogmatism Scale		
Kerlinger & Rokeach (1966)	F Scale	.65	537 undergraduates
	Dogmatism Scale	.70	371 undergraduates
		.77	331 adult part-time undergraduates
Plant (1960)	F Scale	.75	1007 male undergraduates
	Dogmatism Scale	.70	1343 female undergraduates
	E Scale	.57	1007 male undergraduates
	Dogmatism Scale	.61	1343 female undergraduates
Pyron (1966)	28-item F Scale	.53	80 undergraduates
	Dogmatism Scale		
Rokeach (1956)	F Scale	.77	60 English workers
	Dogmatism Scale	.62	80 English undergraduates
	E Scale	.53	60 English workers
	Dogmatism Scale	.32	80 English undergraduates
Rokeach & Fruchter (1956)	29-item F scale	.64	207 undergraduates
	Early 30-item Dogmatism Scale		
Rule & Hewitt (1970)	28-item F Scale	.45	91 male undergraduates
	Dogmatism Scale	.56	113 female undergraduates
Schroder & Streufert (1962)	30-item F Scale	.56	147 male high-school students
	Dogmatism Scale		

Table 7.1 (Continued)

Study	Instruments	Correlation	Sample
Sheikh (1968)	E Scale (?) Dogmatism Scale (?)	.65	25 undergraduates
Thompson & Michel (1972)	F Scale Modified Dogmatism Scale	.64	379 undergraduates
Zippel & Norman (1966)	29-item F Scale Dogmatism Scale	.67	381 undergraduates and other young adults
2. Authoritarianism × Cognitive Complexity			
Bieri (1965)	F Scale Modified Rep Test	.45 NS	Females, unspecified Males, unspecified
Pyron (1966)	28-item F Scale Modified Rep Test	NS	80 undergraduates
Vannoy (1965)	10 original and 10 reversed F-Scale items Modified Bieri Rep Test	.20	113 male undergraduates
3. Authoritarianism × Integrative Complexity			
Harvey (1966)	F Scale TIB Test	As expected	Summary
Rule & Hewitt (1970)	28-item F Scale ITI	.39 .29	91 male undergraduates 113 female undergraduates
Schroder, Driver, & Streufert (1967)	F Scale SCT or IFT	.25–.55	Summary

Study	Measures	Result	Sample
Schroder & Streufert (1962)	30-item F Scale SCT	.34	147 male high-school students
Streufert & Driver (1967)	F Scale IFT	.18	124 male undergraduates
Vannoy (1965)	10 original & 10 reversed F-Scale items SCT	NS	113 male undergraduates
4. Authoritarianism × Field Dependence			
Rudin & Stagner (1958)	30 items from F Scales RFT	.45	34 male undergraduates
	30 items from F Scales Thurstone EFT	NS	34 male undergraduates
Stuart (1965)	F Scale EFT short form	NS	31 vocational studies undergraduates
		NS	42 undergraduates
5. Dogmatism × Cognitive Complexity			
Bieri (1965)	Dogmatism Scale Modified Rep Test	.27	Females, unspecified Males, unspecified
Pyron (1966)	Dogmatism Scale Modified Rep Test	NS	80 undergraduates
Starbird & Biller (1976)	Dogmatism Scale Bieri Rep Test	NS (F Test)	180 undergraduates
6. Dogmatism × Integrative Complexity			
Harvey (1966)	Dogmatism Scale TIB Test	As expected	Summary

Table 7.1 (Continued)

Study	Instruments	Correlation	Sample
Rule & Hewitt (1970)	Dogmatism Scale ITI	.23 NS	91 male undergraduates 113 female undergraduates
Schroder, Driver, & Streufert (1967)	Dogmatism Scale SCT or IFT	Low	Summary
Schroder & Streufert (1962)	Dogmatism Scale SCT	NS	147 male high-school students
Streufert & Driver (1967)	Dogmatism Scale IFT	NS	124 male undergraduates
7. Dogmatism × Field Dependence			
Hellkamp & Marr (1965)	Dogmatism Scale Automated RFT	NS	38 undergraduates
Levy & Rokeach (1960)	Dogmatism Scale Jackson short-form EFT	NS	33 undergraduates
Victor (1976)	Dogmatism Scale HFT	NS	50 master's-level students
8. Cognitive Complexity × Integrative Complexity			
Harvey (1966)	Rep Test TIB Test	As expected	Summary
Hunt (1962b)	Adaptation of Rep Test SIE	.37	136 6th–12th-grade boys

218

Study	Measures	Result	Sample
Epting & Wilkins (1974)	Bieri Rep Test Conceptual Systems Test	.31	90 undergraduates
	Bieri Rep Test PCT	−.31	90 undergraduates
Smith & Leach (1972)	Bieri Rep Test TIB Test	NS	27 unspecified
	Hierarchical measure of cognitive complexity TIB Test	Significant (Mann–Whitney $U = .50$)	27 unspecified
Streufert (1970)	Rep Test	Low and sometimes negative	Summary
Vannoy (1965)	Modified Bieri Rep Test SCT	NS	113 male undergraduates

9. Cognitive Complexity × Field Dependence

Study	Measures	Result	Sample
Elliott (1961)	Modified Bieri Rep Test RFT	NS	128 male undergraduates
	Modified Bieri Rep Test EFT	NS	128 male undergraduates

10. Integrative Complexity × Field Dependence

Study	Measures	Result	Sample
Stewin (1976)	ITI, PCT, TIB Test Group EFT	NS	100 11th-graders
Wolfe, Egelston, & Powers (1972)	PCT EFT	NS	32 undergraduates

On the basis of these studies, then, there appears to be some commonality among the various measures of cognitive style reviewed in this book. However, before any definitive statement could be made, it would be necessary to examine additional data, especially regarding the relationship of measures of field dependence and the other measures. As noted, the lack of unidimensionality may assist in the prediction of behavior when two or more of these instruments are used.

RELATIONSHIPS OF THE FIVE INDICES OF COGNITIVE STYLE TO INTELLIGENCE

In the preceding section some data were presented indicating that the indices of cognitive style considered here have some overlap. In seeking to dimensionalize the construct of cognitive style, it is important to compare the relationships of the various indices to various dependent variables.

Measures of the five approaches to cognitive style relate differentially to intelligence, although for authoritarianism and dogmatism the data are scant. The highest relationships hold for field dependence and intelligence, where there has been some controversy regarding the independence of field dependence from intelligence. Cognitive complexity clearly seems to be independent of intelligence. For authoritarianism and integrative complexity, correlations are generally significant, but rather low. In virtually every case in which there is a significant relationship reported between cognitive style and intelligence, across all five areas of measurement, high intelligence is related to less authoritarian, more abstract functioning.

RELIABILITY

With the possible exception of measures of cognitive complexity, the reliability for the various measures of cognitive style appears to be satisfactory. Since alternate forms of the various measures are generally nonexistent, the reliability studies are either interjudge (integrative complexity) or test-retest over a short period of time. In the area of cognitive complexity, different stimuli have been used to develop alternate forms of the Rep Test that yield scores that are moderately intercorrelated.

RESPONSE SETS

The question of the relationship of acquiescence response set to cognitive style was raised early in the work on authoritarianism. In reviewing the extensive literature relating to this issue, it was concluded that subjects scoring high on the F Scale are likely to score high on indices of acquiescence. It was also noted that this was not a particularly serious difficulty, since acquiescence appears to be a characteristic of the authoritarian individual; the variance attributable to acquiescence on the F Scale is not a confounding factor. A similar situation exists with regard to the measurement of dogmatism.

There has been little interest in the relationship of acquiescence to cognitive complexity, integrative complexity, or field dependence. In one study it was found that subjects low in cognitive complexity tend to be acquiescent. This finding is consistent with those summarized above.

A few attempts have been made to relate cognitive style to social desirability response set. The mixture of positive, negative, and nonsignificant correlations makes it difficult to establish a clear relationship between cognitive style and social desirability.

CHANGES IN COGNITIVE STYLE WITH AGE

For each of the five approaches to the measurement of cognitive style there are data relevant to the relationship between cognitive style and age. Most studies of the development of cognitive style during the precollege years are in the area of field dependence. The data indicate that field independence increases until about the age of 17 years. Scattered studies in authoritarianism and dogmatism are consistent with these results. No such data exist for cognitive complexity. For integrative complexity, where developmental considerations are of special theoretical importance, most of the studies failed to find relationships with age.

There has been some interest in changes in cognitive style during the college years. Most of the studies here are in the area of dogmatism, where it appears that decreases in dogmatism during these years may be a function of either age or education. There is also some evidence that authoritarianism will decrease and cognitive complexity will increase during the college years. The data generally indicate no changes in field dependence between the age of 17 years and advanced age and infirmity, at which time a decrease in field independence occurs.

CHILD-REARING CORRELATES OF COGNITIVE STYLE

The data are rather consistent in indicating that parental child-rearing techniques of control are associated with lower levels of complexity of cognitive style. There are also a number of studies that indicate that cold, rejecting parents foster simple cognitive structures in their children. Although the results in this area are consistent, the magnitude of the correlations involved is not very high. Also, it appears that child-rearing practices designed to encourage autonomy in the child are associated with the development of field independence.

RIGIDITY

One of the earliest lines of research between authoritarianism and an aspect of cognitive style was the series of studies on Einstellung rigidity. There was some concern with the adequacy of the Einstellung water jar problems as a measure of rigidity and that the relationships between authoritarianism and Einstellung rigidity were not consistent. This was also true when other measures of rigidity were related to authoritarianism. One exception to this was the series of studies concerned with perceptual rigidity, where high-authoritarian subjects evidenced greater rigidity than low-authoritarian subjects.

There are some data that indicate that dogmatic subjects tend to be rigid. Openness to novel information may also be considered an aspect of rigidity. There are some data that indicate that high-dogmatic subjects are less accepting of novel stimuli than low-dogmatic subjects. The data regarding field dependence are more consistent, indicating that field-dependent individuals are more rigid than field-independent individuals.

INTOLERANCE OF AMBIGUITY

Data regarding the relationship between authoritarianism and intolerance of ambiguity are fairly clear. In studies involving perceptual measures of intolerance of ambiguity (e.g., the autokinetic phenomenon), paper-and-pencil measures of intolerance of ambiguity (the Walk and Budner scales), and impression formation tasks, authoritarian subjects are generally found to be less tolerant of ambiguity than subjects low in authoritarianism.

Although fewer data exist for the relationship between dogmatism and intolerance of ambiguity, the studies that have been done suggest a similar relationship. This relationship also holds for field dependence.

ANALYTIC AND SYNTHESIZING ABILITY

Rokeach's interest in analysis and synthesis appears to be a forerunner of the interest of Harvey, Hunt, and Schroder in differentiation and integration. Rokeach's hypothesis that high-dogmatic subjects would not differ from low-dogmatic subjects in analytic ability, but would perform worse in tasks involving synthesis was generally supported by research using the Doodlebug problem. However, this relationship received less support when other measures of analysis and synthesis were used.

In the related area of discrimination and synthesis, the data indicate poorer performance by field-dependent than field-independent individuals.

CONFORMITY

Rokeach hypothesized that subjects low in dogmatism would be able to differentiate the information value of a message from the source of the message. The results of several studies generally supported this hypothesis by showing that high-dogmatic subjects are more likely to be influenced by the authority of the source person than are low-dogmatic subjects.

A number of investigators studied the relationship between conformity and field dependence and found some evidence for the existence of such a relationship.

CREATIVITY

The creative person appears to be one who is open to new information, able to synthesize, and flexible. Thus one would expect subjects low in dogmatism to be more creative than those high in dogmatism. There is little support for this hypothesis. Further, there is little evidence of a relationship between field dependence and creativity.

ACCURACY OF JUDGMENT

To the extent that individuals are influenced by irrelevant factors in the stimulus field, the accuracy of their judgments should be adversely affected. Such a relationship appears to hold with regard to dogmatism. In the area of cognitive complexity, a number of studies generally fail to document greater accuracy in the perception of others by subjects high in cognitive complexity compared to subjects low in cognitive complexity.

Although there have been a number of studies concerned with differences in social perception of authoritarian and nonauthoritarian subjects (e.g., Scodel & Mussen, 1953; Scodel & Freedman, 1956; Crockett & Meidinger 1956; Lipetz, 1960), on the basis of these studies it is difficult to make a summary statement about differences in the accuracy of perceptions of members of the two groups.

EFFECTS OF STRESS

There are some data to indicate that the rigidity of high authoritarian subjects increases under conditions of stress (often defined as high ego involvement). This finding was not replicated with regard to intolerance of ambiguity.

In some studies involving integrative complexity, stress was equated with information overload (e.g., war in an internation simulation). At other times it was equated with low levels of information (e.g., sensory deprivation). Stress was often found to lower the levels of integrative complexity. There is only partial support for the hypothesis that stress affects field-dependent subjects more than it does field-independent subjects.

CONSISTENCY

Data regarding the relationship between dogmatism and consistency do not indicate a clear relationship between the two variables. There is some evidence that individuals high in cognitive complexity are better able to integrate inconsistent information than subjects low in cognitive complexity. However, as Shaffer (1975) concluded from his review, the details of the relationship between cognitive style and consistency are unclear.

ENVIRONMENTAL COMPLEXITY

One particularly worthwhile endeavor is to study the relationship between cognitive style and performance in various environments. Except for work on integrative complexity, research in this area is almost nonexistent. In the area of integrative complexity, a number of studies have indicated differential adverse effects of environments of low and high complexity on subjects differing in levels of integrative complexity. There is clearly sufficient promise in this line of research to warrant its extension to other areas of cognitive style.

A FINAL WORD

Each of the five approaches to the study of cognitive style has been shown to relate to behavior of one sort or another. Additional work on instruments and the use of multivariate statistical procedures should further clarify these relationships. In particular, research directed toward the examination of the interaction between levels of cognitive style and environmental dimensions appears especially important.

References

Acker, M., & McReynolds, P. (1965). The obscure figures test: An instrument for measuring "cognitive innovation." *Perceptual and Motor Skills, 21,* 815–821.

Adams, H. E., & Vidulich, R. N. (1962). Dogmatism and belief congruence in paired-associate learning. *Psychological Reports, 10,* 91–94.

Adams-Webber, J. R. (1969). Cognitive complexity and sociality. British *Journal of Social and Clinical Psychology, 8,* 211–216.

Adams-Webber, J. R. (1970a). Actual structure and potential chaos: Relational aspects of progressive variations within a personal construct system. In D. Bannister (Ed.), *Perspectives in personal construct theory.* New York: Academic.

Adams-Webber, J. R. (1970b). An analysis of the discriminate validity of several repertory grid indices. *British Journal of Psychology, 61,* 83–90.

Adams-Webber, J. B. (1970c). Elicited verus provided constructs in repertory grid technique: A review. *British Journal of Medical Psychology, 43,* 349–354.

Adams-Webber, J. R. (1973). The complexity of the target as a factor in interpersonal Judgement. *Social Behavior and Personality, 1,* 35–38.

Adams-Webber, J. R., Schwenker, B., & Barbeau, D. (1972). Personal constructs and the perception of individual differences. *Canadian Journal of Behavioural Science, 4,* 218–224.

Adelson, J. (1953). A study of minority group authoritarianism. *Journal of Abnormal and Social Psychology, 48,* 477–485.

Adevai, G., & McGough, W. E. (1968). Retest reliability of rod-and-frame scores during early adulthood. *Perceptual and Motor Skills, 26,* 1306.

Adevai, G., Silverman, A. J., & McGough, W. E. (1968). Perceptual correlates of the Rod-and-Frame Test. *Perceptual and Motor Skills, 26,* 1055–1065.

Adorno, T. W., Frenkel-Brunswik, E., Levinson, D. J., & Sanford, R. N. (1950). *The authoritarian personality.* New York: Harper & Row.

Allard, M., & Carlson, E. R. (1963). The generality of cognitive complexity. *Journal of Social Psychology, 59,* 73–75.

Allport, G. W. (1937). *Personality: A psychological interpretation.* New York: Holt.

Alter, R. D., & White, B. J. (1966). Some norms for the Dogmatism Scale. *Psychological Reports, 19,* 967–969.

Anderson, A. R., & Moore, O. K. (1960). Autotelic folk-models. *Sociological Quarterly, 1,* 203–216.

Anderson, C. C. (1962). A developmental study of dogmatism during adolescence with reference to sex differences. *Journal of Abnormal and Social Psychology, 65,* 132–135.

227

Angyal, A. F. (1948). The diagnosis of neurotic traits by means of a new perceptual test. *Journal of Psychology, 25,* 105–135.

Applezweig, D. G. (1954). Some determinants of behavioral rigidity. *Journal of Abnormal and Social Psychology, 49,* 224–228.

Arbuthnot, J. (1972). Cautionary note on measurement of field independence. *Perceptual and Motor Skills, 35,* 479–488.

Asch, S. E. (1946). Forming impressions of personality. *Journal of Abnormal and Social Psychology, 41,* 258–290.

Asher, J. W. (1961). Comment on "The relationship between rigidity–flexibility in children and their parents." *Child Development, 32,* 607–608.

Athanasiou, R. (1968). Technique without mystique: A study of authoritarianism in engineering students. *Educational and Psychological Measurement, 28,* 1181–1188.

Ault, R. L., Mitchell, C., & Hartmann, D. P. (1976). Some methodological problems in reflection–impulsivity research. *Child Development, 47,* 227–231.

Axelrod, S., & Cohen, L. D. (1961). Senescence and embedded-figures performance in vision and touch. *Perceptual and Motor Skills, 12,* 283–288.

Ayers, J. B., & Turck, M. J., Jr. (1976). Longitudinal study of change in teacher dogmatism. *College Student Journal, 10,* 84–87.

Baer, D. J. (1964). Factors in perception and rigidity. *Perceptual and Motor Skills, 19,* 563–570.

Bailes, D. W., & Guller, I. B. (1968). *Dogmatism and attitudes toward the Viet Nam War.* Paper presented at meeting of the American Psychological Association, Washington, D.C.

Bailes, D., & Guller, I. (1970). Dogmatism and attitudes towards the Vietnam War. *Sociometry, 33,* 140–146.

Baldwin, B. A. (1972). Autonomic stress resolution in prepressors and sensitizers following microcounseling. *Psychological Reports, 31,* 743–749.

Bales, R. F., & Couch, A. (1956). *A factor analysis of values.* Unpublished manuscript, Laboratory of Social Relations, Harvard University.

Bannister, D., & Fransella, F. (1971). *Inquiring man.* Baltimore: Penguin.

Bannister, D., & Mair, J. M. M. (1968). *The evaluation of personal constructs.* New York: Academic.

Banta, T., Sciarra, J., Sinclair, D., Jett, J., & Gilbert, M. (1969). *Cincinnati Autonomy Test Battery.* Cincinnati: University of Cincinnati.

Banta, T. J. (1970). Tests for the evaluation of early childhood education: The Cincinnati Autonomy Test Battery (CATB). In J. Hellmuth (Ed.), *Cognitive studies,* Vol. 1. New York: Brunner/Mazel.

Barclay, A., & Cusumano, D. R. (1967). Father absence, cross-sex identity, and field-dependent behavior in male adolescents. *Child Development, 38,* 243–250.

Bard, C. (1972). The relation between perceptual style and physical activities. *International Journal of Sport Psychology, 3,* 107–113.

Barker, E. N. (1963). Authoritarianism of the political right, center, and left. *Journal of Social Issues, 19,* 63–74.

Barrett, G. V., Cabe, P. A., & Thornton, C. L. (1968). Relation between hidden figures test and rod and frame test measures of perceptual style. *Educational and Psychological Measurement, 28,* 551–554.

Bass, B. M. (1955). Authoritarianism or acquiescence? *Journal of Abnormal and Social Psychology, 51,* 616–623.

Bauman, G. (1951). *The stability of the individual's mode of perception, and perception-personality relationships.* Unpublished doctoral dissertation, New York University.

Bavelas, J. B., Chan, A. S., & Guthrie, J. A. (1976). Reliability and validity of traits measured by Kelly's repertory grid. *Canadian Journal of Behavioural Science, 8,* 23–38.

Becker, G. (1967). Ability to differentiate message from source as a curvilinear function of scores on Rokeach's Dogmatism Scale. *Journal of Social Psychology, 72,* 265–273.

Becker, G., & DiLeo, D. T. (1967). Scores on Rokeach's Dogmatism Scale and the response set to present a positive social and personal image. *Journal of Social Psychology, 71,* 287–293.

Bender, M. P. (1974). Provided versus elicited constructs: An explanation of Warr & Coffman's (1970) anomalous finding. *British Journal of Social and Clinical Psychology, 13,* 329.

Bendig, A. W. (1959). An inter-item factor analysis of the California F (authoritarianism) Scale. *Journal of Psychological Studies, 11,* 22–26.

Bendig, A. W. (1960). A further factor analysis of the California F Scale. *Journal of Psychological Studies, 11,* 248–252.

Berdie, R. F. (1974). College courses and changes in dogmatism. *Research in Higher Education, 2,* 133–143.

Berkowitz, N. H., & Wolkon, G. H. (1964). A forced-choice form of the F Scale—free of acquiescent response set. *Sociometry, 27,* 54–65.

Berlyne, D. E. (1960). *Conflict, arousal, and curiosity.* New York: McGraw-Hill.

Bernhardson, C. S. (1967). Dogmatism, defense mechanisms, and social desirability responding. *Psychological Reports, 20,* 511–513.

Bernhardson, C. S. (1971). Acquiescence and the F Scale: New analysis not supporting Samelson and Yates. *Canadian Journal of Behavioral Science, 3,* 11–17.

Bettinghaus, E., Miller, G., & Steinfatt, T. (1970). Source evaluation, syllogistic content, and judgments of logical validity by high- and low-dogmatic persons. *Journal of Personality and Social Psychology, 16,* 238–244.

Bhushan, L. I. (1971). A study of leadership preference in relation to authoritarianism and intolerance of ambiguity. *Journal of the Indian Academy of Applied Psychology, 8,* 34–38.

Bieri, J. (1955). Cognitive complexity-simplicity and predictive behavior. *Journal of Abnormal and Social Psychology, 51,* 263–268.

Bieri, J. (1965). *Cognitive complexity: Assessment issues in the study of cognitive structure.* Unpublished manuscript.

Bieri, J. (1966). Cognitive complexity and personality development. In O. J. Harvey (Ed.), *Experience, structure and adaptability.* New York: Springer.

Bieri, J. (1968). Cognitive complexity and judgment of inconsistent information. In R. P. Abelson, E. Aronson, W. J. McGuire, T. M. Newcomb, M. J. Rosenberg, & P. E. Tannenbaum (Eds.), *Theories of cognitive consistency: A sourcebook.* Chicago: Rand McNally.

Bieri, J. (1969). Category width as a measure of discrimination. *Journal of Personality, 37,* 513–521.

Bieri, J. (1971). Cognitive structures in personality. In H. M. Schroder & P. Suedfeld (Eds.), *Personality theory and information processing.* New York: Ronald.

Bieri, J. (1960). Parental identification, acceptance of authority and within-sex differences in cognitive behavior. *Journal of Abnormal and Social Psychology, 60,* 76–79.

Bieri, J., Atkins, A. L., Briar, S., Leaman, R. L., Miller, H., & Tripodi, T. (1966). *Clinical and social judgment: The discrimination of behavioral information.* New York: Wiley.

Bieri, J., & Blacker, E. (1956). The generality of cognitive complexity in the perception of people and inkblots. *Journal of Abnormal and Social Psychology, 53,* 112–117.

Bieri, J., Bradburn, W., & Galinsky, M. D. (1958). Sex differences in perceptual behavior. *Journal of Personality, 26,* 1–12.

Bieri, J., & Lobeck, R. (1959). Acceptance of authority and parental identification. *Journal of Personality, 27,* 74–86.

Bigelow, G. S. (1971). Field dependence-field independence in 5- to 10-year old children. *Journal of Educational Research, 64,* 397–400.

Bishop, D. W., & Chace, C. A. (1971). Parental conceptual systems, home play environment, and potential creativity in children. *Journal of Experimental Child Psychology, 12,* 318–338.

Blackman, S. (1966). The application of multidimensional scaling to the measurement of cognitive patterning. In J. L. Kennedy, B. L. Koslin, H. M. Schroder, S. Blackman, J. D. Ramsey, & C. E. Helm, Cognitive patterning of complex stimuli: A symposium. *Journal of General Psychology, 74,* 25–49.

Blasi, E. R., Cross, H. A., & Hebert, J. A. (1972). Effects of field-independency on weight comparisons. *Perceptual and Motor Skills, 35,* 111–114.

Block, J. (1955). Personality characteristics associated with fathers' attitudes toward child rearing. *Child Development, 26,* 41–48.

Block, J., & Block, J. (1951). An investigation of the relationship between intolerance of ambiguity and ethnocentrism. *Journal of Personality, 19,* 303–311.

Block, J., Block, J. H., & Harrington, D. M. (1974). Some misgivings about the Matching Familiar Figures Test as a measure of reflection—impulsivity. *Developmental Psychology, 10,* 611–632.

Block, J., Block, J. H., & Harrington, D. M. (1975). Comment on the Kagan-Messer reply. *Developmental Psychology, 11,* 249–252.

Blowers, G. H. (1974). Field dependence and distraction in a simple psychomotor task with a constant foreperiod. *Perceptual and Motor Skills, 39,* 1239–1244.

Blowers, G. H. (1976). Field dependence and distraction revisited. *Perceptual and Motor Skills, 42,* 295–297.

Blum, A. (1959). The relationship between rigidity–flexibility in children and their parents. *Child Development, 30,* 297–304.

Bodden, J. L. (1970). Cognitive complexity as a factor in appropriate vocational choice. *Journal of Counseling Psychology, 17,* 364–368.

Bodden, J. L., & James, L. E. (1976). Influence of occupational information giving on cognitive complexity. *Journal of Counseling Psychology, 23,* 280–282.

Bodden, J. L., & Klein, A. J. (1973). Cognitive differentiation and affective stimulus value in vocational judgments. *Journal of Vocational Behavior, 3,* 75–79.

Bonarius, J. C. J. (1965). Research in the personal construct theory of George A. Kelly: Role Construct Repertory Test and basic theory. In B. A. Maher (Ed.), *Progress in experimental personality research,* Vol. 2. New York: Academic.

Bone, R. N., & Choban, M. C. (1972). Sensation-seeking scale, form IV, and field independence. *Perceptual and Motor Skills, 34,* 634.

Bottenberg, E. H. (1969). Instrumental characteristics and validity of the Paragraph Completion Test (PCT) as a measure of integrative complexity. *Psychological Reports, 24,* 437–438.

Bowd, A. D. (1974). Retest reliability of the Children's Embedded Figures Test for young children. *Perceptual and Motor Skills, 39,* 442.

Bowd, A. D. (1976a). Absence of sex differences on the Children's Embedded-Figures Test. *Perceptual and Motor Skills, 43,* 729–730.

Bowd, A. D. (1976b). Item difficulty on the Children's Embedded-Figures Test. *Perceptual and Motor Skills, 43*, 134.

Breskin, S. (1968). Measurement of rigidity, a non-verbal test. *Perceptual and Motor Skills, 27*, 1203–1206.

Breskin, S., & Gorman, B. S. (1969). On rigidity and field dependence. *Perceptual and Motor Skills, 29*, 541–542.

Brierley, D. W. (1967). *The use of personality constructs by children of three different ages.* Unpublished doctoral dissertation, London University.

Brightman, H. J., & Urban, T. F. (1974). The influence of the dogmatic personality upon information processing: A comparison with a Bayesian information processor. *Organizational Behavior and Performance, 11*, 266–276.

Brody, N. (1972). *Personality research and theory.* New York: Academic.

Broverman, D. M. (1960a). Cognitive style and intra-individual variation in abilities. *Journal of Personality, 28*, 240–256.

Broverman, D. M. (1960b). Dimensions of cognitive style. *Journal of Personality, 28*, 167–185.

Brown, D. R., & Datta, L. (1959). Authoritarianism, verbal ability, and response set. *Journal of Abnormal and Social Psychology, 58*, 131–133.

Brown, R. (1965). *Social psychology.* New York: Free Press.

Brown, R. W. (1953). A determinant of the relationship between rigidity and authoritarianism. *Journal of Abnormal and Social Psychology, 48*, 469–476.

Bruner, J. S. (1956). A cognitive theory of personality. *Contemporary Psychology, 1*, 355–357.

Bruner, J. S., Goodnow, J., & Austin, G. A. (1956). *A study of thinking.* New York: Wiley.

Budner, S. (1962). Intolerance of ambiguity as a personality variable. *Journal of Personality, 30*, 29–50.

Burke, W. W. (1966). Social perception as a function of dogmatism. *Perceptual and Motor Skills, 23*, 863–868.

Busch, J. C., & DeRidder, L. M. (1973). Conformity in preschool disadvantaged children as related to field-dependence, sex, and verbal reinforcement. *Psychological Reports, 32*, 667–673.

Busch, J. C., & Simon, L. H. (1972). *Methodological variables in the study of field dependent behavior of young children.* Paper presented at the meeting of the American Educational Research Association, Chicago.

Busse, T. V. (1968). Establishment of the flexible thinking factor in fifth-grade boys. *Journal of Psychology, 69*, 93–100.

Byrne, D. (1965). Parental antecedents of authoritarianism. *Journal of Personality and Social Psychology, 1*, 369–373.

Campbell, D. R., Dyer, F. N., & Boersma, F. J. (1967). Field dependency and picture recognition ability. *Perceptual and Motor Skills, 25*, 713–716.

Campbell, D. T., Siegman, C. R., & Rees, M. B. (1967). Direction-of-wording effects in the relationships between scales. *Psychological Bulletin, 68*, 293–303.

Campbell, V. N. (1960). *Assumed similarity, perceived sociometric balance, and social influence.* Unpublished doctoral dissertation, University of Colorado.

Canavan, D. (1969). *Field dependence in children as a function of grade, sex, and ethnic group membership.* Paper presented at the meeting of the American Psychological Association, Washington, D.C.

Caracena, F. K., & King, G. (1962). Generality of individual differences in complexity. *Journal of Clinical Psychology, 18*, 234–236.

Carr, J. E. (1965a). Cognitive complexity: Construct descriptive terms vs. cognitive process. *Psychological Reports, 16,* 133–134.

Carr, J. E. (1965b). The role of conceptual organization in interpersonal discrimination. *Journal of Psychology, 59,* 159–176.

Carr, J. E. (1969). Differentiation as a function of source characteristics and judge's conceptual structure. *Journal of Personality, 37,* 378–386.

Cattell, R. B., Eber, H. W., & Tatsouka, M. M. (1970). *Handbook for the sixteen personality factors questionnaire (16 P.F.) in clinical, educational, and research psychology.* Champaign, Ill.: Institute for Personality and Ability Testing.

Cattell, R. B., & Tiner, L. G. (1949). The varieties of structural rigidity. *Journal of Personality, 17,* 321–341.

Cegalis, J. A., & Young, R. (1974). Effect of inversion-induced conflict on field dependence. *Journal of Abnormal Psychology, 83,* 373–379.

Chabassol, D. J., & Thomas, D. (1975). Needs for structure, tolerance of ambiguity and dogmatism in adolescents. *Psychological Reports, 37,* 507–510.

Chapko, M. K., & Lewis, M. H. (1975). Authoritarianism and *All in the Family. Journal of Psychology, 90,* 245–248.

Chapman, L. J., & Bock, R. D. (1958). Components of variance due to acquiescence and content in the F Scale measure of authoritarianism. *Psychological Bulletin, 55,* 328–333.

Chapman, L. J., & Campbell, D. T. (1957). Response set in the F Scale. *Journal of Abnormal and Social Psychology, 54,* 129–132.

Chapman, L. J., & Campbell, D. T. (1959). The effect of acquiescence response-set upon relationships among the F-Scale, ethnocentrism, and intelligence. *Sociometry, 22,* 153–161.

Child, I. L. (1965). Personality correlates of ethnic judgment in college students. *Journal of Personality, 33,* 476–511.

Chown, S. M. (1959). Rigidity: A flexible concept. *Psychological Bulletin, 56,* 195–223.

Christie, R. (1952). Changes in authoritarianism as related to situational factors. *American Psychologist, 7,* 307–308. (Abstract)

Christie, R. (1954). Authoritarianism re-examined. In R. Christie & Jahoda (Eds.), *Studies in the scope and method of "The authoritarian personality."* New York: Free Press.

Christie, R. (1956a). Eyesenck's treatment of the personality of communists. *Psychological Bulletin, 53,* 411–430.

Christie, R. (1966). Some abuses of psychology. *Psychological Bulletin, 54,* 439–451.

Christie, R., & Cook, P. (1958). A guide to published literature relating to the authoritarian personality through 1956. *Journal of Psychology, 45,* 171–199.

Christie, R., & Garcia, J. (1951). Subcultural variation in authoritarian personality. *Journal of Abnormal and Social Psychology, 46,* 457–469.

Christie, R., Havel, J., & Seidenberg, B. (1958). Is the F Scale irreversible? *Journal of Abnormal and Social Psychology, 56,* 143–159.

Christie, R., & Jahoda, M. (Eds.). (1954). *Studies in the scope and method of "The authoritarian personality."* New York: Free Press.

Clarke, P., & James, J. (1967). The effects of situation, attitude, intensity and personality on information-seeking. *Sociometry, 30,* 235–245.

Clark, S. L. (1968). Authoritarian attitudes and field dependence. *Psychological Reports, 22,* 309–310.

Claunch, N. C. (1964). *Cognitive and motivational characteristics associated with con-*

crete and abstract levels of conceptual complexity. Unpublished doctoral dissertation, Princeton University.

Clayton, M. B., & Jackson, D. N. (1961). Equivalence range, acquiescence, and over-generalization. *Educational and Psychological Measurement, 21,* 371–382.

Coates, S. (1974). Sex differences in field dependence-independence between the ages of 3 and 6. *Perceptual and Motor Skills, 39,* 1307–1310.

Coates, S. (1975). Field independence and intellectual functioning in preschool children. *Perceptual and Motor Skills, 41,* 251–254.

Coates, S. W. (1972). *The Preschool Embedded Figures Test Manual.* Palo Alto: Consulting Psychologists Press.

Coates, S. Lord, M., & Jakabovics, E. (1975). Field dependence-independence, social-non-social play and sex differences in preschool children. *Perceptual and Motor Skills, 40,* 195–202.

Cohen, H. S., & Feldman, J. M. (1975). *On the domain specificity of cognitive complexity: An alternative approach.* Paper presented at the meeting of the American Psychological Association, Chicago.

Cohen, J. (1965). Some statistical issues in psychological research. In B. B. Wolman (Ed.), *Handbook of clinical psychology.* New York: McGraw-Hill.

Cohn, T. S. (1952). Is the F Scale indirect? *Journal of Abnormal and Social Psychology, 47,* 732.

Cohn, T. S. (1953). The relation of the F Scale to a response set to answer positively. *American Psychologist, 8,* 335. (Abstract)

Cohn, T. S. (1956). Relation of the F Scale to a response set to answer positively. *Journal of Social Psychology, 44,* 129–133.

Cohn, T. S., & Carsch, H. (1954). Administration of the F Scale to a sample of Germans. *Journal of Abnormal and Social Psychology, 49,* 471.

Comalli, P. E., Jr. (1965). Cognitive functioning in a group of 80- to 90-year-old men. *Journal of Gerontology, 20,* 14–17.

Comrey, A. L., Backer, T. E., & Glaser, E. M. (1973). *A sourcebook for mental health measures.* Unpublished manuscript, Human Interaction Research Institute, Los Angeles.

Constantinople, A. (1974). Analytical ability and perceived similarity to parents. *Psychological Reports, 35,* 1335–1345.

Coop, A. H., & Sigel, I. E. (1971). Cognitive style: Implications for learning and instruction. *Psychology in the Schools, 2,* 152–161.

Cooper, J. B., & Blair, M. A. (1959). Parent evaluations as a determiner of ideology. *Journal of Genetic Psychology, 94,* 93–100.

Cooper, J. B., & Lewis, J. H. (1962). Parent evaluation as related to social ideology and academic achievement. *Journal of Genetic Psychology, 101,* 135–143.

Corah, N. L. (1965a). Differentiation in children and their parents. *Journal of Personality, 33,* 300–308.

Corah, N. L. (1965b). Effects of the visual field upon perception of change in spatial orientation. *Journal of Experimental Psychology, 70,* 598–601.

Corfield, V. K. (1971). *An attempt to predict academic stability of university freshmen.* Paper presented at the meeting of the Canadian Guidance and Counsellor Association, Toronto.

Couch, H., & Keniston, K. (1960). Yeasayers and naysayers: Agreeing response set as a personality variable. *Journal of Abnormal and Social Psychology, 60,* 151–174.

Cox, G. B. (1974). A comparison of two measures of cognitive complexity and their relationships with intelligence, sex, age, and race. JSAS *Catalog of Selected Documents in Psychology, 4,* 80.

Crandall, V. J., & Lacey, W. (1972). Children's perceptions of inter-external control in intellectual-academic situations and their Embedded Figures Test performance. *Child Development, 43,* 1123–1124.

Crandall, V. J., & Sinkeldam, C. (1964). Children's dependent and achievement behaviors in social situations and their perceptual field dependence. *Journal of Personality, 32,* 1–22.

Crano, W. D., & Schroder, H. M. (1967). Complexity of attitude structure and processes of conflict resolution. *Journal of Personality and Social Psychology, 5,* 110–114.

Crano, W. D., & Sigal, J. A. (1968). The effect of dogmatism upon pattern of response to attitudinally discrepant information. *Journal of Social Psychology, 75,* 241–247.

Crockett, W. H. (1965). Cognitive complexity and impression formation. In B. A. Maher (Ed.), *Progress in experimental personality research,* Vol. 2. New York: Academic.

Crockett, W. H., & Meidinger, T. (1956). Authoritarianism and interpersonal perception. *Journal of Abnormal and Social Psychology, 53,* 378–380.

Cronbach, L. J. (1956). Assessment of individual differences. *Annual Review of Psychology, 7,* 173–176.

Cross, H. J. (1964). *A manual for scoring responses to interview on child rearing.* Unpublished manuscript, University of Connecticut.

Cross, H. J. (1966). The relation of parental training conditions to conceptual level in adolescent boys. *Journal of Personality, 34,* 348–365.

Crowne, D. P., & Marlowe, D. (1964). *The approval motive.* New York: Wiley.

Crutchfield, R. S. (1954). Social psychology and group processes. *Annual Review of Psychology, 5,* 171–202.

Crutchfield, R. S., Woodworth, D. G., & Albrecht, R. E. (1958). *Perceptual performance and the effective person.* USAF WADC Technical Note, No. 58-60.

Curry, D. J., & Menasco, M. (1977). *An assessment of the Construct Role Repertory Test* (Bureau of Business and Economic Research, Working Paper Series No. 77-11). Iowa City: University of Iowa.

Davids, A. (1955). Some personality and intellectual correlates of intolerance of ambiguity. *Journal of Abnormal and Social Psychology, 51,* 415–420.

Davids, A. (1956). The influence of ego-involvement on relations between authoritarianism and intolerance of ambiguity. *Journal of Consulting Psychology, 20,* 179–184.

Davis, T. B., Frye, R. L., & Joure, S. (1975). Perceptions and behaviors of dogmatic subjects in a T-group setting. *Perceptual and Motor Skills, 41,* 375–381.

Dawson, J. L. (1967). Cultural and physiological influences upon spatial-perceptual processes in West Africa: Part I. *International Journal of Psychology, 2,* 115–128.

Day, H. (1966). Looking time as a function of stimulus variables and individual differences. *Perceptual and Motor Skills, 22,* 423–428.

Deaux, K., & Farris, E. (1975). Complexity, extremity, and affect in male and female judgments. *Journal of Personality, 43,* 379–389.

Delia, J. G., Clark, R. A., & Switzer, D. E. (1974). Cognitive complexity and impression formation in formal social interaction. *Speech Monographs, 41,* 299–308.

Denmark, F. L., Havlena, R. A., & Murgatroyd, D. (1971). Reevaluation of some measures of cognitive styles. *Perceptual and Motor Skills, 33,* 133–134.

Dershowitz, Z. (1971). Jewish subcultural patterns and psychological differentiation. *International Journal of Psychology, 6,* 223–231.

Dickstein, L. S. (1968). Field independence in concept attainment. *Perceptual and Motor Skills, 27,* 635–642.

DiRenzo, G. J. (1967). Professional politicians and personality structures. *American Journal of Sociology, 73,* 217–225.

DiRenzo, G. J. (1968). Dogmatism and presidential preferences in the 1964 elections. *Psychological Reports, 22,* 1197–1202.

DiRenzo, G. J. (1971). Dogmatism and presidential preferences: A 1968 replication. *Psychological Reports, 29,* 109–110.

Domash, L., & Balter, L. (1976). Sex and psychological differentiation in preschoolers. *Journal of Genetic Psychology, 128,* 77–84.

Dommert, E. M. (1967). *An adaptation of Rokeach's Dogmatism Scale for use with elementary school children.* Unpublished master's thesis, Texas Women's University.

Dreyer, A. S., Dreyer, C. A., & Nebelkopf, E. B. (1971). Portable Rod-and-Frame Test as a measure of cognitive style in kindergarten children. *Perceptual and Motor Skills, 33,* 775–781.

Dreyer, A. S., Hulac, V., & Rigler, D. (1971). Differential adjustment to pubescence and cognitive style patterns. *Developmental Psychology, 4,* 456–462.

Dreyer, A. S., Nebelkopf, E. B., & Dreyer, C. A. (1969). A note concerning stability of cognitive style measures in young children. *Perceptual and Motor Skills, 28,* 933–934.

Droppleman, L. F., & Schaefer, E. S. (1963). Boys' and girls' reports of maternal and paternal behavior. *Journal of Abnormal and Social Psychology, 67,* 648–654.

Dubois, T. E., & Cohen, W. (1970). Relationship between measures of psychological differentiation and intellectual ability. *Perceptual and Motor Skills, 31,* 411–416.

Duck, S. W. (1972). Friendship, similarity and the Rep Test. *Psychological Reports, 31,* 231–234.

Duck, S. W., & Spencer, C. (1972). Personal constructs and friendship formation. *Journal of Personality and Social Psychology, 23,* 40–45.

Dumsha, T. C., Minard, J., & McWilliams, J. (1973). Comparison of two self-administered field dependency measures. *Perceptual and Motor Skills, 36,* 252–254.

Durand, R. M., & Lambert, Z. V. (1975). Dogmatism and exposure to political candidates. *Psychological Reports, 36,* 423–429.

Durand, R. M., & Lambert, Z. V. (1976). Generalizability of cognitive differentiation across product and social domains. *Psychological Reports, 39,* 665–666.

Dyer, F. N. (1973). The Stroop phenomenon and its use in the study of perceptual, cognitive, and response processes. *Memory and Cognition, 1,* 106–120.

Dyk, R. B. (1969). An exploratory study of mother-child interaction in infancy as related to the development of differentiation. *Journal of The American Academy of Child Psychiatry, 8,* 657–691.

Dyk, R. B., & Witkin, H. A. (1965). Family experiences related to the development of differentiation in children. *Child Development, 36,* 21–55.

Egeland, B., & Weinberg, R. A. (1976). The Matching Familiar Figures Test: A look at its psychometric credibility. *Child Development, 47,* 483–491.

Ehri, L. C., & Muzio, I. M. (1974). Cognitive style and reasoning about speed. *Journal of Educational Psychology, 66,* 569–571.

Ehrlich, D. (1965). "Intolerance of ambiguity," Walk's A Scale: Historical comment. *Psychological Reports, 17,* 591–594.

Ehrlich, H. J. (1961). Dogmatism and learning. *Journal of Abnormal and Social Psychology, 62,* 148–149.

Ehrlich, H. J., & Lee, D. (1969). Dogmatism, learning, and resistance to change: A review and a new paradigm. *Psychological Bulletin, 71,* 249–260.

Eisner, D. A. (1972). Developmental relationships between field independence and fixity-mobility. *Perceptual and Motor Skills, 34,* 767–770.

Eisner, D. A., & Williams, E. J. (1973). Assessment of perceptual field independence in freshman and senior undergraduates. *Perceptual and Motor Skills, 37,* 794.

Ekehammar, B. (1974). Interactionism in personality from a historical perspective. *Psychological Bulletin, 81,* 1026–1048.

Elkind, D. (1964). Ambiguous pictures for study of perceptual development and learning. *Child Development, 35,* 1391–1396.

Elliott, R. (1961). Interrelationships among measures of field dependence, ability, and personality traits. *Journal of Abnormal and Social Psychology, 63,* 27–36.

Epting, F. (1975). Order of presentation of construct poles: What are the factors to be considered? A reply. *British Journal of Social and Clinical Psychology, 14,* 427–428.

Epting, F., & Wilkins, G. (1974). Comparison of cognitive structural measures for predicting person perception. *Perceptual and Motor Skills, 38,* 727–730.

Epting, F. R. (1972). The stability of cognitive complexity in construing social issues. *British Journal of Social and Clinical Psychology, 11,* 122–125.

Epting, F. R., Wilkins, G., & Margulis, S. T. (1972). Relationship between cognitive differentiation and level of abstraction. *Psychological Reports, 31,* 367–370.

Erginel, A. (1972). The relation of cognitive style and intelligence to achievement and errors in thinking. *Hacettepe Bulletin of Social Sciences and Humanities, 4,* 8–20.

Erikson, E. H. (1942). Hitler's imagery and German youth. *Psychiatry, 5,* 475–493.

Escalona, S., & Leitch, M. (1953). *Early phases of personality development: A nonnormative study of infant behavior.* Evanston, Ill.: Child Development.

Evans, F. J. (1969). Effects of practice on the validity of a group-administered embedded figures test. *Acta Psychologica* (Amsterdam), *29,* 172–180.

Eysenck, H. J. (1954). *The psychology of politics.* London: Routledge & Kegan Paul.

Eysenck, H. J., & Coulter, T. T. (1972). The personality and attitudes of working- class British communists and fascists. *Journal of Social Psychology, 87,* 59–73.

Eysenck, H. J., & Eysenck, S. B. G. (1973). *Eysenck Personality Questionnaire (EPQ).* San Diego: Educational and Industrial Testing Service.

Farley, F. H. (1974). Sensation-seeking motive and field independence. *Perceptual and Motor Skills, 38,* 330.

Feather, N. T. (1969a). Cognitive differentiation, attitude strength, and dogmatism. *Journal of Personality, 37,* 111–126.

Feather, N. T. (1969b). Preference for information in relation to consistency, novelty, intolerance of ambiguity, and dogmatism. *Australian Journal of Psychology, 21,* 235–249.

Feather, N. T. (1971). Value difference in relation to ethnocentrism, intolerance of ambiguity, and dogmatism. *Personality, 2,* 349–366.

Feather, N. T. (1973). Cognitive differentiation, cognitive isolation, and dogmatism: Rejoinder and further analysis. *Sociometry, 36,* 221–236.

Felker, D. W., & Treffinger, D. J. (1970). Some evidence concerning the validity of an elementary school form of the Dogmatism Scale. *Journal of Experimental Education, 39,* 24–26.

Fenchel, C. H. (1958). *Cognitive rigidity as a behavioral variable manifested in intellectual and perceptual tasks by an outpatient population.* Unpublished doctoral dissertation, New York University.

Fertig, E. S., & Mayo, C. (1970). Impression formation as a function of trait consistency and cognitive complexity. *Journal of Experimental Research in Personality, 4,* 190–197.

Fiebert, M. (1967). Cognitive styles in the deaf. *Perceptual and Motor Skills, 24,* 319–329.

Figert, R. S., Jr. (1968). An elementary school form of the Dogmatism Scale. *Journal of Experimental Education, 37,* 19–23.

Fillenbaum, S., & Jackman, A. (1961). Dogmatism and anxiety in relation to problem solving—an extension of Rokeach's results. *Journal of Abnormal and Social Psychology, 63,* 212–214.

Fine, B. J. (1973). Field-dependence–independence as "sensitivity" of the nervous system: Supportive evidence with color and weight discrimination. *Perceptual and Motor Skills, 37,* 287–295.

Fisher, S. (1950). Patterns of personality rigidity and some of their determinants. *Psychological Monographs, 64* (1, Whole No. 307).

Fjeld, S. P., & Landfield, A. W. (1961). Personal construct consistency. *Psychological Reports, 8,* 127–129.

Forster, N. C., Vinacke, W. E., & Digman, J. M. (1955). Flexibility and rigidity in a variety of problem situations. *Journal of Abnormal and Social Psychology, 50,* 211–216.

Foulds, M. L., Guinan, J. F., & Warehime, R. G. (1974). Marathon group: Changes in a measure of dogmatism. *Small Group Behavior, 5,* 387–392.

Foulkes, D., & Foulkes, S. H. (1965). Self-concept, dogmatism and tolerance of trait inconsistency. *Journal of Personality and Social Psychology, 2,* 104–110.

Franklin, B. J., & Carr, R. A. (1971). Cognitive differentiation, cognitive isolation, and dogmatism. *Sociometry, 34,* 230–237.

Fransella, F., & Joyston-Bechal, M. P. (1971). An investigation of conceptual process and pattern change in a psychotherapy group over one year. *British Journal of Psychiatry, 119,* 199–206.

Fraser, C. O. (1976). Cognitive strategies and multidimensional scaling. *British Journal of Psychology, 67,* 399–406.

Frauenfelder, K. J. (1974a). A cognitive determinant of favorability of impression. *Journal of Social Psychology, 94,* 71–81.

Frauenfelder, K. J. (1974b). Integrative complexity and extreme responses. *Psychological Reports, 34,* 770.

French, E. G. (1955). Interrelation among some measures of rigidity under stress and nonstress conditions. *Journal of Abnormal and Social Psychology, 51,* 114–118.

Frenkel-Brunswik, E. (1948). A study of prejudice in children. *Human Relations, 1,* 295–306.

Frenkel-Brunswik, E. (1949). Intolerance of ambiguity as an emotional and perceptual personality variable. *Journal of Personality, 18,* 108–143.

Frenkel-Brunswik, E. (1951). Patterns of social and cognitive outlooks in children and parents. *American Journal of Orthopsychiatry, 21,* 543–558.

Frenkel-Brunswik, E. (1954). Further explorations by a contributor to "The Authoritarian Personality." In R. Christie & M. Jahoda (Eds.), *Studies in the scope and method of "The Authoritarian Personality."* New York: Free Press.

Fromm, E. (1936). A social psychological approach to "authority and family." In M. Horkheimer (Ed.), *Studien über Autorität und Familie.* Paris: Librairie Felix Alcan.

Fromm, E. (1941). *Escape from freedom.* New York: Farrar & Rinehart.

Fruchter, B., Rokeach, M., & Novak, E. G. (1958). A factorial study of dogmatism, opinionation, and related scales. *Psychological Reports, 4,* 19–22.

Gaensslen, H., May, F., & Wolpert, F. (1973). Relation between dogmatism and anxiety. *Psychological Reports, 33,* 955–958.

Gage, N. L., Leavitt, G. S., & Stone, G. C. (1957). The psychological meaning of acquiescence set for authoritarianism. *Journal of Abnormal and Social Psychology, 55,* 98–103.

Gallagher, J. J. (1957). Authoritarianism and attitudes toward children. *Journal of Social Psychology, 45,* 107–111.

Gardiner, G. S., & Schroder, H. M. (1972). Reliability and validity of the Paragraph Completion Test: Theoretical and empirical notes. *Psychological Reports, 31,* 959–962.

Gardner, R. W. (1953). Cognitive styles in categorizing behavior. *Journal of Personality, 22,* 214–233.

Gardner, R. W. (1959). Cognitive control principles and perceptual behavior. *Bulletin of the Menninger Clinic, 23,* 241–248.

Gardner, R. W. (1962). Cognitive controls in adaptation: Research and measurement. In S. Messick & J. Ross (Eds.), *Measurement in personality and cognition.* New York: Wiley.

Gardner, R. W. (1970). Cognitive structure formation, organismic equilibration, and individuality of conscious experience. *Journal for the Study of Consciousness, 3,* 119–136.

Gardner, R. W. (1973). Contrast reactivity: Situational and temporal stability of cognitive control. *Perceptual and Motor Skills, 36,* 617–618.

Gardner, R. W., Holzman, P. S., Klein, G. S., Linton, H. B., & Spence, D. P. (1959). Cognitive control: A study of individual consistencies in cognitive behavior. *Psychological Issues, 1* (4, Whole No. 4).

Gardner, R. W., Jackson, D. N., & Messick, S. J. (1960). Personality organization in cognitive controls and intellectual abilities. *Psychological Issues, 2* (4, Whole No. 8).

Gardner, R. W., Lohrenz, L., & Schoen, R. (1968). Cognitive control of differentiation in the perception of persons and objects. *Perceptual and Motor Skills, 26,* 311–330.

Gardner, R. W., & Long, R. I. (1960a). Cognitive controls as determinants of learning and remembering. *Psychologia, 3,* 165–171.

Gardner, R. W., & Long, R. I. (1960b). Leveling—sharpening and serial learning. *Perceptual and Motor Skills, 10,* 179–185.

Gardner, R. W., & Long, R. I. (1962a). Cognitive controls of attention and inhibition: A study of individual consistencies. *British Journal of Psychology, 53,* 381–388.

Gardner, R. W., & Long, R. I. (1962b). Control, defense and centration effect: A study of scanning behavior. *British Journal of Psychology, 53,* 129–140.

Gardner, R. W., & Moriarty, A. (1968). Dimensions of cognitive control at preadolescence. In R. Gardner (Ed.), *Personality development at preadolescence.* Seattle: University of Washington Press.

Gardner, R. W., & Schoen, R. A. (1962). Differentiation and abstraction in concept formation. *Psychological Monographs, 76,* (41, Whole No. 560).

Gerard, H. A. (1969). *Factors contributing to adjustment and achievement.* Progress Report of a Joint Project at Riverside Unified School District and the University of California, Riverside.

Gibson, H. B. (1962). The lie scale of the Maudsley Personality Inventory. *Acta Psychologica, 20,* 18–23.

Gibson, M. (1975). An illustration of the effect of the order of presentation of construct poles on Bieri's measure of cognitive complexity. *British Journal of Social and Clinical Psychology, 14,* 425–426.

Goldberger, L., & Bendich, S. (1972). Field-dependence and social responsiveness as determinants of spontaneously produced words. *Perceptual and Motor Skills, 34,* 883–886.

Golden, C. J. (1975). A group version of the Stroop Color and Word Test. *Journal of Personality Assessment, 39,* 386–388.

Goldstein, A., & Chance, J. (1965). Effects of practice on sex-related differences in performance on embedded figures. *Psychonomic Science, 3,* 361–362.

Goldstein, H. S., & Peck, R. (1973). Maternal differentiation, father absence, and cognitive differentiation in children. *Archives of General Psychiatry, 29,* 370–373.

Goldstein, K. M., & Blackman, S. (1976). Cognitive complexity, maternal child rearing, and acquiescence. *Social Behavior and Personality, 4,* 97–103.

Gollin, E. S. (1954). Forming impressions of personality. *Journal of Personality, 23,* 65–76.

Goodenough, D. R. (1976). The role of individual differences in field dependence as a factor in learning and memory. *Psychological Bulletin, 83,* 675–694.

Goodenough, D. R., & Eagle, C. J. (1963). A modification of the Embedded Figures Test for use with young children. *Journal of Genetic Psychology, 103,* 67–74.

Goodenough, D. R., & Karp, S. A. (1961). Field dependence and intellectual functioning. *Journal of Abnormal and Social Psychology, 63,* 241–246.

Goodenough, D. R., & Witkin, H. A. (1977). *Origins of the field-dependent and field-independent cognitive styles.* (ETS RB-77-9). Princeton: Educational Testing Service.

Goodman, B. (1960). *Field dependence and closure factors.* Unpublished manuscript.

Gormly, M. V., & Clore, C. L. (1969). Attraction, dogmatism, and attitude similarity-dissimilarity. *Journal of Experimental Research in Personality, 4,* 9–13.

Gottschaldt, K. (1926). Über den Einfluss der Erfahrung auf die Wahrnehmung von Figuren, I; Über den Einfluss gehaüfter Einpragung von Figuren auf ihre Sichtbarkeit in umfassenden Konfigurationen. *Psychologische Forschung, 8,* 261–317.

Gough, H. G. (1951). Studies of social intolerance: I. Some psychological and sociological correlates of anti-Semitism. *Journal of Social Psychology, 33,* 237–246.

Gough, H. G., Harris, D. B., Martin, W. E., & Edwards, M. (1950). Children's ethnic attitudes: I. Relationship to certain personality factors. *Child Development, 21,* 83–91.

Gough, H. G., & Lazzari, R. (1974). A 15-item form of the F Scale and a cross-cultural application. *Journal of Psychology, 88,* 39–46.

Gough, H. G., & Olton, R. M. (1972). Field independence as related to nonverbal measures of perceptual performance and cognitive ability. *Journal of Consulting and Clinical Psychology, 38,* 338–342.

Gough, H. G., & Sanford, R. N. (1952). *Rigidity as a psychological variable.* Unpublished manuscript, University of California, Institute of Personality Assessment and Research.

Granberg, D., & Corrigan, G. (1972). Authoritarianism, dogmatism and orientations toward the Vietnam War. *Sociometry, 35,* 468–476.

Greaves, G. (1971). Harvey's "This I Believe" test: Studies of reliability. *Psychological Reports, 28,* 387–390.

Greaves, G. (1972). Conceptual system functioning and selective recall of information. *Journal of Personality and Social Psychology, 21,* 327–332.

Greenberg, H., & Fare, D. (1959). An investigation of several variables and determinants of authoritarianism. *Journal of Social Psychology, 49,* 105–111.

Greenberg, H., Guerino, R., Lashen, M., Mayer, D., & Piskowski, D. (1963). Order of birth as a determinant of personality and attitudinal characteristics. *Journal of Social Psychology, 60,* 221–230.

Greene, L. R. (1976). Effects of field dependence on affective reactions and compliance in dyadic interactions. *Journal of Personality and Social Psychology, 34,* 569–577.

Grippin, P. C., & Ohnmacht, F. W. (1972). Relationship of field independence and dogmatism with an hierarchically arranged concept learning task. *Perceptual and Motor Skills, 34,* 983–986.

Gruenfeld, L., & Arbuthnot, J. (1969). Field independence as conceptual framework for prediction of variability in ratings of others. *Perceptual and Motor Skills, 28,* 31–44.

Gruenfeld, L., Weissenberg, P., & Loh, W. (1973). Achievement values, cognitive style and social class: A cross-cultural comparison of Peruvian and U.S. students. *International Journal of Psychology, 8,* 41–49.

Guertin, W. H. (1973). SORTO: Factor analyzing Q sorts of Kelly's personal construct productions. *Journal of Personality, 37,* 69–77.

Guetzkow, H. (1951). An analysis of the operation of set in problem-solving behavior. *Journal of General Psychology, 45,* 219–244.

Guilford, J. P. (1956). The structure of the intellect. *Psychological Bulletin, 53,* 267–293.

Guilford, J. P. (1959). *Personality.* New York: McGraw-Hill.

Gulo, E. V., & Lynch, M. D. (1973). Evidence on the validity of Rokeach Dogmatism Scale (DS) Form E. *College Student Journal, 7,* 62–67.

Gump, P. (1955). *Relation of efficiency of recognition to personality variables.* Unpublished doctoral dissertation, University of Colorado.

Haiman, F. S. (1964). A revised scale for the measurement of open-mindedness. *Speech Monographs, 31,* 97–102.

Haiman, F. S., & Duns, D. F. (1964). Validations in communicative behavior of attitude-scale measures of dogmatism. *Journal of Social Psychology, 64,* 287–297.

Halverson, C. F., Jr. (1970). Interpersonal perception: Cognitive complexity and trait implication. *Journal of Consulting and Clinical Psychology, 34,* 86–90.

Hampton, J. D. (1968). Intolerance of ambiguity: A coping mechanism or mode of evaluation? *Revista Interamericana de Psicologia, 9,* 43–49.

Handel, A. (1972). Perception of verticality of a modified portable Rod-and-Frame Test. *Perceptual and Motor Skills, 34,* 459–468.

Hanson, D. J. (1968). Dogmatism and authoritarianism. *Journal of Social Psychology, 76,* 89–95.

Hanson, D. J. (1973). Dogmatism and attitude extremity. *Journal of Social Psychology, 89,* 155–156.

Hanson, D. J. (1974). Dogmatism and authoritarianism: A bibliography of master's theses. JSAS *Catalog of Selected Documents in Psychology, 4,* 128.

Hanson, D. J. (1975a). Authoritarianism as a variable in political research. *Il Politico, 40,* 700–705.

Hanson, D. J. (1975b). Dogmatism and authoritarianism: A bibliography of doctoral dissertations. JSAS *Catalog of Selected Documents in Psychology, 5,* 329.

Hanson, D. J. (1976). Dogmatism and ideological orientation. *International Review of History and Political Science, 8,* 77–88.

Hanson, D. J., & Clune, M. (1973). Dogmatism and anxiety in relation to childhood experience. *Journal of Social Psychology, 91,* 157–158.

Hanson, D. J., & White, B. J. (1973). Authoritarianism and candidate preference in the 1972 presidential election. *Psychological Reports, 32,* 1158.

Harris, D. B., Gough, H. G., & Martin, W. E. (1950). Children's ethnic attitudes: II. Relationships to parental beliefs concerning child training. *Child Development, 21,* 169–181.

Hart, I. (1957). Maternal child rearing practices and authoritarian ideology. *Journal of Abnormal and Social Psychology, 55*, 232–237.

Harvey, J., & Hays, D. G. (1972). Effect of dogmatism and authority of the source of communication upon persuasion. *Psychological Reports, 30,* 119–122.

Harvey, O. J. (1963a). Authoritarianism and conceptual functioning in varied conditions. *Journal of Personality, 31*, 462–470.

Harvey, O. J. (1963b). *Cognitive determinants of role playing* (Technical Report No. 3, Contract Nonr 1147(07)). Boulder: University of Colorado.

Harvey, O. J. (1964). Some cognitive determinants of influencibility. *Sociometry, 27*, 208–221.

Harvey, O. J. (1965). Some situational and cognitive determinants of dissonance resolution. *Journal of Personality and Social Psychology, 1*, 349–355.

Harvey, O. J., Ed. (1966a). *Experience, structure and adaptability.* New York: Springer.

Harvey, O. J. (1966b). System structure flexibility and creativity. In O. J. Harvey (Ed.), *Experience, structure and adaptability.* New York: Springer.

Harvey, O. J., & Beverly, G. D. (1961). Some personality correlates of concept change through role playing. *Journal of Abnormal and Social Psychology, 63,* 125–130.

Harvey, O. J., & Felknor, C. (1970). Parent-child relations as an antecedent to conceptual functioning. In R. A. Hoppe, G. A. Milton, & E. C. Simmel (Eds.), *Early experiences and the processes of socialization.* New York: Academic.

Harvey, O. J., Hunt, D. E., & Schroder, H. M. (1961). *Conceptual systems and personality organization.* New York: Wiley.

Harvey, O. J., Prather, M., White, B. J., & Hoffmeister, J. K. (1968). Teachers' beliefs, classroom atmosphere and student behavior. *American Educational Research Journal, 5,* 151–166.

Harvey, O. J., Reich, J., & Wyer, R. S. (1968). Attitudinal direction, intensity and personality as determinants of differentiation. *Journal of Personality and Social Psychology, 10,* 472–478.

Harvey, O. J., & Schroder, H. M. (1963). Cognitive aspects of self and motivation. In O. J. Harvey (Ed.), *Motivation and social interaction.* New York: Ronald.

Harvey, O. J., & Ware, R. (1967). Personality differences in dissonance resolution. *Journal of Personality and Social Psychology, 7,* 227–230.

Heikkinen, C. A., & German, S. C. (1975). Change of counselor attitudes: Complications due to closed-mindedness. *Journal of Counseling Psychology, 22,* 170–172.

Hellkamp, D. T., & Marr, J. N. (1965). Dogmatism and field-dependency. *Perceptual and Motor Skills, 20,* 1046–1048.

Herkowitz, J. (1972). Moving Embedded Figures Test. *Research Quarterly, 43,* 479–488.

Hess, H. F. (1966). Additional evidence on the generality of cognitive complexity. *Perceptual and Motor Skills, 23,* 857–858.

Hession, E., & McCarthy, E. (1975). Human performance in assessing subjective probability distribution. *Irish Journal of Psychology, 3,* 31–46.

Hewitt, D. (1972). Conceptual complexity, environment complexity, communication salience and an attitude change. *European Journal of Social Psychology, 2,* 285–305.

Higgins, J. (1965). Authoritarianism and candidate preference. *Psychological Reports, 16,* 603–604.

Higgins, J., & Kuhlman, D. (1967). Authoritarianism and candidate preference: II. *Psychological Reports, 20,* 572.

Hill, E., & Feigenbaum, K. D. (1966). Altering field dependence through stress. *Perceptual and Motor Skills, 23,* 1200.

Hill, K., & Kuiken, D. (1975). Conceptual complexity and concept learning of painting styles. *Journal of Personality and Social Psychology, 32,* 154–159.

Himelhoch, J. (1947). Is there a bigot personality? *Commentary, 3,* 277–284.

Hinkle, D. N. (1970). The game of personal constructs. In D. Bannister (Ed.), *Perspectives in personal construct theory.* New York: Academic.

Hochman, S. H. (1971). Field independence and Stroop color-word performance. *Perceptual and Motor Skills, 33,* 782.

Hoffer, E. (1951). *The true believer.* New York: Harper.

Hoffman, C., & Kagan, S. (1977). Field dependence and facial recognition. *Perceptual and Motor Skills, 44,* 119–124.

Hofstaetter, P. R. (1952). A factorial study of prejudice. *Journal of Personality, 21,* 228–239.

Hogan, H. W. (1975). Validity of a symbolic measure of authoritarianism. *Psychological Reports, 37,* 539–543.

Hollander, E. P. (1954). Authoritarianism and leadership choice in a military setting. *Journal of Abnormal and Social Psychology, 49,* 365–370.

Hollingworth, H. (1913). The central tendency of judgment in experimental studies of judgment. *Archives of Psychology, 29,* 44–52.

Holzman, P. S., & Klein, G. S. (1954). Cognitive system—principles of leveling and sharpening: Individual differences in assimilation effects in visual time-error. *Journal of Psychology, 37,* 105–122.

Holtzman, W. H., Thorpe, J. S., Swartz, J. D., & Herron, E. W. (1961). *Inkblot perception and personality: Holtzman Inkblot techniques.* Austin: University of Texas.

Honess, T. (1976). Cognitive complexity and social prediction. *British Journal of Social and Clinical Psychology, 15,* 23–31.

Hornsby, J. R. (1964). *Social concept attainment and cognitive complexity.* Progress Report, Public Health Grant MH-08334-02.

Houston, B. K. (1969). Field independence and performance in distraction. *Journal of Psychology, 72,* 65–69.

Hritzuk, J., & Taylor, L. (1973). A relationship between field-dependency–independency and set: A Western and Soviet view. *Social Behavior and Personality, 1,* 23–28.

Hunt, D. E. (1951). *Studies in the role concept repertory: Conceptual consistency.* Unpublished master's thesis, Ohio State University.

Hunt, D. E. (1962a). *Manual for scoring sentence completion responses for ages 10–16.* Unpublished manuscript, Syracuse University.

Hunt, D. E. (1926b). *Personality patterns in adolescent boys.* Progress report No. 7, Grant No. M-3517, Syracuse University.

Hunt, D. E., & Dopyera, J. (1966). Personality variation in lower-class children. *Journal of Psychology, 62,* 47–54.

Hunt, D. E., & Halverson, C. (1964). *Manual for scoring sentence completion responses for adolescents.* Unpublished manuscript, Syracuse University.

Hunt, D. E., & Sullivan, E. V. (1974). *Between psychology and education.* Hinsdale, Ill.: Dryden.

Hunt, M. F., Jr., & Miller, G. R. (1968). Open- and closed-mindedness, belief-discrepant communication behavior, and tolerance for cognitive inconsistency. *Journal of Personality and Social Psychology, 8,* 35–37.

Hurley, J. T. (1972). Development of group measures of the rod & frame test and the slanting disc effect. *Psychology, 9,* 49–52.

Hyman, H. H., & Sheatsley, P. B. (1954). "The Authoritarian Personality"—A methodological critique. In R. Christie & M. Jahoda (Eds.), *Studies in the scope and method of "The Authoritarian Personality."* New York: Free Press.

Immergluck, L. (1968). Comment on "Figural after-effects, illusions and the dimension of field dependence." *Psychonomic Science, 11,* 363.

Irwin, M., Tripodi, T., & Bieri, J. (1967). Affective stimulus value and cognitive complexity. *Journal of Personality and Social Psychology, 5,* 444–448.

Iverson, M., & Schwab, H. G. (1967). Ethnocentric dogmatism and binocular fusion of sexually and radically discrepant stimuli. *Journal of Personality and Social Psychology, 7,* 73–81.

Jackson, D. N. (1956). A short form of Witkin's Embedded Figures Test. *Journal of Abnormal and Social Psychology, 53,* 254–255.

Jackson, D. N., & Messick, S. J. (1957). A note on "ethnocentrism" and acquiescent response sets. *Journal of Abnormal and Social Psychology, 54,* 132–134.

Jackson, D. N., Messick, S., & Myers, C. T. (1962). *The role of memory and color in group and individual embedded-figures measures of field independence.* Educational Testing Service, Princeton.

Jackson, D. N., Messick, S., & Myers, C. T. (1964). Evaluation of group and individual forms of embedded-figures measures of field-independence. *Educational and Psychological Measurement, 24,* 177–192.

Jackson, D. N., Messick, S. J., & Solley, C. M. (1957). How "rigid" is the "authoritarian?" *Journal of Abnormal and Social Psychology, 54,* 137–140.

Jacobson, F. N., & Rettig, S. (1959). Authoritarianism and intelligence. *Journal of Social Psychology, 50,* 213–219.

Jacobson, G. H. (1973). *An examination of possible changes in authoritarianism, values, and cognitive complexity, with their implications for business.* Unpublished doctoral dissertation, University of Southern California.

Jacoby, J. (1967). Open-mindedness and creativity. *Psychological Reports, 20,* 822.

Jacoby, J. (1971). Interpersonal perceptual accuracy as a function of dogmatism. *Journal of Experimental Social Psychology, 7,* 221–236.

Jahoda, M. (1954). Introduction. In R. Christie & M. Jahoda (Eds.), *Studies in the scope and method of "The Authoritarian Personality."* New York: Free Press.

Jensen, A. R. (1965). Scoring the Stroop test. *Acta Psychologica, 24,* 398–408.

Jensen, A. R., & Rohwer, W. D., Jr. (1966). The Stroop Color-Word Test: A review. *Acta Psychologica, 25,* 36–93.

Johnson, O. G., & Bommarito, J. W. (1971). *Tests and measurements in child development: A handbook.* San Francisco: Jossey-Bass.

Jones, J. M. (1973). Dogmatism and political preferences. *Psychological Reports, 33,* 640.

Jones, M. B. (1955). Authoritarianism and intolerance of fluctuation. *Journal of Abnormal and Social Psychology, 40,* 125–126.

Jones, R. E. (1961). Identification in terms of personal constructs. *Journal of Consulting Psychology, 25,* 276.

Kagan, J., & Henker, B. (1966). Developmental psychology. *Annual Review of Psychology, 17,* 1–50.

Kagan, J., & Kogan, N. (1970). Individual variation in cognitive processes. In P. H. Mussen (Ed.), *Carmichael's manual of child psychology,* Vol. 1. New York: Wiley.

Kagan, J., & Messer, S. B. (1975). A reply to "Some misgivings about the Matching Familiar Figures Test as a measure of reflection-impulsivity." *Developmental Psychology, 11,* 244–248.

Kagan, J., Moss, H. A., & Sigel, I. E. (1963). Psychological significance of styles of conceptualization. In J. C. Wright & J. Kagan (Eds.), *Basic cognitive process in children. Monographs of the Society for Research in Child Development, 28* (2, Serial No. 86).

Kagan, J., Rosman, B., Day, D., Albert, J., & Phillips, W. (1964). Information processing in the child: Significance of analytic and reflective attitudes. *Psychological Monographs, 78* (1, Whole No. 578).

Kahoe, R. D. (1974). Personality and achievement correlates of intrinsic and extrinsic religious orientations. *Journal of Personality and Social Psychology, 29,* 812–818.

Kaplan, M. F., & Singer, E. (1963). Dogmatism and sensory alienation: An empirical investigation. *Journal of Consulting Psychology, 27,* 486–491.

Karabenick, S. A., & Wilson, W. (1969). Dogmatism among war hawks and peace doves. *Psychological Reports, 25,* 419–422.

Karlins, M. (1967). Conceptual complexity and remote-associative proficiency as creativity variables in a complex problem-solving task. *Journal of Personality and Social Psychology, 6,* 264–278.

Karlins, M., Coffman, T., Lamm, H., & Schroder, H. M. (1967). The effect of conceptual complexity on information search in a complex problem-solving task. *Psychonomic Science, 7,* 137–138.

Karlins, M., & Lamm, H. (1967). Information search as a function of conceptual structure in a complex problem-solving task. *Journal of Personality and Social Psychology, 5,* 456–459.

Karlins, M., & Schroder, H. M. (1967). Discovery learning, creativity, and the inductive teaching program. *Psychological Reports, 20,* 867–876.

Karp, S. A. (1963). Field dependence and overcoming embeddedness. *Journal of Consulting Psychology, 27,* 294–302.

Karp, S. A. (1967). Field dependence and occupational activity in the aged. *Perceptual and Motor Skills, 24,* 603–609.

Karp, S. A., & Konstadt, N. (1963). *Manual for the Children's Embedded-figures Test: Cognitive tests.* Unpublished manuscript.

Kates, S. L., & Diab, L. N. (1955). Authoritarian ideology and attitudes on parent-child relationships. *Journal of Abnormal and Social Psychology, 51,* 13–16.

Kelly, G. A. (1955). *The psychology of personal constructs* (2 vols.). New York: Norton.

Kelly, G. A. (1970). A brief introduction to personal construct theory. In D. Bannister (Ed.), *Perspectives in personal construct theory.* New York: Academic.

Kelly, J. V. (1964). *A program for processing George Kelly's Rep grids on the 1620 IBM computer.* Unpublished manuscript, Ohio State University.

Kelman, H. C., & Barclay, J. (1963). The F Scale as a measure of breadth of perspective. *Journal of Abnormal and Social Psychology, 67,* 608–615.

Kemp, C. G. (1960). Changes in values in relation to open-closed systems. In M. Rokeach, *The open and closed mind.* New York: Basic Books.

Kemp, C. G., & Kohler, E. W. (1965). Suitability of the Rokeach Dogmatism Scale for high school use. *Journal of Experimental Education, 33,* 383–385.

Kenny, D. T., & Ginsberg, R. (1958). Authoritarianism submission, intolerance of ambiguity and aggression. *Canadian Journal of Psychology, 21,* 121–126.

Keogh, B. K., & Ryan, S. R. (1971). Use of three measures of field organization with young children. *Perceptual and Motor Skills, 33,* 466.

Keogh, B. K., & Tardo, K. (1975). Measurement of field-independence–dependence in children: A methodological note. *Perceptual and Motor Skills, 40,* 743–746.

Keogh, B. K., Welles, M. F., & Weiss, A. L. (1972). *Field independence–dependence, re-*

flection–impulsivity, and problem-solving styles of preschool children. Tech. Rep. SERP 1972-A1. Los Angeles: University of California, Graduate School of Education.

Kerlinger, F., & Rokeach, M. (1966). The factorial nature of the F and D scales. *Journal of Personality and Social Psychology, 4,* 391–399.

Kerpelman, L. C. (1968). Personality and attitude correlates of political candidate preference. *Journal of Personality and Social Psychology, 2,* 219–226.

Kessler, M. R., & Kronenberger, E. J. (1967). Dogmatism and perceptual synthesis. *Perceptual and Motor Skills, 24,* 179–182.

Kidd, A. H., & Kidd, R. M. (1971). Relation of Holtzman scores to rigidity. *Perceptual and Motor Skills, 32,* 1003–1010.

Kidd, A. H., & Kidd, R. M. (1972). Relation of F-test scores to rigidity. *Perceptual and Motor Skills, 34,* 239–243.

Kirscht, J. P., & Dillehay, R. C. (1967). *Dimensions of authoritarianism.* Lexington: University of Kentucky Press.

Kirtley, D., & Harkless, R. (1969). Some personality and attitudinal correlates of dogmatism. *Psychological Reports, 24,* 851–854.

Kleck, R. E., & Wheaton, J. (1967). Dogmatism and responses to opinion-consistent and opinion-inconsistent information. *Journal of Personality and Social Psychology, 5,* 249–252.

Klein, E. B. (1965). A factor analysis of the F and reversed F scales in three regional samples. *Journal of Social Psychology, 65,* 127–134.

Klein, G. S. (1954). Need and regulation. In M. R. Jones (Ed.), *Nebraska Symposium on Motivation.* Lincoln: University of Nebraska Press.

Klein, G. S. (1970). *Perception, motives, and personality.* New York: Knopf.

Klein, G. S., Barr, H. L:, & Wolitzky, D. L. (1967). Personality. *Annual Review of Psychology, 18,* 467–560.

Klein, G. S., Gardner, R. W., & Schlesinger, H. J. (1962). Tolerance of unrealistic experiences: A study of the generality of a cognitive control. *British Journal of Psychology, 53,* 41–55.

Klein, G. S., & Schlesinger, H. J. (1951). Perceptual attitudes toward instability: I. Prediction of apparent movement experiences from Rorschach responses. *Journal of Personality, 19,* 289–302.

Klyman, F. I., & Kruckenberg, J. (1974). A methodology for assessing citizen perceptions of police. *Journal of Criminal Justice, 2,* 219–233.

Koenig, F. (1971). Positive affective stimulus value and accuracy of role perception. *British Journal of Social and Clinical Psychology, 10,* 385–386.

Koenig, F. (1975). Group affective stimulus value and cognitive complexity. *Journal of Social Psychology, 97,* 143–144.

Koenig, F., & Edmonds, D. (1972). Cognitive complexity and affective value of literary stimuli. *Perceptual and Motor Skills, 33,* 947–948.

Koenig, F., & Seaman, J. (1974). Vigilance and justification as explanations of complex cognition. *Journal of Social Psychology, 93,* 75–80.

Kogan, N. (1973). Creativity and cognitive style: A life span perspective. In P. Baltes & K. W. Schaie (Eds.), *Life span developmental psychology: Personality and socialization.* New York: Academic.

Kogan, N. (1976). *Cognitive styles in infancy and early childhood.* Hillsdale, N.J.: Lawrence Erlbaum Associates.

Kohn, P. M. (1972). The authoritarianism-rebellion scale: A balanced F Scale with left-wing reversals. *Sociometry, 35,* 176–189.

Korn, H. A., & Giddan, N. S. (1964). Scoring methods and construct validity of the Dogmatism Scale. *Educational and Psychological Measurement, 24,* 867–874.

Kornhauser, A., Sheppard, H. L., and Mayer, A. J. (1956). *When labor votes.* New York: University Books.

Kropp, R. P., & Stoker, H. W. (1966). *The construction and validation of tests of the cognitive processes as described in the "Taxonomy of Educational Objectives."* Cooperative Research Project No. 2177. Tallahassee: University of Florida.

Krug, R. E. (1961). An analysis of the F Scale: 1. Item factor analysis. *Journal of Social Psychology, 53,* 285–291.

Kuna, D. P., & Williams, D. C. (1976). Threatening behavior and complex judgments: A test of the vigilance and Pollyanna hypotheses. *Representative Research in Social Psychology, 7,* 6–12.

Kutner, B. (1958). Patterns of mental functioning associated with prejudice in children. *Psychological Monographs, 72* (7, Whole No. 460).

Kutner, B., & Gordon, N. B. (1964). Cognitive functioning and prejudice: A nine-year follow-up study. *Sociometry, 27,* 66–74.

Kuusinen, J., & Nystedt, L. (1972a). Individual versus provided constructs, cognitive complexity and extremity of ratings in person perception. *Scandinavian Journal of Psychology, 16,* 137–148.

Kuusinen, J., & Nystedt, L. (1972b). The convergent validity of four indices of cognitive complexity in person perception: A multi-index multimethod and factor analytical approach. *Scandinavian Journal of Psychology, 16,* 131–136.

Kuusinen, J., & Nystedt, L. (1972c). *Relation of social intelligence and spatial ability to cognitive complexity in person perception.* Reports No. 372. University of Stockholm, Psychological Laboratories.

Laird, J. D., & Berglas, S. (1975). Individual differences in the effects of engaging in counter-attitudinal behavior. *Journal of Personality, 43,* 286–304.

Lambert, Z. V., & Durand, R. M. (1977). Purchase information acquisition and cognitive style. *Journal of Psychology, 97,* 3–13.

Landfield, A. W. (1977). Interpretive man: The enlarged self-image. In A. W. Landfield (Ed.), *Nebraska Symposium on Motivation* (Vol. 24). Lincoln: University of Nebraska Press.

Landfield, A. W., & Barr, M. A. (1976). *Ordination: A new measure of concept organization.* Unpublished manuscript, University of Nebraska, Lincoln.

Larsen, K. (1969). Authoritarianism, hawkishness and attitudes change as related to high and low status communications. *Perceptual and Motor Skills, 28,* 114.

Larsen, K. S. (1971). Affectivity, cognitive style, and social judgment. *Journal of Personality and Social Psychology, 19,* 119–123.

Lasry, J., & Dyne, L. (1974). Administration procedures and correlations between Witkin's tests of field dependence. *Perceptual and Motor Skills, 38,* 216–218.

Lavrakas, P. J., Buri, J. R., & Mayzner, M. S. (1976). A perspective on the recognition of other-race faces. *Perception and Psychophysics, 20,* 475–481.

Leavitt, H. J., Hax, H., & Roche, J. H. (1955). "Authoritarianism" and agreement with things authoritative. *Journal of Psychology, 40,* 215–221.

Leckart, B. T., & Wagner, J. F. (1967). Stimulus familiarity, dogmatism, and the duration of attention. *Perception and Psychophysics, 2,* 268–270.

Lee, R., & Warr, P. (1969). The development and standardization of a balanced F scale. *Journal of General Psychology, 81,* 109–129.

Lefever, M., & Ehri, L. C. (1976). The relationship between field independence and sentence disambiguation ability. *Journal of Psycholinguistic Research, 5,* 99–106.

Lehmann, I. J. (1963). Changes in critical thinking, attitudes, and values from freshman to senior years. *Journal of Educational Psychology, 54*, 305–315.

Leitner, L. M., Landfield, A. W., & Barr, M. A. (1974). *Cognitive complexity: A review and elaboration within personal construct theory.* Unpublished manuscript, University of Nebraska.

Lesser, H., & Steininger, M. (1975). Family patterns in dogmatism. *Journal of Genetic Psychology, 126,* 155–156.

Lester, G. (1968). The Rod-and-Frame Test: Some comments on methodology. *Perceptual and Motor Skills, 26,* 1307–1314.

Leventhal, H. (1957). Cognitive processes and interpersonal predictions. *Journal of Abnormal Social Psychology, 55,* 176–180.

Leventhal, H., Jacobs, R. L., & Kudirka, N. Z. (1964). Authoritarianism, ideology and political candidate choice. *Journal of Abnormal and Social Psychology, 69,* 539–549.

Leventhal, H., & Singer, D. L. (1964). Cognitive complexity, impression formation, and impression change. *Journal of Personality, 32,* 210–226.

Levine, B. E. (1976). Curvilinear relation of schematizing test scores and their statistical treatment. *Perceptual and Motor Skills, 42,* 1175–1180.

Levine, F. J. (1976). Influence of field-independence and study habits on academic performance of black students in a predominantly white university. *Perceptual and Motor Skills, 42,* 1101–1102.

Levinson, D. J. (1949). An approach to the theory and measurement of ethnocentric ideology. *Journal of Psychology, 28,* 19–39.

Levinson, D. J., & Huffman, P. E. (1955). Traditional family ideology and its relation to personality. *Journal of Personality, 23,* 251–273.

Levinson, D. J., & Sanford, R. N. (1944). A scale for the measurement of anti-Semitism. *Journal of Psychology, 17,* 339–370.

Levitt, E. E. (1953). Studies in intolerance of ambiguity: I. The Decision-Location Test with grade school children. *Child Development, 24,* 263–268.

Levitt, E. E. (1956). The water-jar Einstellung test as a measure of rigidity. *Psychological Bulletin, 53,* 347–370.

Levitt, E. E., & Zelen, S. L. (1953). The validity of the Einstellung test as a measure of rigidity. *Journal of Abnormal and Social Psychology, 48,* 573–580.

Levitt, E. E., & Zelen, S. L. (1955). An investigation of the water-jar extinction problem as a measure of rigidity. *Psychological Reports, 1,* 331–334.

Levitt, E., & Zuckerman, M. (1959). The water-jar test revisited: The replication of a review. *Psychological Reports, 5,* 365–380.

Levy, J. M., & Rokeach, M. (1960). The formation of new perceptual systems. In M. Rokeach, *The open and closed mind.* New York: Basic Books.

Levy, L. H., & Dugan, R. D. (1956). A factorial study of personal constructs. *Journal of Consulting Psychology, 20,* 53–57.

Lewin, K. (1935). *A dynamic theory of personality.* New York: McGraw-Hill.

Lewin, K., Lippitt, R., & White, R. (1939). Patterns of aggressive behavior in experimentally created "social climates." *Journal of Social Psychology, 10,* 271–299.

Lichtenstein, E., Quinn, R., & Hover, G. (1961). Dogmatism and acquiescent response set. *Journal of Abnormal and Social Psychology, 63,* 636–638.

Lindstrom, D. R., & Shipman, V. C. (1972). Sigel Object Categorization Test. In V. C. Shipman (Ed.), *Disadvantaged children and their first school experiences.* Princeton: Educational Testing Service.

Linton, H. (1955). Dependence on external influence: Correlates in perception, attitudes, and judgment. *Journal of Abnormal and Social Psychology, 51,* 502–507.

Lipetz, M. E. (1960). Effects of information on the assessment of attitudes by authoritarians and nonauthoritarians. *Journal of Abnormal and Social Psychology, 60,* 95–99.

Lippett, R., & White, R. K. (1943). The social climate of children's groups. In R. G. Barker, J. S. Kounin, & H. F. Wright (Eds.), *Child behavior and development.* New York: McGraw-Hill.

Little, B. R. (1969). Sex differences and comparability of three measures of cognitive complexity. *Psychological Reports, 24,* 607–609.

Long, B. H., & Ziller, R. C. (1965). Dogmatism and predecisional information search. *Journal of Applied Psychology, 49,* 376–378.

Long, G. M. (1973). The Rod-and-Frame Test: Further comments on methodology. *Perception and Motor Skills, 36,* 624–626.

Long, G. M. (1974). Reported correlates of perceptual style: A review of the field dependency-independency dimension. JSAS *Catalog of Selected Documents in Psychology, 4,* 3 (Ms. No. 540).

Loo, R., & Cauthen, N. R. (1976). Anxiety and perceptual articulation. *Perceptual and Motor Skills, 43,* 403–408.

Luchins, A. S. (1942). Mechanization in problem-solving. *Psychological Monographs, 54* (6, Whole No. 248).

Luchins, A. S. (1949). Rigidity and ethnocentrism: A critique. *Journal of Personality, 17,* 449–466.

Luchins, A. S. (1951). The Einstellung test of rigidity: Its relation to concreteness of thinking. *Journal of Consulting Psychology, 15,* 303–310.

Luck, J., & Gruner, C. (1970). Another note on political candidate preference and authoritarianism. *Psychological Reports, 26,* 594.

Lundy, R. M., & Berkowitz, L. (1957). Cognitive complexity and assimilative projection in attitude change. *Journal of Abnormal and Social Psychology, 55,* 34–37.

Lyda, L., & Fillenbaum, S. (1964). Dogmatism and problem solving: An examination of the Denny Doodlebug problem. *Psychological Reports, 14,* 99–102.

Lyle, W. H., Jr., & Levitt, E. E. (1955). Punitiveness, authoritarianism, and parental discipline of grade-school children. *Journal of Abnormal and Social Psychology, 51,* 42–46.

MacDonald, A. P., Jr. (1970). Revised scale for ambiguity tolerance: Reliability and validity. *Psychological Reports, 26,* 791–798.

MacKinnon, A. A. (1972). Eskimo and Caucasian: A discordant note on cognitive-perceptual abilities. *Proceedings at the 80th Annual Convention of the American Psychological Association, 7,* 303–304. (Summary)

MacKinnon, W. J., & Centers, R. (1956). Authoritarianism and urban stratification. *American Journal of Sociology, 61,* 610–620.

MacNeil, L. W., & Rule, B. G. (1970). Effects of conceptual structure on information preference under sensory-deprivation conditions. *Journal of Personality and Social Psychology, 16,* 530–535.

Macrae, J. A. (1969). Interpersonal perception—some determinants and variables. *Papers in Psychology, 3.*

Mahoney, M. J. (1977). Reflections on the cognitive–learning trend in psychotherapy. *American Psychologist, 32,* 5–13.

Marcus, E. H. (1964). Dogmatism and the medical profession. *Journal of Nervous and Mental Disease, 138,* 114–118.

Markus, E. J. (1971). Perceptual field dependence among aged persons. *Perceptual and Motor Skills, 33,* 175–178.

Markus, E. J., Blenkner, M., Bloom, M., & Downs, T. (1970). Relocation stress and the aged. In T. Blumenthal (Ed.), *Interdisciplinary topics in gerontology,* Vol. 7. Basel: Karger.

Markus, E. J., & Nielsen, M. (1973). Embedded Figures Test scores among five samples of aged persons. *Perceptual and Motor Skills, 36,* 455–459.

Marlowe, D., & Gergen, K. J. (1969). Personality and social interaction. In G. Lindzey & E. Aronson (Eds.), *The handbook of social psychology* (Vol. 3). Reading, Mass.: Addison-Wesley.

Martin, J. G., & Westie, F. R. (1959). The tolerant personality. *American Sociological Review, 24,* 521–528.

Marx, D. J. (1970). Intentional and incidental concept formation as a function of conceptual complexity, intelligence, and task complexity. *Journal of Educational Psychology, 61,* 207–304.

Massari, D. J. (1975). The relation of reflection-impulsivity to field dependence-independence and internal-external control in children. *Journal of Genetic Psychology, 126,* 61–67.

Massari, D. J., & Massari, J. A. (1973). Sex differences in the relationship of cognitive style and intellectual functioning in disadvantaged preschool children. *Journal of Genetic Psychology, 122,* 175–181.

Mausner, B., & Graham, J. (1970). Field dependence and prior reinforcement as determinants of social interaction in judgment. *Journal of Personality and Social Psychology, 16,* 486–493.

Mayo, C. W., & Crockett, W. H. (1964). Cognitive complexity and primacy-recency effects in impression formation. *Journal of Abnormal and Social Psychology, 68,* 335–338.

Mazis, M. B. (1973). Cognitive tuning and receptivity to novel information. *Journal of Experimental Social Psychology, 9,* 307–319.

McCandless, B. R. (1961). *Children and adolescents.* New York: Holt, Rinehart & Winston.

McGinnies, E., & Altman, I. (1959). Discussion as a function of attitudes and content of a persuasive communication. *Journal of Applied Psychology, 43,* 53–59.

McKeachie, W. J. (1976). Psychology in America's bicentennial year. *American Psychologist, 31,* 819–833.

McLeish, J., & Park, J. (1973). Outcomes associated with direct and vicarious experience in training groups. II. Attitudes, dogmatism. *British Journal of Social and Clinical Psychology, 12,* 353–358.

Mebane, D., & Johnson, D. L. (1970). A comparison of the performance of Mexican boys and girls on Witkin's cognitive tasks. *Interamerican Journal of Psychology, 4,* 3–4.

Mednick, S. A. (1962). The associative basis of the creative process. *Psychological Review, 69,* 220–232.

Mednick, S. A., & Mednick, M. T. (1967). *Examiner's manual: Remote Associates Test.* Boston: Houghton Mifflin.

Melikian, L. H. (1956). Some correlates of authoritarianism in two cultural groups. *Journal of Psychology, 42,* 237–248.

Melvin, D. (1955). *An experimental and statistical study of two primary social attitudes.* Unpublished doctoral dissertation, University of London.

Menasco, M. B. (1976). Experienced conflict in decision-making as a function of level of cognitive complexity. *Psychological Reports, 39,* 923–933.

Messer, S. B. (1976). Reflection-impulsivity: A review. *Psychological Bulletin, 83,* 1026–1052.

Messick, S. (1964). *Speed of color discrimination test.* Unpublished manuscript, Educational Testing Service.

Messick, S. (1970). The criterion problem in the evaluation of instruction: Assessing possible, not just intended, outcomes. In M. C. Wittrock & D. Wiley (Eds.), *The evaluation of instruction: Issues and problems.* New York: Holt, Rinehart, & Winston.

Messick, S. (1976). Personality consistencies in cognition and creativity. In S. Messick and associates, *Individuality in learning.* San Francisco: Jossey-Bass.

Messick, S., and associates. (1976). *Individuality in learning.* San Francisco: Jossey-Bass.

Messick, S., & Damarin, F. (1964). Cognitive styles and memory for faces. *Journal of Abnormal and Social Psychology, 69,* 313–318.

Messick, S., & Fredericksen, N. (1958). Ability, acquiescence, and authoritarianism. *Psychological Reports, 4,* 687–697.

Messick, S., Jackson, D. N. (1956). *The measurement of authoritarian attitudes.* Research Memorandum, RM-56-5. Princeton: Educational Testing Service.

Metcalf, R. J. (1974). Own vs. provided constructs in a Rep test measure of cognitive complexity. *Psychological Reports, 35,* 1305–1306.

Meyers, B. (1964). *An analysis of factors relating to cognitive complexity in three high school groups.* Unpublished manuscript.

Miklich, D. R. (1970). Item ambiguity in the authoritarianism scales. *Psychological Reports, 27,* 414.

Mikol, B. (1960). The enjoyment of new musical systems. In Rokeach, M., *The open and closed mind.* New York: Basic Books.

Miller, A. G. (1968). Psychological stress as a determinant of cognitive complexity. *Psychological Reports, 23,* 635–639.

Miller, A. G. (1969). Amount of information and stimulus valence as determinants of cognitive complexity. *Journal of Personality, 37,* 141–157.

Miller, A. G., & Harvey, O. J. (1973). Effects of concreteness-abstractness and anxiety on intellectual and motor performance. *Journal of Consulting and Clinical Psychology, 40,* 444–451.

Miller, G. R., & Bacon, P. (1971). Open- and closed-mindedness and recognition of visual humor. *Journal of Communication, 21,* 150–159.

Miller, H., & Bieri, J. (1965). Cognitive complexity as a function of the significance of the stimulus objects being judged. *Psychological Reports, 16,* 1203–1204.

Millon, T. (1957). Authoritarianism, intolerance of ambiguity, and rigidity under ego- and task-involving conditions. *Journal of Abnormal and Social Psychology, 55,* 29–33.

Milton, O. (1952). Presidential choice and performance on a scale of authoritarianism. *American Psychologist, 7,* 597–598.

Minard, J. G., & Mooney, W. (1969). Psychological differentiation and perceptual defense: Studies of the separation of perception from emotion. *Journal of Abnormal Psychology, 74,* 131–139.

Mischel, T. (1964). Personal constructs, rules, and the logic of clinical activity. *Psychological Review, 71,* 180–192.

Mischel, W. (1973). Toward a cognitive social learning reconceptualization of personality. *Psychological Review, 80,* 252–283.

Mischel, W. (1977). On the future of personality measurement. *American Psychologist, 32*, 246–254.

Montgomery, R. L., Hinkle, S. W., & Enzie, R. F. (1976). Arbitrary norms and social change in high- and low-authoritarian societies. *Journal of Personality and Social Psychology, 33*, 698–708.

Moore, S. F., Gleser, G. C., & Warm, J. S. (1970). Cognitive style in the organization and articulation of ambiguous stimuli. *Psychonomic Science, 21*, 243–244.

Mosher, D. L., & Mosher, J. B. (1965). Relationships between authoritarian attitudes in delinquent girls and the authoritarian attitudes and authoritarian rearing practices of their mothers. *Psychological Reports, 16*, 23–30.

Mosher, D. L., & Scodel, A. (1960). Relationships between ethnocentrism in children and the ethnocentrism and authoritarian rearing practices of their mothers. *Child Development, 31*, 369–376.

Mouw, J. T. (1969). Effect of dogmatism on levels of cognitive processes. *Journal of Educational Psychology, 60*, 363–369.

Mueller, W. S. (1974). Cognitive complexity and salience of dimensions in person perception. *Australian Journal of Psychology, 26*, 173–182.

Murray, C. (1974). Item analysis of the elementary school form of the Dogmatism Scale. *Journal of Experimental Education, 42*, 50–54.

Muuss, R. E. (1959). A comparison of "high causally" and "low causally" oriented sixth grade children on personality variables indicative of mental health. *Proceedings of the Iowa Academy of Science, 66*, 388–394.

Naditch, S. F. (1976). Sex differences in field dependence: The role of social influence. In *Determinants of gender differences in cognitive functioning.* Symposium presented at the meeting of the American Psychological Association, Washington, D.C.

Nebelkopf, E. B., & Dreyer, A. S. (1970). Perceptual structuring: Cognitive style differences in the perception of ambiguous stimuli. *Perceptual and Motor Skills, 30*, 635–639.

Nevill, D. (1974). Experimental manipulation of dependency motivation and its effect on eye contact and measures of field dependency. *Journal of Personality and Social Psychology, 29*, 72–79.

Nickel, T. (1971). The reduced size Rod-and-Frame Test as a measure of psychological differentiation. *Educational and Psychological Measurement, 31*, 555–559.

Nidorf, L. J. (1961). *Individual differences in impression formation.* Unpublished doctoral dissertation, Clark University.

Niyekawa, A. M. (1960). *Factors associated with authoritarianism in Japan.* Unpublished doctoral dissertation, New York University.

Norton, R. W. (1975). Measurement of ambiguity tolerance. *Journal of Personality Assessment, 39*, 607–619.

Nye, R. D. (1973). Authoritarianism and the formation and change of impressions. JSAS *Catalog of Selected Documents in Psychology, 3*, 11 (Ms. No. 301).

O'Connor, P. (1952). Ethnocentrism, "intolerance of ambiguity," and abstract reasoning ability. *Journal of Abnormal and Social Psychology, 47*, 526–530.

Ohnmacht, F. W. (1966). Effects of field independence and dogmatism on reversal and non-reversal shifts in concept formation. *Perceptual and Motor Skills, 22*, 491–497.

Ohnmacht, F. W., & McMorris, R. F. (1971). Creativity as a function of field independence and dogmatism. *Journal of Psychology, 79*, 165–168.

Okonji, M. O. (1969). The differential effects of rural and urban upbringing on the development of cognitive styles. *International Journal of Psychology, 4*, 293–305.

Oltman, P. (1968). A portable rod-and-frame apparatus. *Perceptual and Motor Skills, 26,* 503–506.

Oltman, P. K., Goodenough, D. R., Witkin, H. A., Freedman, N., & Friedman, F. (1975). Psychological differentiation as a factor in conflict resolution. *Journal of Personality and Social Psychology, 32,* 730–736.

O'Neil, W. M., & Levinson, D. J. (1954). A factorial exploration of authoritarianism and some of its ideological concomitants. *Journal of Personality, 22,* 449–463.

O'Reilly, C. T., & O'Reilly, E. J. (1954). Religious beliefs of Catholic college students and their attitudes toward minorities. *Journal of Abnormal and Social Psychology, 49,* 378–380.

Osborn, W. P. (1973). Dogmatism, tolerance for cognitive inconsistency, and persuasibility under three conditions of message involvements. *Proceedings of the 81st Annual Convention of the American Psychological Association,* Montreal, Canada, *8,* 365–366. (Summary)

Pannes, E. D. (1963). The relationship between self acceptance and dogmatism in junior-senior high school students. *Journal of Educational Sociology, 36,* 419–426.

Parrott, G. (1971). Dogmatism and rigidity: A factor analysis. *Psychological Reports, 29,* 135–140.

Parrott, G., & Brown, L. (1972). Political bias in the Rokeach Dogmatism Scale. *Psychological Reports, 30,* 805–806.

Peabody, D. (1961). Attitude content and agreement set in scales of authoritarianism, dogmatism, anti-semitism, and economic conservatism. *Journal of Abnormal and Social Psychology, 63,* 1–11.

Peabody, D. (1962). Two components in bipolar scales: Direction and extremeness. *Psychological Review, 69,* 65–73.

Peabody, D. (1966). Authoritarianism scales and response bias. *Psychological Bulletin, 65,* 11–23.

Pearson, P. R. (1972). Field dependence and social desirability response set. *Journal of Clinical Psychology, 28,* 166–167.

Pedersen, F. A. (1958). *Consistency data on the role construct repertory test.* Unpublished manuscript, Ohio State University.

Pedersen, F. A., & Wender, P. H. (1968). Early social correlates of cognitive functioning in six-year-old boys. *Child Development, 39,* 185–193.

Pedhazur, E. J. (1971). Factor structure of the Dogmatism Scale. *Psychological Reports, 28,* 735–740.

Pelletier, K. R. (1974). Influence of transcendental meditation upon autokinetic perception. *Perceptual and Motor Skills, 39,* 1031–1034.

Perney, V. H. (1976). Effects of race and sex on field dependence–independence in children. *Perceptual and Motor Skills, 42,* 975–980.

Perry, A., & Cunningham, W. H. (1975). A behavioral test of three F subscales. *Journal of Social Psychology, 96,* 271–275.

Pervin, L. A. (1973). On construing our constructs. *Contemporary Psychology, 18,* 110–112.

Petronko, M. R., & Perin, C. T. (1970). A consideration of cognitive complexity and primacy-recency effects in impression formation. *Journal of Personality and Social Psychology, 15,* 151–157.

Pettigrew, T. F. (1958). The measurements and correlates of category width as a cognitive variable. *Journal of Personality, 26,* 532–544.

Pilisuk, M. (1963). Anxiety, self-acceptance and open-mindedness. *Journal of Clinical Psychology, 19,* 387–391.

Pitcher, B., & Stacey, C. L. (1954). Is Einstellung rigidity a general trait? *Journal of Abnormal and Social Psychology, 49,* 3–6.

Pizzamiglio, C. L., & Pizzamiglio, L. (1974). Psychometric data of some tests of field dependence related to an Italian population of children four and a half to ten and a half years old. *Archivio di Psicologia Neurologia e Psichiatria, 35,* 127–143.

Plant, W. T. (1960). Rokeach's Dogmatism Scale as a measure of general authoritarianism. *Psychological Reports, 6,* 164.

Plant, W. T. (1965a). Longitudinal changes in intolerance and authoritarianism for subjects differing in amount of college education over four years. *Genetic Psychology Monographs, 72,* 247–287.

Plant, W. T. (1965b). Personality changes associated with college attendance. *Human Development, 8,* 142–151.

Plant, W. T., & Telford, C. W. (1966). Changes in personality for groups completing different amounts of college over two years. *Genetic Psychology Monographs, 74,* 3–36.

Pohl, R. L., & Pervin, L. A. (1968). Academic performance as a function of task requirements and cognitive style. *Psychological Reports, 22,* 1017–1020.

Poley, W. (1974). Dimensionality in the measurement of authoritarian and political attitudes. *Canadian Journal of Behavioral Science, 6,* 81–94.

Powell, F. A. (1962). Open- and closed-mindedness and the ability to differentiate message from source. *Journal of Abnormal and Social Psychology, 65,* 61–64.

Press, A. N., Crockett, W. H., & Delia, J. G. (1975). Effects of cognitive complexity and of perceivers set upon the organization of impressions. *Journal of Personality and Social Psychology, 32,* 865–872.

Pressey, A. (1968). A reply to comments on "Figural aftereffects, illusions and the dimension of field dependence." *Psychonomic Science, 11,* 364.

Pritchard, D. A. (1975). Leveling-sharpening revisited. *Perceptual and Motor Skills, 40,* 111–117.

Prothro, E. T., & Keehn, J. D. (1956). The structure of social attitudes in Lebanon. *Journal of Abnormal and Social Psychology, 53,* 157–160.

Pulos, L., & Spilka, B. (1961). Perceptual selectivity, memory, and anti-Semitism. *Journal of Abnormal and Social Psychology, 62,* 690–692.

Pyron, B. (1966). A factor-analytic study of simplicity-complexity of social ordering. *Perceptual and Motor Skills, 22,* 259–272.

Pyron, B., & Kafer, J., Jr. (1967). Recall of nonsense and attitudinal rigidity. *Journal of Personality and Social Psychology, 5,* 463–466.

Ramirez, M., & Price-Williams, D. (1974). Cognitive styles in children: Two Mexican communities. *Journal of Interamerican Psychology, 8,* 93–101.

Ravenette, T. (1964). Some attempts at developing the use of the repertory grid technique in a child guidance clinic. In N. Warren (Ed.), *Brunel Construct Theory Seminar Report.* Brunel University.

Ray, J. J. (1970). The development and validation of a balanced Dogmatism Scale. *Australian Journal of Psychology, 22,* 253–260.

Ray, J. J. (1972). A new balanced F Scale and its relation to social class. *Australian Psychologist, 7,* 155–166.

Ray, J. J. (1974). Balanced dogmatism scales. *Australian Journal of Psychology, 26,* 9–14.

Ray, J. J., & Martin, J. (1974). How desirable is dogmatism? *Australian and New Zealand Journal of Sociology, 10,* 143–144.

Rebhun, M. T. (1967). Parental attitudes and the closed belief-disbelief system. *Psychological Reports, 20,* 260–262.

Reich, W. (1945). *Character analysis*. New York: Orgone Institute Press.

Reid, W. A., & Holley, B. J. (1972). An application of repertory grid techniques to the study of choice of university. *British Journal of Educational Psychology, 42,* 52–59.

Reinking, R., Goldstein, G., & Houston, B. K. (1974). Cognitive style, proprioceptive skills, task set, stress, and the Rod-and-Frame Test of field orientation. *Journal of Personality and Social Psychology, 30,* 807–811.

Reker, G. T. (1974). Interpersonal conceptual structures of emotionally disturbed and normal boys. *Journal of Abnormal Psychology, 83,* 380–386.

Renna, M., & Zenhausern, R. (1976). The Group Embedded-Figures Test: Normative data. *Perceptual and Motor Skills, 43,* 1176–1178.

Rigney, J., Bieri, J., & Tripodi, T. (1964). Social concept attainment and cognitive complexity. *Psychological Reports, 15,* 503–509.

Riley, J., & Armlin, N. J. (1965). The Dogmatism Scale and flexibility in maze performance. *Perceptual and Motor Skills, 21,* 914.

Riley, R. T., & Denmark, F. L. (1974). Field independence and measures of intelligence: Some reconsiderations. *Social Behavior and Personality, 2,* 25–29.

Robbins, G. E. (1975). Dogmatism and information gathering in personality impression formation. *Journal of Research in Personality, 9,* 74–84.

Robbins, L. C. (1963). The accuracy of parental recall of aspects of child development and of child-rearing practices. *Journal of Abnormal and Social Psychology, 66,* 261–270.

Roberts, A. H. (1962). Intra-test variability as a measure of generalized response set. *Psychological Reports, 11,* 793–799.

Robinson, J. P., & Shaver, P. R. (1973). *Measures of social psychological attitudes* (Rev. ed.). Ann Arbor: Survey Research Center, Institute for Social Research.

Rogers, C. R. (1956). Intellectualized psychotherapy. *Contemporary Psychology, 1,* 357–358.

Rokeach, M. (1948). Generalized mental rigidity as a factor in ethnocentrism. *Journal of Abnormal and Social Psychology, 43,* 259–278.

Rokeach, M. (1949). Rigidity and ethnocentrism: A rejoinder. *Journal of Personality, 17,* 467–474.

Rokeach, M. (1951a). A method for studying individual differences in "narrow-mindedness." *Journal of Personality, 20,* 219–233.

Rokeach, M. (1951b). Prejudice, concreteness of thinking, and reification of thinking. *Journal of Abnormal and Social Psychology, 46,* 83–91.

Rokeach, M. (1954). The nature and meaning of dogmatism. *Psychological Review, 61,* 194–204.

Rokeach, M. (1956). Political and religious dogmatism: An alternative to the authoritarian personality. *Psychological Monographs, 70* (18, Whole No. 425).

Rokeach, M. (1960). *The open and closed mind.* New York: Basic Books.

Rokeach, M. (1963). The double agreement phenomenon: Three hypotheses. *Psychological Review, 70,* 304–309.

Rokeach, M. (1967). Authoritarianism scale and response bias: Comment on Peabody's paper. *Psychological Bulletin, 67,* 349–355.

Rokeach, M., & Fruchter, B. (1956). A factorial study of dogmatism and related concepts. *Journal of Abnormal and Social Psychology, 53,* 356–360.

Rokeach, M., & Kemp, C. G. (1960). Open and closed systems in relation to anxiety and childhood experience. In M. Rokeach, *The open and closed mind.* New York: Basic Books.

Rokeach, M., McGovney, W. C., & Denny, M. R. (1955). A distinction between dogmatic and rigid thinking. *Journal of Abnormal and Social Psychology, 51,* 87–93.

Rokeach, M., McGovney, W. C., & Denny, M. R. (1960). Dogmatic thinking versus rigid thinking. In M. Rokeach, *The open and closed mind.* New York: Basic Books.

Rokeach, M., & Vidulich, R. N. (1960). The formation of new belief systems: The roles of memory and the capacity to entertain. In M. Rokeach, *The open and closed mind.* New York: Basic Books.

Roodin, P. A., Broughton, A., & Vaught, G. M. (1974). Effects of birth order, sex, and family size on field dependence and locus of control. *Perceptual and Motor Skills, 39,* 671–676.

Rorer, L. G. (1965). The great response-style myth. *Psychological Bulletin, 63,* 129–156.

Rosenblum, L. A., Witkin, H. A., Kaufman, I. C., & Brosgole, L. (1965). Perceptual disembedding in monkeys: Note on method and preliminary findings. *Perceptual and Motor Skills, 20,* 729–736.

Rosenkrantz, P. S. (1961). *Relationships of some conditions of presentation and cognitive differentiation to impression formation.* Unpublished doctoral dissertation, Clark University.

Rosenman, M. F. (1967). Dogmatism and the movie "Dr. Strangelove." *Psychological Reports, 20,* 942.

Rosner, S. (1957). Consistency in response to group pressure. *Journal of Abnormal and Social Psychology, 55,* 145–146.

Rosnow, R. L., Gitter, A. G., & Holz, R. F. (1969). Some determinants of postdecisional information preferences. *Journal of Social Psychology, 79,* 235–245.

Rubenowitz, S. (1963). *Emotional flexibility-rigidity as a comprehensive dimension of mind.* Stockholm: Almqvist & Wiksell.

Rudin, S. A., & Stagner, R. (1958). Figure-ground phenomena in the perception of physical and social stimuli. *Journal of Psychology, 45,* 213–225.

Rule, B. G., & Hewitt, D. (1970). Factor structure of anti-Semitism, self-concept and cognitive structure. *Personality, 1,* 319–332.

Rusch, R., & Lis, D. (1977). Reliability and trend for field independence as measured by the portable rod-and-frame. *Perceptual and Motor Skills, 44,* 51–61.

Rushton, J. P., & Wiener, J. (1975). Altruism and cognitive development in children. *British Journal of Social and Clinical Psychology, 14,* 341–349.

Russell, G. W., & Sandilands, M. L. (1973). Some correlates of conceptual complexity. *Psychological Reports, 33,* 587–593.

Rydell, S. T., & Rosen, E. (1966). Measurement and some correlates of need-cognition. *Psychological Reports, 19,* 139–165.

Saarni, C. I. (1973). Piagetian operations and field independence as factors in children's problem-solving performance. *Child Development, 44,* 338–345.

Sales, S. M., & Friend, K. E. (1973). Success and failure as determinants of level of authoritarianism. *Behavioral Science, 18,* 163–172.

Salmon, P. (1967). *A study of the social values and differential conformity on primary schoolboys, as a function of maternal attitude.* Unpublished doctoral dissertation, University of London.

Salmon, P. (1970). A psychology of personal growth. In D. Bannister (Ed.), *Perspectives in personal construct theory.* New York: Academic.

Samelson, F., & Yates, J. F. (1967). Acquiescence and the F Scale: Old assumptions and new data. *Psychological Bulletin, 68,* 91–103.

Sanford, R. N. (1954). Recent developments in connection with the investigation of the authoritarian personality. *Sociological Review, 2,* 11–33.

Sanford, N. (1956). The approach of The Authoritarian Personality. In J. L. McCary (Ed.), *Psychology of personality.* New York: Grove.

Santostefano, S. G. (1964). A developmental study of the cognitive control "Leveling-Sharpening." *Merrill-Palmer Quarterly of Behavior and Development, 10,* 343–360.

Santostefano, S., & Paley, E. (1964). Development of cognitive controls in children. *Child Development, 35,* 939–949.

Santostefano, S., Rutledge, L., & Randall, D. (1965). Cognitive styles and reading disability. *Psychology in the Schools, 2,* 57–62.

Sarris, V., Heineken, E., & Peters, H. (1976). Effect of stress on field dependence. *Perceptual and Motor Skills, 43,* 121–122.

Satterly, D. J. (1976). Cognitive styles, spatial ability and school achievement. *Journal of Educational Psychology, 68,* 36–42.

Schaefer, E. S. (1959). A circumplex model for maternal behavior. *Journal of Abnormal and Social Psychology, 59,* 226–235.

Schaefer, E. S. (1965). Children's reports of parental behavior: An inventory. *Child Development, 36,* 413–424.

Schaefer, E. S., & Bell, R. Q. (1958). Development of a parental attitude research instrument. *Child Development, 29,* 339–361.

Schaefer, E. S., & Bell, R. Q. (1960). *Father Form of the Parental Attitude Research Instrument.* Unpublished manuscript, National Institute of Mental Health.

Scheerer, M. (1954). Cognitive theory. In G. Lindzey (Ed.), *Handbook of social psychology,* Vol. 1. Reading, Mass.: Addison-Wesley.

Schimek, J. G., & Wachtel, P. L. (1969). Exploration of effects of distraction, competing tasks and cognitive style on attention deployment. *Perceptual and Motor Skills, 28,* 567–574.

Schleifer, M., & Douglas, V. I. (1973). Moral judgments, behaviour and cognitive style in young children. *Canadian Journal of Behavioural Science, 5,* 133–144.

Schooler, C. (1972). Social antecedents of adult psychological functioning. *American Journal of Sociology, 78,* 299–322.

Schroder, H. M. (1971). Conceptual complexity and personality organization. In H. M. Schroder & P. Suedfeld (Eds.), *Personality theory and information processing.* New York: Ronald.

Schroder, H. M., Driver, M. J., & Streufert, S. (1967). *Human information processing.* New York: Holt, Rinehart, & Winston.

Schroder, H. M., & Harvey, O. J. (1963). Conceptual organization and group structure. In O. J. Harvey (Ed.), *Motivation and social interaction: Cognitive determinants.* New York: Ronald.

Schroder, H. M., & Streufert, S. (1962). *The measurement of four systems of personality structure varying in level of abstractness (Sentence Completion Method).* Tech. Rep. No. 11, ONR. Princeton: Princeton University.

Schultz, C. B., & DiVesta, F. J. (1972). Effects of expert endorsement of beliefs on problem-solving behavior of high and low dogmatics. *Journal of Educational Psychology, 63,* 194–201.

Schulze, R. H. K. (1962). A shortened version of the Rokeach Dogmatism Scale. *Journal of Psychological Studies, 13,* 93–97.

Schwartz, D. W., & Karp, S. A. (1967). Field dependence in a geriatric population. *Perceptual and Motor Skills, 24,* 495–504.

Schwendiman, G., Larsen, K., & Cope, S. (1970). Authoritarian traits as predictors of candidate preference in the 1968 U.S. presidential election. *Psychological Reports, 27,* 629–630.

Scodel, A., & Freedman, M. (1956). Additional observations on the social perceptions of authoritarians and non-authoritarians. *Journal of Abnormal and Social Psychology, 52,* 92–95.

Scodel, A., & Mussen, P. (1953). Social perceptions of authoritarians and nonauthoritarians. *Journal of Abnormal and Social Psychology, 48,* 181–184.

Scott, W. A. (1963). Cognitive complexity and cognitive balance. *Sociometry, 26,* 66–74.

Seaman, J. M., & Koenig, F. (1974). A comparison of measures of cognitive complexity. *Sociometry, 37,* 375–390.

Sears, R. R., Maccoby, E. E., & Levin, H. (1957). *Patterns of child-rearing.* Evanston, Ill.: Row, Peterson.

Sechrest, L., & Jackson, D. N. (1961). Social intelligence and accuracy of interpersonal predictions. *Journal of Personality, 29,* 167–182.

Segal, S. J., & Barr, H. L. (1969). Effect of instructions on phi phenomenon, criterion task of "tolerance for unrealistic experiences." *Perceptual and Motor Skills, 29,* 483–486.

Shaffer, D. R. (1975). The effects of cognitive style upon the inconsistency process. JSAS *Catalog of Selected Documents in Psychology, 5,* 283 (MS. No. 1017).

Shaw, M. E., & Wright, J. M. (1967). *Scales for the measurement of attitudes.* New York: McGraw-Hill.

Sheikh, A. A. (1968). Stereotypy in interpersonal perception and intercorrelation between some attitude measures. *Journal of Social Psychology, 76,* 175–179.

Shelley, H. P. (1956). Response set and the California attitude scales. *Educational and Psychological Measurement, 16,* 63–67.

Sherif, M. (1936). *The psychology of social norms.* New York: Harper.

Shikiar, R. (1975). Authoritarianism and political behavior: The 1973 election. *Psychological Reports, 36,* 874.

Shils, E. A. (1954). Authoritarianism: "Right" and "left." In R. Christie & M. Jahoda (Eds.), *Studies in the scope and method of "The Authoritarian Personality."* New York: Free Press.

Shoben, E. J. (1949). The assessment of parental attitudes in relation to child adjustment. *Genetic Psychology Monographs, 39,* 101–148.

Shupe, D. R., & Wolfer, J. A. (1966). Comparative reliability of the Dogmatism Scale with 2 and 6 scale points. *Psychological Reports, 19,* 284–286.

Sieber, J. E., & Lanzetta, J. T. (1964). Conflict and conceptual structure as determinant of decision-making behavior. *Journal of Personality, 32,* 622–641.

Sieber, J. E., & Lanzetta, J. T. (1966). Some determinants of individual differences in predecision information-processing behavior. *Journal of Personality and Social Psychology, 4,* 100–103.

Siegel, S. (1954). Certain determinants and correlates of authoritarianism. *Genetic Psychology Monographs, 49,* 187–230.

Siegel, A. E., & Siegel, S. (1957). Reference groups, membership groups, and attitude change. *Journal of Abnormal and Social Psychology, 55,* 360–364.

Sigel, I. E. (1967). *SCST manual: Instructions and scoring guide.* Detroit: Merrill-Palmer Institute.

Sigel, I. E., & Olmsted, P. (1970). Modification of cognitive skills among lower-class Black children. In J. Hellmuth (Ed.), *The disadvantaged child,* Vol. 3. New York: Brunner-Mazel.

Simon, G., Langmeyer, D., & Boyer, R. K. (1974). Perceptual style as a determinant in the solution of a group task. *Personality and Social Psychology Bulletin, 1,* 252–255.

Slater, P. (1969). Theory and technique of the repertory grid. *British Journal of Psychiatry, 115,* 1287–1296.

Slater, P., Ed. (1976). *Explorations of intrapersonal space: The measurement of intrapersonal space by grid technique,* Vol. 1. New York: Wiley.

Sloane, H. N., Gorlow, L., & Jackson, D. N. (1963). Cognitive styles in equivalence range. *Perceptual and Motor Skills, 16,* 389–404.

Small, M. M. (1973). Modification of performance on the Rod-and-Frame Test. *Perceptual and Motor Skills, 36,* 715–720.

Smith, D. D. (1968). Dogmatism, cognitive consistency, and knowledge of conflicting facts. *Sociometry, 31,* 259–277.

Smith, G. J. W., & Klein, G. S. (1953). Cognitive controls in serial behavior patterns. *Journal of Personality, 22,* 188–213.

Smith, M. B. (1950). Review of The Authoritarian Personality. *Journal of Abnormal and Social Psychology, 45,* 775–779.

Smith, S., & Leach, C. (1972). A hierarchical measure of cognitive complexity. *British Journal of Psychology, 63,* 561–568.

Smith, T. V. G. (1971). Acculturation and field dependence among the Xhosa. *Journal of Behavioral Science, 1,* 121–123.

Snoek, J., & Dobbs, M. F. (1967). Galvanic skin responses to agreement and disagreement in relation to dogmatism. *Psychological Reports, 20,* 195–198.

Solar, D., Davenport, G., & Bruehl, D. (1969). Social compliance as a function of field dependence. *Perceptual and Motor Skills 29,* 299–306.

Soucar, E. (1971). Vigilance and the perceptions of teachers and students. *Perceptual and Motor Skills, 32,* 83–86.

Soucar, E., & DuCette, J. (1971). Cognitive complexity and political preferences. *Psychological Reports, 29,* 373–374.

Spotts, J. XV., & Mackler, B. (1967). Relationships of field-dependent and field-independent cognitive styles to creative test performance. *Perceptual and Motor Skills, 24,* 239–268.

Stager, D. P. (1967). Conceptual level as a composition variable in small-group decision making. *Journal of Personality and Social Psychology, 5,* 152–161.

Stagner, R. (1965). *Psychology of personality.* New York: McGraw-Hill.

Standing, T. E. (1973). Satisfaction with the work itself as a function of cognitive complexity. *Proceedings of the 81st Annual Convention of the American Psychological Association, 8,* 605–606. (Summary)

Stanes, D. (1973). Analytic responses to Conceptual Style Test as a function of instructions. *Child Development, 44,* 389–391.

Stanley, G., & Martin, J. (1964). How sincere is the dogmatist? *Psychological Review, 71,* 331–334.

Starbird, D. H., & Biller, H. B. (1976). An exploratory study of the interaction of cognitive complexity, dogmatism, and repression-sensitization among college students. *Journal of Genetic Psychology, 128,* 227–232.

Steffensmeier, D. J. (1974). Levels of dogmatism and attitudes toward law and order. *Psychological Reports, 34,* 151–153.

Steiner, I. D. (1954). Ethnocentrism and "tolerance of trait inconsistency." *Journal of Abnormal and Social Psychology, 49,* 349–354.

Steiner, I. D., & Johnson, H. H. (1963). Authoritarianism and "tolerance of trait inconsistency." *Journal of Abnormal and Social Psychology, 67,* 388–391.

Steininger, M. P., Durso, B. E., & Pasquariello, C. (1972). Dogmatism and attitudes. *Psychological Reports, 30,* 151–157.

Steininger, M., & Eisenberg, E. (1976). Order effects and individual differences in impression formation. *Journal of Psychology, 92,* 45–51.

Steininger, M., & Lesser, H. (1974). Dogmatism, dogmatism factors, and liberalism-conservatism. *Psychological Reports, 35,* 15–21.

Stewart, D., & Hoult, T. (1959), A social-psychological theory of the authoritarian personality. *American Journal of Sociology, 65,* 274–279.

Stewin, L. (1976). Integrative complexity: Structure and correlates. *Alberta Journal of Educational Research, 22,* 226–236.

Stewin, L., & Anderson, C. C. (1974). Cognitive complexity as a determinant of information processing. *Alberta Journal of Educational Research, 20,* 233–243.

Stimpson, D. V., & D'Alo, J. (1974). Dogmatism, attitude extremity, and attitude intensity as determinants of perceptual displacement. *Journal of Psychology, 86,* 87–91.

Struefert, S. (1969). Increasing failure and response rate in complex decision making. *Journal of Experimental Social Psychology, 5,* 310–323.

Streufert, S. (1970). Complexity and complex decision making. *Journal of Experimental Social Psychology, 6,* 494–509.

Streufert, S. (1972). Success and response rate in complex decision making. *Journal of Experimental Social Psychology, 8,* 389–403.

Streufert, S., & Castore, C. H. (1971). Information search and the effects of failure: A test of complexity theory. *Journal of Experimental Social Psychology, 7,* 125–143.

Streufert, S., Clardy, M. A., Driver, M. J., Karlins, M., Schroder, H. M., & Suedfeld, P. (1965). A tactical game for the analysis of complex decision making in individuals and groups. *Psychological Reports, 17,* 723–729.

Streufert, S., & Driver, M. J. (1965). Conceptual structure, information load and perceptual complexity. *Psychonomic Science, 3,* 249–250.

Streufert, S., & Driver, M. J. (1967). Impression formation as a measure of the complexity of conceptual structure. *Educational and Psychological Measurement, 27,* 1025–1039.

Streufert, S., Driver, M., & Haun, K. (1967). Components of response rate in complex decision making. *Journal of Experimental Social Psychology, 3,* 286–295.

Streufert, S., & Schroder, H. M. (1962). *The measurement of varying levels of abstractness in personality structure (Impression Formation Method).* Unpublished manuscript, Princeton University.

Streufert, S., & Streufert, S. C. (1969). Effects of conceptual structure, failure and success on attribution of causality and interpersonal attitudes. *Journal of Personality and Social Psychology, 11,* 138–147.

Streufert, S., Suedfeld, P., & Driver, M. J. (1965). Conceptual structure, information search, and information utilization. *Journal of Personality and Social Psychology, 2,* 736–740.

Streufert, S. C. (1973). Effects of information relevance on decision making in complex environments. *Memory and Cognition, 1,* 224–228.

Stringer, P. (1972). Psychological significance in personal and supplied construct systems: A defining experiment. *European Journal of Social Psychology, 2,* 437–447.

Stroop, J. R. (1935). Studies of interference in serial verbal reactions. *Journal of Experimental Psychology, 18,* 643–662.

Stuart, I. R. (1967). Perceptual style and reading ability: Implications for an instructional approach. *Perceptual and Motor Skills, 24,* 135–138.

Stuart, I. R. (1965). Field dependency, authoritarianism, and perception of the human figure. *Journal of Social Psychology, 66,* 209–214.

Stuart, I. R., & Murgatroyd, D. (1971). Field research model of the Rod-and-Frame Test. *Perceptual and Motor Skills, 32,* 671–674.

Suedfeld, P. (1963). *Conceptual and environmental complexity as factors in attitude change.* Unpublished docoral dissertation, Princeton University.

Suedfeld, P. (1964a). Attitude manipulation in restricted environments: I. Conceptual structure and response to propaganda. *Journal of Abnormal and Social Psychology, 68,* 242–246.

Suedfeld, P. (1964b). Conceptual structure and subjective stress in sensory deprivation. *Perceptual and Motor Skills, 19,* 896–898.

Suedfeld, P. (1968). Verbal indices of conceptual complexity. Manipulation by instruction. *Psychonomic Science, 12,* 377.

Suedfeld, P. (1971). Information processing as a personality model. In H. M. Schroder & P. Suedfeld (Eds.), *Personality theory and information processing.* New York: Ronald.

Suedfeld, P., & Hagen, R. L. (1966). Measurement of information complexity: I. Conceptual structure and information pattern as factors in information processing. *Journal of Personality and Social Psychology, 4,* 233–236.

Suedfeld, P., & Rank, A. D. (1976). Revolutionary leaders: Long-term success as a function of changes in conceptual complexity. *Journal of Personality and Social Psychology, 34,* 169–178.

Suedfeld, P., & Streufert, S. (1966). Information search as a function of conceptual and environmental complexity. *Psychonomic Science, 4,* 351–353.

Suedfeld, P., Tomkins, S. S., & Tucker, W. H. (1969). On relations among perceptual and cognitive measures of information processing. *Perception and Psychophysics, 6,* 45–46.

Suedfeld, P., & Vernon, J. (1966). Attitude manipulation in restricted environments: II. Conceptual structure and the internalization of propaganda received as a reward for compliance. *Journal of Personality and Social Psychology, 3,* 586–589.

Sullivan, E. V., McCullogh, G., & Stager, M. (1970). A developmental study of the the relationship between conceptual, ego, and moral development. *Child Development, 41,* 399–411.

Sumner, W. G. (1906). *Folkways.* Boston: Ginn.

Sundberg, N. D., & Bachelis, W. D. (1956). The fakability of two measures of prejudice: The California F Scale and Gough's Pr. scale. *Journal of Abnormal and Social Psychology, 52,* 140–142.

Supnick, J. J. (1964). *An examination of change in categorization of others following a college course in personality development.* Unpublished senior honors thesis, Clark University.

Taft, R. (1956). Intolerance of ambiguity and ethnocentrism. *Journal of Consulting Psychology, 20,* 153–154.

Taylor, I. A. (1960). Similarities in the structure of extreme social attitudes. *Psychological Monographs, 74* (Whole No. 489).

Taylor, J. A. (1953). A personality scale of manifest anxiety. *Journal of Abnormal and Social Psychology, 48,* 285–290.

Taylor, R. N., & Dunnette, M. D. (1970). Influence of dogmatism, risk-taking propensity, and intelligence on decision-making strategies for a sample of industrial managers. *Journal of Applied Psychology, 59,* 420–423.

Templer, A. J. (1972). The relationship between field dependence–independence and concept attainment. *Psychologia Africana, 14,* 121–129.

Thompson, R. C., & Michel, J. B. (1972). Measuring authoritarianism: A comparison of the F and D scales. *Journal of Personality, 40,* 180–190.

Thurstone, L. L. (1944). A factorial study of perception. *Psychometric Monographs* (No. 4). Chicago: University of Chicago Press.

Titus, H. E. (1968). F Scale validity considered against peer nomination criteria. *Psychological Record, 18,* 395–403.

Titus, H. E., & Hollander, E. P. (1957). The California F Scale in psychological research: 1950–1955. *Psychological Bulletin, 54,* 47–64.

Torcivia, J. M., & Laughlin, P. R. (1968). Dogmatism and concept-attainment strategies. *Journal of Personality and Social Psychology, 8,* 397–400.

Touhey, J. C. (1973). Category width and expectancies: Risk conservatism or generalization? *Journal of Research in Personality, 7,* 173–178.

Tramer, R. R., & Schludermann, E. H. (1974). Cognitive differentiation in a geriatric population. *Perceptual and Motor Skills, 39,* 1071–1075.

Tripodi, T., & Bieri, J. (1963). Cognitive complexity as a function of own and provided constructs. *Psychological Reports, 13,* 26.

Tripodi, T., & Bieri, J. (1964). Information transmission in clinical judgments as a function of stimulus dimensionality and cognitive complexity. *Journal of Personality, 32,* 119–137.

Tripodi, T., & Bieri, J. (1966). Cognitive complexity, perceived conflict, and certainty. *Journal of Personality, 34,* 144–153.

Troldahl, V. C., & Powell, F. A. (1965). A short-form Dogmatism Scale for use in field studies. *Social Forces, 44,* 211–214.

Tuckman, B. W. (1964). Personality structure, group composition and group functioning. *Sociometry, 27,* 469–487.

Tuckman, B. W. (1966). Integrative complexity: Its measurement and relation to creativity. *Educational and Psychological Measurement, 26,* 369–382.

Turck, M. J. (1969). A look at dogmatism at Tennessee Technological University. *Tennessee Tech Journal, 4,* 1–7.

Turner, R., & Tripodi, T. (1968). Cognitive complexity as a function of type of stimulus object and affective stimulus value. *Journal of Consulting and Clinical Psychology, 32,* 182–185.

Uhes, M. J., & Shaver, J. P. (1970). Dogmatism and divergent-convergent abilities. *Journal of Psychology, 75,* 3–11.

Uznadze, D. N. (1961). *Eksperimental'nye Osnovy Psikhologii Ustanovkii.* Tbilisi: Academy of Sciences. (Cited by Hritzuk & Taylor, 1973)

Vacc, N. A. (1974). Cognitive complexity in resident assistants and their accuracy in predicting student academic performance. *Journal of College Student Personnel, 15,* 194–197.

Vacc, N. A., & Greenleaf, W. (1975). Sequential development of cognitive complexity. *Perceptual and Motor Skills, 41,* 319–322.

Vacc, N. A., & Vacc, N. E. (1973). An adaptation for children of the modified Role Reportory Test—A measure of cognitive complexity. *Psychological Reports, 33,* 771–776.

Vacchiano, R. B., Schiffman, D. C., & Strauss, P. S. (1967). Factor structure of the Dogmatism Scale. *Psychological Reports, 20,* 847–852.

Vacchiano, R. B., Strauss, P. S., & Hochman, L. (1969). The open and closed mind: A review of dogmatism. *Psychological Bulletin, 71,* 261–273.

Vannoy, J. S. (1965). Generality of cognitive complexity-simplicity as a personality construct. *Journal of Personality and Social Psychology, 2,* 385–396.

Vaught, G. (1968). Expected scores in the Rod-and-Frame Test: Fuel for the Immergluck-Pressey fire. *Psychonomic Science, 13,* 248.

Vaught, G. M., & Auguston, B. (1967a). Field dependence and form discrimination in females. *Psychonomic Science, 7,* 333–334.

Vaught, G. M., & Augustson, B. (1967b). Field dependence and form discrimination in males. *Psychonomic Science, 8,* 233–234.

Vaught, G. M., & Ellinger, J. (1966). Field dependence and form discrimination. *Psychonomic Science, 6,* 357–358.

Vaught, G. M., Pittman, M. D., & Roodin, P. A. (1975). Developmental curves for the portable Rod-and-Frame Test. *Bulletin of the Psychonomic Society, 5,* 151–152.

Vaught, G. M., & Roodin, P. A. (1973). Cognitive style performance and form discrimination. *Social Behavior and Personality, 1,* 17–22.

Victor, J. B. (1976). Peer judgments of teaching competence as a function of field independence and dogmatism. *Journal of Experimental Education, 44,* 10–13.

Vidulich, R. N., & Kaiman, I. P. (1961). The effects of information source status and dogmatism upon conformity behavior. *Journal of Abnormal and Social Psychology, 63,* 639–642.

Vojtisek, J. E., & Magaro, P. A. (1974). The two factors present in the Embedded Figures Test and a suggested short form for hospitalized psychiatric patients. *Journal of Consulting and Clinical Psychology, 42,* 554–558.

Wachtel, P. L. (1971). Cognitive style, attention, and learning. *Perceptual and Motor Skills, 32,* 315–318.

Wachtel, P. L. (1972). Field dependence and psychological differentiation: Reexamination. *Perceptual and Motor Skills, 35,* 179–189.

Walk, R. D. (1950). *Perception and personality: A pretest.* Unpublished manuscript, Social Relations Library, Harvard University.

Ware, R., & Harvey, O. J. (1967). A cognitive determinant of impression formation. *Journal of Personality and Social Psychology, 5,* 38–44.

Warr, P. B., & Coffman, T. L. (1970). Personality, involvement and extremity of judgment. *British Journal of Social and Clinical Psychology, 9,* 108–121.

Warr, P. B., Lee, R. E., & Jöreskog, K. G. (1969). A note on the factorial nature of the F and D scales. *British Journal of Psychology, 60,* 119–123.

Warr, P. B., & Rogers, C. (1974). Some personality effects on extreme responding and on the relative weighting of items in combination. *British Journal of Social and Clinical Psychology, 13,* 347–357.

Warr, P. B., Schroder, H. M., & Blackman, S. (1969a). A comparison of two techniques for the measurement of international judgment. *International Journal of Psychology, 4,* 135–140.

Warr, P. B., Schroder, H. M., & Blackman, S. (1969b). The structure of political judgment. *British Journal of Social and Clinical Psychology, 8,* 32–43.

Warr, P. B., & Sims, A. (1965). A study of cojudgment processes. *Journal of Personality, 33,* 598–604.

Watson, J. P. (1970). A repertory grid method of studying groups. *British Journal of Psychiatry, 117,* 309–318.

Weatherley, D. (1961). Anti-Semitism and the expression of fantasy aggression. *Journal of Abnormal and Social Psychology, 62,* 454–457.

Weatherley, D. (1963). Maternal response to childhood aggression and subsequent anti-Semitism. *Journal of Abnormal and Social Psychology, 66,* 183–185.

Webster, H. (1956). Some quantitative results. *Journal of Social Issues, 12,* 29–43.

Webster, H., Sanford, N., & Freedman, M. (1955). A new instrument for studying authoritarianism. *Journal of Psychology, 40,* 73–84.

Weissenberg, P. (1973). Concurrent validity of Hidden Figures Test (CF-1). *Perceptual and Motor Skills, 36,* 460–462.

Weisz, J. R., O'Neill, P., & O'Neill, P. C. (1975). Field dependence–independence on the Children's Embedded Figures Test: Cognitive style or cognitive level? *Developmental Psychology, 11,* 539–540.

Westbrook, M. (1974). Judgment of emotion: Attention versus accuracy. *British Journal of Social and Clinical Psychology, 13,* 383–389.

White, B. J., & Alter, R. D. (1965). Dogmatism authoritarianism, and contrast effects in judgment. *Perceptual and Motor Skills, 20,* 99–101.

White, B. J., Alter, R. D., & Rardin, M. (1965). Authoritarianism, dogmatism, and usage of conceptual categories. *Journal of Personality and Social Psychology, 2,* 293–295.

Whiting, W. M., & Child, I. L. (1953). *Child training and personality: A cross-cultural study.* New Haven: Yale University Press.

Wicker, A. (1969). Cognitive complexity, school size, and participation in school behavior settings: A test of the frequency of interaction hypothesis. *Journal of Educational Psychology, 60,* 200–203.

Wilkins, G., Epting, F., & Van De Riet, H. (1972). Relationship between repression-sensitization and interpersonal cognitive complexity. *Journal of Consulting and Clinical Psychology, 39,* 448–450.

Williams, E. I., Jr., & Williams, C. D. (1963). Relationships between authoritarian attitudes of college students, estimation of parents' attitudes, and actual parental attitudes. *Journal of Social Psychology, 61,* 43–48.

Williams, J. D., Harlow, S. D., & Borgen, J. S. (1971). Creativity, dogmatism, and arithmetic achievement. *Journal of Psychology, 78,* 217–222.

Willoughby, R. H. (1967). Field-dependence and locus of control. *Perceptual and Motor Skills, 24,* 671–672.

Wilson, W., Dennns, L., & Wadsworth, A. P., Jr. (1976). "Authoritarianism" of the left and the right. *Bulletin of the Psychonomic Society, 7,* 271–274.

Witkin, H. A. (1950). Individual differences in ease of perception of embedded figures. *Journal of Personality, 19,* 1–15.

Witkin, H. A. (1964). Origins of cognitive style. In C. Sheerer (Ed.), *Cognition: Theory, research, promise.* New York: Harper & Row.

Witkin, H. A., Cox, P. W., & Friedman, F. (1976). *Field-dependence–independence and psychological differentiation.* Supplement No. 2 (ETS RB-76-28). Princeton: Educational Testing Service.

Witkin, H. A., Cox, P. W., Friedman, F., Hrishikesan, A. G., & Siegel, K. N. (1974). *Field-dependence–independence and psychological differentiation.* Supplement No. 1 (ETS RB-74-42). Princeton: Educational Testing Service.

Witkin, H. A., Dyk, R. B., Faterson, H. F., Goodenough, D. R., & Karp, S. A. (1962). *Psychological differentiation.* New York: Wiley.

Witkin, H. A., & Goodenough, D. R. (1976). *Field dependence and interpersonal behavior.* ETS RB-76-12. Princeton: Educational Testing Service.

Witkin, H. A., Goodenough, D. R., & Karp, S. A. (1967). Stability of cognitive style from childhood to young adulthood. *Journal of Personality and Social Psychology, 7,* 291–300.

Witkin, H. A., Lewis, H. B., Hertzman, M., Machover, K., Meissner, P. B., & Wapner, S. (1954). *Personality through perception.* New York: Harper.

Witkin H. A., Oltman, P. K., Cox, P. W., Ehrlichman, E., Hamm, R. M., & Ringler, R. W.

(1973). *Field-dependence–independence and psychological differentiation.* ETS RB73-62. Princeton: Educational Testing Service.

Witkin, H. A., Oltman, P. K., Raskin, E., & Karp, S. A. (1971). *A manual for the embedded figures tests.* Palo Alto: Consulting Psychologists Press.

Wolfe, R. (1963). The role of conceptual systems in cognitive functioning at varying levels of age and intelligence. *Journal of Personality, 31,* 108–123.

Wolfe, R., Egelston, R., & Powers, J. (1972). Conceptual structure and conceptual tempo. *Perceptual and Motor Skills, 35,* 331–337.

Wolfer, J. A. (1967). Changes in dogmatism scores of high and low dogmatics as a function of instructions. *Psychological Reports, 20,* 947–950.

Wolitzky, D. L. (1973). Cognitive controls and person perception. *Perceptual and Motor Skills, 36,* 619–623.

Wrightsman, L. (1974). Authoritarianism—back again? *Contemporary Psychology, 19,* 209–210.

Yarrow, M. R. (1963). Problems of methods in parent-child research. *Child Development, 34,* 215–226.

Young, D. V., Beier, E. G., Beier, P., & Barton, C. (1975). Is chivalry dead? *Journal of Communication, 25,* 57–64.

Young, H. H. (1959). A test of Witkin's field dependence hypothesis. *Journal of Abnormal and Social Psychology, 59,* 188–192.

Zacker, J. (1973). Authoritarian avoidance of ambiguity. *Psychological Reports, 33,* 901–902.

Zagona, S. V., & Kelly, M. A. (1966). The resistance of the closed mind to a novel and complex audio-visual experience. *Journal of Social Psychology, 70,* 123–131.

Zagona, S. V., & Zurcher, L. A. (1965). Notes on the reliability and validity of the Dogmatism Scale. *Psychological Reports, 16,* 1234–2136.

Zajonc, R. B. (1968). Cognitive theories in social psychology. In G. Lindzey & E. Aronson (Eds.), *The handbook of social psychology,* Vol. 1. Reading, Mass.: Addison-Wesley.

Zaks, M. S. (1954). *Perseveration of set: A determinant in problem-solving rigidity.* Unpublished master's thesis, Roosevelt College of Chicago.

Zigler, E. (1963a). A measure in search of a theory. *Contemporary Psychology, 8,* 133–135.

Zigler, E. (1963b). Reply to Witkin. *Contemporary Psychology, 8,* 459–461.

Zimring, F. M. (1971). Cognitive simplicity–complexity: Evidence for disparate processes. *Journal of Personality, 39,* 1–9.

Zippel, B., & Norman, R. D. (1966). Party switching, authoritarianism, and dogmatism in the 1964 election. *Psychological Reports, 19,* 667–670.

Zuckerman, M., & Eisen, B. (1962). Relationship of acquiescence response set to authoritarianism and dependency. *Psychological Reports, 10,* 95–102.

Zuckerman, M., Kolin, A., Price, L., & Zoob, I. (1964). Development of a sensation-seeking scale. *Journal of Consulting Psychology, 28,* 477–482.

Zuckerman, M., & Link, K. (1968). Construct validity for the sensation-seeking scale. *Journal of Consulting and Clinical Psychology, 32,* 420–426.

Zuckerman, M., Norton, J., & Sprague, D. S. (1958). Acquiescence and extreme sets and their role in tests of authoritarianism and parental attitudes. *Psychiatric Research Reports, 10,* 28–45.

Zuckerman, M., & Oltean, M. (1959). Some relationships between maternal attitude factors and authoritarianism, personality needs, psychopathology, and self-acceptance. *Child Development, 30,* 27–36.

Author Index

Subject Index